ETHICS
in the
PRESENT TENSE

ETHICS
in the
PRESENT TENSE

Readings from Christianity and Crisis

1966–1991

Edited by
LEON HOWELL
and
VIVIAN LINDERMAYER

Friendship Press • **New York**

Copyright © 1991 by Friendship Press

Editorial Offices:
475 Riverside Drive, New York, NY 10115

Distribution Offices:
P.O. Box 37844, Cincinnati, OH 45222-0844

Manufactured in the United States of America

Library of Congress Cataloging-in-Publication Data

Ethics in the present tense : readings from Christianity and crisis,
1966-1991 / edited by Leon Howell and Vivian Lindermayer.
   p. cm.
  ISBN 0-377-00230-5
  1. Theology—20th century. 2. Christian ethics. 3. Social
ethics. 4. Christianity and politics. 5. Sex—Religious aspects—
Christianity. 6. Christianity—20th century. I. Howell, Leon.
II. Lindermayer, Vivian. III. Christianity and crisis.
BR123.E74 1991
241—dc20   91-21730
                                                    CIP

To

WAYNE H. COWAN

With appreciation for
the vision, dedication and persistence
that sustained *Christianity and Crisis*
for thirty-one years

Contents

Part 3
Religion and Politics

Part 4
Faith and Empire

Part 5
Sexual Politics/AIDS

Foreword

FOR ME, the word "crisis" in *Christianity and Crisis*'s title has always carried ambiguous overtones. In one of my lexicons "crisis" signifies a particularly difficult time, one fraught — as the familiar homiletical adage puts it — "with both challenge and opportunity." In this way of thinking, crises are perilous but periodic. They eventually pass and we all return to some kind of quotidian normalcy. A crisis is by definition something you eventually get through.

But, given my theological formation, "crisis" conveys another and more supercharged meaning as well. It recalls the steely theology of Karl Barth, Dietrich Bonhoeffer, and Reinhold Niebuhr, who taught my generation that the proclamation of the Gospel should always be expected to create a crisis. The Word, rightly proclaimed, should interrupt, confront, and dislocate. It should subvert conventional categories and shatter normal expectations. Where there is no crisis, this theology insisted, the Gospel produces one.

When I first started writing for *Christianity and Crisis* three decades ago these two meanings were more or less fused in my mind. God knows the world was in crisis. The building of the Berlin wall, the Cuban missile crisis, the initial American moves to shore up South Vietnam, the dogs and firehoses of Birmingham — all generated the distinct impression of old patterns coming unstuck and lethal new dangers looming.

I was living in Berlin as an ecumenical fraternal worker, crossing three or four times a week through Checkpoint Charley into the Communist-controlled Eastern sector of the riven city. This kind of commuting, although technically legal at the time under the "Four Power" administration of Berlin, was frowned on by the East Germans and deemed risky and inadvisable by American military authorities. The white-helmeted GI's at the western entrance to the checkpoint dutifully informed me during each crossing that I was now passing beyond their sphere of protection. They were right; if the East German regime happened to decide it needed a spy to exchange one day, I might find myself sitting in a prison until the swap could be arranged. Consequently I was always in something of a crisis mood.

But so was the whole city. Clusters of housewives lined up at stores along the Bundesallee to buy potatoes on the day President Kennedy issued his ultimatum to the USSR about the Cuban missiles. We had all been warned to expect a Russian countermove against Berlin, then an island in Soviet controlled territory. A U.S. military official at the American base in Dahlem had told me that, yes, there was an evacuation plan, but no, the handful of American civilians living in Berlin could probably not expect to be on the list of evacuees. As it turned out, the "missile crisis" itself passed, but the mood of the crisis, or at least my sense of living every day on the edge, did not.

Back in Boston in 1963 I wrote a couple of articles on the church in Eastern Europe, but they had hardly appeared in *Christianity and Crisis* before I found myself in the middle of my country's own internal cold war. Rosa Parks, it seemed, had violated a checkpoint in Alabama. Along with many others, I responded to Martin Luther King, Jr.'s call to march and demonstrate in various picturesque locations in the south — like Selma and St. Augustine — and later in Chicago and Boston itself (where, incidentally, the crowds of hecklers were often nastier than they were in Dixie). Never jailed in East Germany, I did get locked up briefly in the U.S.A. (for "parading without a permit").

In those days no one had to remind us then that we were living in a crisis. Nor could we doubt that "Christianity" — the churches and individual Christians — was addressing the crisis. We were sometimes tardy, and frequently scared, and often inept; but we had a sense that the "and" that linked Christianity with crisis was dialectical and not merely conjunctive.

It is sometimes hard for those who have no personal memory of the 1960s to realize that we did not experience their tumultuous qualities sequentially. For us, civil rights, the Beatles, the Vietnam war, *The Secular City*, the Prague spring, assassinations, psychedelia, the French student revolt, Vatican II, the ghetto uprisings, *Honest to God*, the Medellín conference, all seemed to be happening at once. Throughout that period and into the 1970s and 1980s *Christianity and Crisis* documented, illustrated, sharpened, and informed the excitement, the rhythm, and the dashed hopes. It kept us in touch.

Now that the 1990s are upon us, can we still talk about a "crisis"? For some the word itself has become trite and redundant. Brandished so heatedly and so repeatedly, it has lost its zing. If everything is a crisis, then — ho hum — nothing is a crisis. Yet paradoxically, as we witness the rapid disintegration of India, the USSR, and whole regions of Latin America, and as American cities lurch toward chaos and nihilism, while the middle class shops and the homeless queue up for cots, those decades in which "crisis" seemed to describe our reality so accurately now seem almost stable by comparison. Now that the American infant mortality rate exceeds that of the former East Germany where I started out as a *Christianity and Crisis* contributor, and racism is in some ways more rampant than it was in 1968, one has to wonder if we need a new vocabulary.

To make matters more complicated, in those older times, regardless of what the crisis was we usually thought we had at least a pretty good idea of how our Christianity might respond to it. Jim Crow laws? We wanted integration! War in Vietnam? Give peace a chance! Though we often disagreed on strategies — and the pages of *Christianity and Crisis* record our spirited debates — we more or less agreed on the vision itself. Can we say the same today? Does anyone really know for sure what we should do about the six million street kids of Brazil, the drug empires, the public school disaster, the AIDS epidemic?

As we move out of the first half century of *Christianity and Crisis* and into the next one, I doubt that we can now consider our Christianity — if we ever really did — a secure vantage point from which our witness to the social crisis can be carried on. We are more aware now than we once were of how deeply implicated we are as Christians in the societal evils we seek to heal. In the theological as opposed to the sociological sense of the word "crisis," this is not a bad thing at all. It often discourages us, but it also makes us more humble, more receptive.

The Gospel, when rightly grasped, does create a crisis, not only for the culture, but for those of us who live by faith. Not once, but time and time again, the Message subverts our settled views of how things should be — in the church and in the world. It calls us to contrition and pushes us into painful redefinition. God's cleansing judgment, as the prophets knew, always begins with the temple itself. We exist, it would seem, both by faith and in crisis. We live not by any hard-won certainties of our own, but by the constant, surprising, and jarring grace of the One who never ceases to do a New Thing in our midst.

HARVEY COX

Acknowledgments

EMERGING AS IT DOES out of the life of a very special enterprise, this book acknowledges its debt to hosts of peoples and groups. Those cited are representative of what could be hundreds of others.

In the first instance *C&C* is grateful to movements of people around the world who have, in the name of justice, challenged the status quo, to communities and congregations who have embodied their faith. Their voices have always inspired this journal.

We want also to recognize our staff colleagues. Tom Kelly, associate editor, Marilyn Seven, production, J Richard Butler, managing publisher, and Margaret Ferns, office manager, combine wit, intelligence, commitment, talent, and humaneness to sustain and produce *C&C*. Richard Pemberton, student intern, helped locate and duplicate articles for this book. In the process they have all assured that our work together reflects something of what we wish for the wider world.

Three former staff members deserve special comment. This book is dedicated to long-time editor Wayne H. Cowan. Robert Hoyt shared his remarkable editorial gifts and professionalism with *C&C* from 1977 to 1985. Gail Hovey provided spirit, energy, conviction, and wide-ranging contacts from 1984 to 1990.

C&C has twenty contributing editors, writers, thinkers, and doers of unusual talent who maintain a direct editorial relationship to the journal. Seven — John C. Bennett, Robert McAfee Brown, Harvey Cox, Arthur J. Moore, Howard Moody, Roger Shinn, and Rosemary Ruether — have served for most of the twenty-five-year span of this book.

As an independent journal of opinion, *C&C* is sustained legally and corporately by its Board of Directors. Few magazines anywhere have a board that takes as seriously its duties. During the past twenty-five years board presidents have taken on unusual responsibilities. They have included Edith Lerrigo, Robert W. Lynn, B. J. Stiles, Richard Fernandez, Michael McIntyre, Robert J. Harman, Ardith Hays, Roger L. Shinn, Donald E. Wilson, Louis Oliver Gropp, and William S. Ellis.

C & C has always depended on its readers and friends for contributions to supplement its subscription income. More than twelve hundred made donations in 1990. All are appreciated. But Anne Hale Johnson, Harle and Kenneth Montgomery, Luther Tucker, and one couple who wish to remain anonymous have given exceptionally during the past decade.

Agencies within the Presbyterian Church (U.S.A.), the United Methodist Church, the United Church of Christ, the Christian Church (Disciples of Christ), the Evangelical Lutheran Church in America, and the Episcopal Church have also made important contributions, often in relation to specific editorial projects.

Since 1947 C & C has been housed in one building owned, first, by Union Theological Seminary and then, after 1978, by Jewish Theological Seminary. They have provided a dynamic ecumenical setting, and for forty-three years neither demanded full commercial rent. To these, and to scores more, C & C acknowledges its debt and its gratitude.

Introduction

THE PAST TWENTY-FIVE YEARS have been extraordinary. From the heights of the civil rights movement to the depths of the Vietnam era, running through the Johnson, Nixon, Carter, and Reagan years into the Gulf war confusion of 1991, the world has churned.

During this time the United States enjoyed great economic growth, but the gap between the poor and the rich widened sharply. It experienced three energy shocks (to which it has never effectively responded), became the world's single military superpower, and descended from the world's number one creditor to number one debtor nation.

Great euphoria accompanied the end of the cold war and the reduction of the nuclear threat. But fears for the future of the ecosystem — acid rain, ozone holes, and global warming are a few of the ominous phrases — encountered powerful economic and political denial. The AIDS pandemic heightened the stigmatization of gays and the black and Hispanic poor, punctured medical presumptions, and returned dreadful mystery to the center of human life. The terrible economic situation of much of the Third World produced near despair.

But all over the world various groups — South African as well as U.S. blacks, Latin American peasants, gay men and lesbians, women and native peoples — became empowered, and began to speak in their own voices. And in South Africa and Nicaragua, the Philippines and East Germany, oppressed peoples scored significant victories.

The articles in this book — all of which originally appeared in *Christianity and Crisis* — reflect efforts to wrestle with the meaning of these and other historical moments over the past twenty-five years. They differ in style and perspective. But taken together they provide a unique take on recent history and the distinct contribution of an important part of the religious community to the public debate.

Readers not familiar with *C & C* should know this much about it. *C & C* is devoted to "discerning the signs of the times," to analyzing and describing affairs of the state and the church through the eyes of a critical faith. That does not imply that any one article is

1

the "truth," but that the journal's particular perspective and tradition in the mainstream, ecumenical Protestant churches, shaped by fifty years of practice, allow it to perceive and communicate certain truths very powerfully. As former editor Robert Hoyt wrote in 1985,

The particular tradition we've inherited and affirm derives in part from a certain understanding of the Christian Gospel, in part from a certain method of applying the Gospel to social reality.... The tradition reaches deeper than sociological sophistication can in grasping the pervasiveness of social sin, and its ache for justice is stronger by far than a mere penchant for fair play. Once absorbed, these components of the tradition help its bearers recognize realities and raise questions others don't.

The book begins with a few snapshots from 1968, that fateful year when the Tet offensive changed forever U.S. perceptions of the Vietnam War, when Martin Luther King, Jr., and Robert F. Kennedy were assassinated, when the Prague spring was crushed by a brutal Soviet invasion, when the tumultuous Chicago Democratic convention demonstrated profound fissures in U.S. society, when "the movement" soured and fragmented, and when Richard Nixon's election marked the end of the New Deal.

It then takes up various ways in which people began, not so much to pick up the pieces as to find themselves in new configurations, to develop new voices and new approaches.

Take the theological field. By the late 1960s the spectrum had shattered. The comprehensive systems associated with European, largely German, theologians like Barth, Brunner, and Tillich were no longer accepted as the norm. Theologies now were coming from other contexts than Europe, and had names like liberation, black, feminist, womanist, creation, minjung. That insistence on diversity has produced a sometimes bewildering, often threatening, but always rich interplay, a challenge to everyone's parochialisms that offers a much fuller sense of the holy in our midst.

Or look at the women's movement — which reemerged, in the U.S. at least, in the late 1960s to challenge male domination of society and culture. The feminist movement has posed a fundamental challenge to traditional notions of gender, power, and value, and has made rich contributions to theology, ethics, psychology — the list goes on.

An example close to the journal's life illustrates the changes of the last twenty-five years. In 1966, *Christianity and Crisis* put together a similar volume, a collection of essays from its first twenty-five years entitled *Witness to a Generation*. It contained powerful articles and famous names like Barth, Bennett, Bonhoeffer, Paton, Toynbee, Tillich, Cox, Brown, and the Niebuhrs. But every contribution save one, by M. M. Thomas from India, was by a white male. This book is different.

The articles that appear are only a sampling — to the compilers a disturbingly limited sampling — of a more nuanced and varied discussion. Of the various aspects of the feminist movement, for example, we have concentrated on feminist and womanist theology and on abortion. In the international arena, space limits prevent using important material from Nicaragua, Korea, South Africa, the Philippines. We have chosen articles that highlight both the human rights theme that challenged imperial presumptions during the past two decades, and the kind of political analysis and reportage that give weight to the religious community's concern with human rights.

The book also pays attention to the shifting situation of the churches. The mainline churches no longer dominate the culture as they once did; their mission for the future is up for discussion and debate (as are developments in evangelical and other congregations), and so is their global dominance, as the Christian faith becomes more and more rooted in the Third World — by the year 2000, 60 percent of Christians are expected *not* to be found in North America and Europe.

Finally, this book contains several short pieces on the meaning of Christmas and Easter, the central celebrations of the Christian faith. They point to an affirmation that unifies the entire collection. However painful the dilemmas and overpowering the problems, we are not without hope. People of faith act with the confidence that God gives meaning to our history. And by grace, God supports our strivings for justice and nullifies our failures.

Part 1

1968

Just as the events of the early 1940s, when this magazine was born, shook an entire generation loose from its faith in historical progress, so too did the dissonances of the 1960s uproot the realist consensus in both theology and society.

Growing awareness of the depths of racism and, later, sexism in U.S. society undercut talk of a blessed community. Vietnam brought about a loss of American innocence. This, and more, led to calls for new ways to analyze society, for new understandings of Christian symbols.

The two most important developments in twentieth-century theology for North Americans have been fully interpreted in the pages of C&C. The first shift — reflected in the first twenty-five years of the journal's life — was the movement, led in the U.S. by Reinhold Niebuhr and others, toward neo-orthodoxy. It cut through claims of human perfectibility with restatements of the meaning of sin and the mixed motives that accompany even our good acts. The second shift — reflected in the articles that follow — is the challenge to the Western white male-defined consensus by a pluralist world ecumenism.

We begin with the late 1960s. The question at hand, as Tom Driver put it in 1968, was not whether we could be realists but what were the realities. And, as Roger Shinn added and the next section makes clear, the theological spectrum was shattered. "The diversity of theological movements defied classification. Not only was there no one dominant theology; there was not even a clear spectrum....Everything was up for grabs."

Martin Luther King
and Vietnam

May 1, 1967

John David Maguire

John Maguire, president of the Claremont University Center and Graduate School in Cal-
ifornia, is an Alabama native and was a teen-aged friend of Martin Luther King, Jr.
Maguire was provost at Wesleyan University (Conn.) when he wrote this piece.

WE FIND IT DISTURBING that Dr. Martin Luther King's now celebrated April 4 speech on Vietnam evoked so much criticism and
reproach. Most of his comrades-in-arms in the civil rights movement — Roy Wilkins and Whitney Young, for example — and many
other supporters, Ralph Bunche for one, have severely criticized him
for allegedly attempting to merge the peace movement with the civil
rights struggle. As a matter of fact, the speech explicitly denied attempting such a fusion. He did suggest the possibility of a fruitful
interdependence between the movements, and he indicated how the
war diverts funds and efforts from social programs at home, "directing
away money like some demonic suction pump."

In this speech King was not dealing at the level of merging movements, nor was he concerning himself with tactical questions. He was
speaking out of his conviction that nonviolence is a way for all life
and that one cannot counsel nonviolence within a nation at the same
time that nation savagely denies it abroad.

King's colleagues, like most Americans, become anxious and defensive in the presence of such a metaphysical principle, especially
one that is held to govern the whole of life and to be more important than pragmatic, prudential, or political considerations. So they
attack him for tactical naïveté and for splitting the already fractured
rights movement. But, even at the tactical level, they must know that
the war in Vietnam is itself far more destructive of these rights than
King's antiwar statements.

The extent to which King's colleagues-turned-critics have become
like all other Americans is more deeply revealed by their contention
that social leaders should eschew multiple roles and confine themselves to a single area — "either civil rights or peace." To make this
demand is to forget that King was a follower of Gandhi before he became an American civil rights leader. Such a demand is also morally
dubious. His call to be a civil rights leader surely did not entail the
surrender of his right to speak out on other matters. Rather than urg-
ing him to fall silent on war and peace, his colleagues might rather

insist on his right to speak his conscience on all subjects — a right in which they have a very deep stake indeed.

King's dramatic style, to be sure, leaves him vulnerable to misrepresentation in the press. His penchant for drama and aphorism leads him to label America in the Vietnam situation "the greatest purveyor of violence in the world today," to warn of the imminence of "America's soul being totally poisoned," and to liken our testing of new weapons to "the Germans' testing of new medicine and new tortures in the concentration camps of Europe." While these sentences may be hyperbolic, are they altogether untrue? The sermonic mode is certainly not the most appropriate style for political analysis and its premium on the pungent and emotionally evocative encourages simplism.

But why has the press seized on these bits from a speech that was, for the most part, a model of restraint, accuracy, and due qualification?

We see two reasons: King's insistence that America is "on the wrong side of the worldwide revolution" — not just in Vietnam but virtually everywhere — and that nothing short of a new national economic asceticism — a gradual "giving up of the privileges and pleasures that come from the immense profits of overseas investment" — will move us to the right side of the revolution. This surely is far more of a threat than his questioning the U.S. involvement in Vietnam. The fourth estate reacted as if, in the idiom of King's native South, he had "quit preaching and gone to meddling."

The other fact is that, as Nobel Peace Prize holder, Dr. King is the first American of such stature to question so totally, so publicly, our present policy. Rather than reporting King's speech, the press seemed constrained to exploit it. Those who heard it or read it, however, can hardly avoid being haunted by his suggestion that "a nation that continues year after year to spend more money on military defense than on programs of social uplift is approaching spiritual death."

Nor can we rest easily with his closing quotation from John F. Kennedy: "Those who make peaceful revolution impossible will make violent revolution inevitable."

The Mysterious Case of the AFL-CIA

May 29, 1967

Arthur J. Moore

Arthur Moore, a veteran observer of the religious scene and long-time editor of New World Outlook, *is a contributing editor of* Christianity and Crisis.

IN THE RECENT revelations about the Central Intelligence Agency's channeling money to various private groups, nothing is more murky than the relationship between the government and the AFL-CIO. In recent months columnist Drew Pearson, labor expert Paul Jacobs (in the April *Ramparts*) and former CIA executive Thomas Braden (in the May 20 *Saturday Evening Post*) have all charged that CIA money has gone to the labor federation over a period of years. Mr. Braden also included the former CIO through Walter and Victor Reuther.

Walter Reuther has admitted receiving a large sum of money on one occasion to help a needy European union. George Meany, AFL-CIO president, on the other hand, has angrily denied everything and called his various accusers liars. Jay Lovestone and Irving Brown, the AFL agents most directly involved, have maintained a discreet silence. It is this attitude on Mr. Meany's part that is baffling. Certainly these stories are not new. They have been circulating for years among people with even a slight connection with the labor movement.

In the respective cases of these three writers, their motives could not have been more dissimilar. Mr. Braden wrote to defend CIA help to private organizations; Mr. Jacobs, to attack such aid; and Mr. Pearson, well, to be Mr. Pearson. If the charges are untrue, the AFL-CIO should welcome a chance to dispose of them once and for all.

Mr. Meany's attitude raises the suspicion that the charges are true, and this is a very serious matter. For the allegations against Mr. Lovestone are far more than that he served as a neutral conduit for money to prop up anticommunist unions overseas.

On the one hand, it is charged that unions have served as covers for government agents engaged in active subversion, as in the overthrow of the Cheddi Jagan government in British Guiana. On the other hand, it is charged that Lovestone and Irving Brown used government funds and influence to help put into office in European unions people who were not only anticommunist but also sympathetic to their point of view. Finally, it is charged that the AFL-CIO has carried on an anticommunist crusade more rigid than that of the U.S. government. This has involved them with right-wing organizations here and abroad.

If these charges are only partially true, it means that one of our more lauded assets in the free enterprise-Communist competition has lost its credibility, and rightly so. It does not much matter who benefits most when the result is to topple the proud boast of free labor unions divorced from government.

To say this is not to overlook past history, when these same people were rescuing European unionists from Nazi prison camps or doing valiant battle against Communist control of weak unions struggling to get back on their feet after World War II. It is not to overlook the emotional climate of the late 1940s and 1950s when certain excesses looked more like heroic measures needed in a desperate struggle. We do not suggest that Mr. Meany or Mr. Lovestone "come clean" in a confession, McCarthy style, to berate the past.

What we do need to know, however, is whether what might be defended as an extraordinary act has hardened into a system, and even a corrupt system. The question about CIA funds is most acute in this case — in our attempts to fight unscrupulous opponents, have we ended up debauching ourselves? Such arrangements between government and labor unions, if they took place and did so without the consent of either citizens or union members, not only destroy the credibility of both the government and the labor movement but also undermine the democratic system.

The issues here are important enough and the disagreement over facts is sharp enough to warrant further investigation by some governmental body. Here, once again, we run into the lack of accountability of the CIA. Nevertheless, such questions as these are so basic that the curtain of secrecy of intelligence operations should be raised.

The Year of the Raven?

February 5, 1968

C. Eric Lincoln

C. Eric Lincoln is William Rand Kenan Jr. Professor of Religion at Duke University. He is the author, with Lawrence H. Mamiya, of The Black Church in the African-American Experience *and* This Road since Freedom, *a collection of poetry.*

THE YEAR 1967 is consigned to history, but say no requiem for it — and write no epitaph. Not yet. The year just ended is indeed past; but we can scarcely argue that it is dead, except perhaps for the uncritical and for those who live in a world of make-believe. For such, 1967 may indeed be just another year past and gone. For the rest of us, it is not so simple; we have to live in a world of critical realities where the consequences of our acts and failures to act do not end with the ringing of bells and the blowing of whistles but are projected into a future oblivious of the calendar's neat divisions.

In the year we have just survived some of us saw, or thought we saw, some startling and unsettling instances of social interaction that were not characteristic of this society as we have known it, or believe it to be. Others were shaken by the unrestrained public illustrations of the eternal conflict of human values. For the first time in our modern history there was a serious division of national will, and the resulting national schizophrenia brought us perilously close to disaster.

Last year may well be a sign of the times, a prototype of what is yet to come. This society grows increasingly complex, and the demands made upon the individual to make new personal adjustments that mesh more readily with an ever-expanding social machinery grow increasingly refined. That we have reached, or are near the threshold of, toleration seems indicated by the fact that we seem no longer able to contain our frustrations or to relieve them through traditional channels that have widespread social approval. We have, instead, "gone into the streets," a kind of behavior that heretofore has been repugnant to our national ideals and to our self-image as a democratic society. Societies that settled their differences in the streets have evoked in the American mind romantic images of totalitarian regimes beset by the hapless rabble. It was out of the land of storybooks, and it could not happen in democratic America.

But it happened in America in 1967 and it is happening still; and we are called upon to reexamine our thinking about what is totalitarianism and who are the rabble. On this issue, as on so many others, we are sharply divided. In the present instance, it is not essential to social polity that we agree on definitions, but it is essential to our survival as a democratic society that we do not in our frustrations become hysterical over either the definitions, the issues or the people thus defined.

We saw the shadow of hysteria in the streets in 1967. It was the hysteria born of the feeling of powerlessness that led to excesses on a dozen college campuses and in the "Peace March on Washington." And it was the hysteria born of too little black power and too much police power with too little restraint that produced the more unspeakable excesses at Newark and Detroit. Wherever social hysteria exhibits itself, it is ugly and it is dangerous.

If we are to make any progress toward the solution of our problems other than the mere removal of their symptoms, we may as well recognize now that — just as ringing out the old year and ringing in the new didn't take away any of the hard decisions confronting us — neither the removal of the present administration nor the end of the war in Vietnam is going to automatically bring us peace and tranquility, either at home or abroad. The fundamental issue here is *why* we presume to be in that unhappy country rather than the fact that we are there. It is naive to attempt to answer this question in terms of a particular administration, or to seek the ultimate solution in terms of the use or avoidance of this or that military strategy. The answer is somewhat deeper than that.

Inasmuch as this is a political year — and we are conditioned to expect political interest above principle — it is quite probable that something will be done before November to placate those whose anxieties are focused on Vietnam. What then? With due allowances for personal frustrations, the opportunism of subversives, and the inevitable social voyeurs, there is no reason to doubt the genuineness of American moral concern over our involvement in Vietnam.

But the truth is that despite all of the tragedy and suffering we may have exported to Southeast Asia, the more desperate problem facing the American people is the unexported tragedy we keep right around home.

There is reason to suspect that much of this concern with Vietnam is patently displaced, that it really derives, unconsciously perhaps, from a national sense of guilt that we have made so little serious effort to cope with the disastrous effects of race prejudice and poverty at home. Indeed, America has a long history — in politics and in religion — of exporting her concern for the unfortunate to the far places of the earth. Meanwhile the world has looked back at us in wonder and consternation that we have been so unconcerned about our own.

We cannot go on in sweet and innocent oblivion, forever jousting at the same old windmills. It must be brought home to us rather soon that *this society can be destroyed from within perhaps more readily than from without,* and that the seeds of our destruction have long since been sown by our moral lassitude at home.

As we confront the year ahead, it is our common hope that there will be peace in Asia. But 1968 will not necessarily be the Year of the Dove, nor yet the Year of the Hawk. It may well be the Year of the Raven.

The End of an Era

January 6, 1969

Harvey Cox

Harvey Cox is professor of divinity at Harvard Divinity School and a contributing editor of C & C. *Author of the influential* The Secular City (1964) *and many other books, he has drawn on his broad ecumenical experiences and travels to write about important developments in religious experience and their relationships to social and political change.*

WITH THE COMING of Nixon, the New Deal is over. A thirty-five-year epoch in American history, studded with unforgettable accomplishments, has come to a close. *Requiescat in Pace.* True, there was within it the eight-year parenthesis under Eisenhower. But the Eisenhower years served mainly to assure everyone that a kind of cumbersome custodial liberalism was really a bipartisan affair. Ike was a somewhat paler JFK, a somewhat more colorful version of the same basic approach to issues that began in 1933.

The typical solution to any social problem during the era now ending was to create a new Federal agency or beef up an old one, bring the smartest people to Washington to supply it with ideas, give it an energetic administrator and then pour in money. From the New Deal through the Fair Deal to the New Frontier this was the pattern. As a result our new president inherits a labyrinthine pyramid of colossal overlapping governmental structures manned by tired, routine-dulled, civil servants.

Both conservatives and radicals now agree that these elephantine agencies swamped with proposals, guidelines, and coffee cups cannot be relied on to heal the festering sores of poverty, racial enmity, urban putrefaction, or massive citizen alienation. The country is too large and sprawling. The problems, despite surface similarities, differ from region to region. Our massive and rigid bureaucracies simply cannot innovate and, therefore, grow increasingly unresponsive to their public. Welfare has become a cruel technique of repressive social control, and urban school systems function mainly as low-security custodial barracks. In order to fight poverty we feed the horses, hoping the sparrows will eventually benefit.

But none of it works. The Liberal Era, whatever its historic accomplishments, is over. President Nixon cannot and should not try to perpetuate its moribund approach to our social crisis. He has only two choices. First, he could keep the present hierarchical monstrosities and simply feed them less money, hoping they will slim down and become more efficient. They won't. Or, he could move in a wholly new direction, one he hinted at occasionally during his campaign: he could try to restore power, responsibility, and initiative to lower levels of government, to states, cities, and especially to neighborhoods.

If Nixon is a real "conservative," not just a vacuous power seeker, he will choose the latter course. He will not simply do less of what is being done now; he will do something different.

If he chooses the second course he may find allies he never expected. He will not only be supported by those Republicans who are attracted by Rockefeller's ideas for a new kind of decentralized federalism. He will also receive encouragement from some quarters of the New Left where decentralization, community control, neighborhood corporations, and the rebirth of authentic local life are not only intensely discussed but have been tried out here and there with real promise of success.

Last July, for example, thirty-five senators, both Republicans and Democrats, introduced S.3875, the Community Self-Determination Act of 1968. This act would make it possible for thousands of local communities, both rural and urban, to form neighborhood corporations that could eventually take over control of the businesses, public services, schools, and municipal facilities in their area. The potential of this approach has already been demonstrated in the ECCO experiment in Columbus, Ohio, which began its life around an inner-city Lutheran parish.

If community corporations could have access to federally guaranteed development capital and their share of federal procurement contracts (a portion of which are already set aside for small businesses), people might once again begin to take hold of responsibility for the institutions around them. Apathy and alienation might really begin to recede.

Some politicians are also beginning to realize that decentralization is administratively more efficient. It puts decision making closer to the problem, and when errors are made, they do not foul up a whole system. The immediate passage of S.3875 by the new Congress would signal to the nation that Nixon is serious about a new attack on old problems.

Governor Rockefeller has pointed out rightly that the federal government's vast taxing powers could be creatively wed to the imagination and special competence of lower levels of government if federal revenues were redistributed where they are really needed. Of course not all problems can usefully be attacked at lower levels, for example, polluted atmospheres and the urban transit mess. But many — schools, police, mental health, recreation — can. Nor will all units use the money efficiently. But neither does OEO nor HEW. They just use more.

Most Americans in November either voted or refrained because they were against something. Some were against the war, others against the blacks, others against the cops or the kids or both. But few people in America today cherish a real vision of what to be for. What we all need now is a period of radically diverse experimentation, probes, and model building. Only something like the decentralized approach symbolized by the Community Self-Determination Act will allow this new tactic to emerge. If it or its equivalents pass, the next decade may see a period of healthful social change that could restore vitality to the parched and passive grassroots of America. Mr. Nixon, the next move is yours.

Part 2

Liberation Theology and Its Aftermath

Liberation theology burst into the consciousness of North Americans and Europeans with the publication in 1973 of the English translation of Gustavo Gutiérrez's A Theology of Liberation.

At about the same time Christianity and Crisis *featured a debate on liberation theology and Christian realism. At issue: whether liberation theology was a form of the utopian wishfulness that Christian realism criticized or whether Christian realism's claims to oppose sentimental utopianism obscured its uses by certain thinkers to enhance an American ideology.*

The debate over liberation theology, C & C's *editors predicted, would continue for a long time to come. And they concluded that nothing in the debate would obscure the reality that "the center of history is moving away from the West...."*

Today, liberation theologies — and more important the movements for social justice from which they arise — have become key reference points for theological discourse. As liberation theology has been interpreted by specific communities in specific places across the world, it has given rise to a host of voices.

The new currents in the world church include liberal perspectives as well. C & C's *legacy has been liberal, but its commitment to uniting theological imperatives with concrete historical and political analysis has meant its pages are open to a range of theological voices. It has served as a forum for debating key tensions among and within liberal and liberationist approaches. It has given prominence to a multifaceted, ever-shifting pluralism.*

Christian Realism:
Ideology of the Establishment

September 17, 1973

Rubem A. Alves

Rubem A. Alves, Brazilian theologian, poet and, lately, writer of children's books, is the author of A Theology of Human Hope *(1969), one of the pioneering works in liberation theology.*

CHRISTIANITY AND CRISIS asked me to react to its debate on Liberation Theology. I found it strange that the article sent to me did not carry the author's name. But when I finished reading it I was glad. I knew that my irritation was not directed at anyone in particular.

My feelings were mixed. At first, surprise. I had the illusion that — after the Pentagon Papers, Watergate, and the falsification of bombing reports — at least intellectuals would have started questioning the realistic-pragmatic attitudes that have been responsible, apparently, for this country's policies. And then, irritation. What irritated me most was not *what* was said, but *how* it was said. When empirical and logical matters are at stake, it is possible to argue rationally. But when the tone of a statement is more important than the statement itself, how is one to react?

I know that North Americans like to see us Latin Americans as highly emotional types, who speak more out of our guts than out of our brains. So I decided to let the article rest for a few days on my desk. Maybe I would be able, then, to produce a cool and, hopefully, scholarly reply. However, when I finished reexamining it this morning, I came to the conclusion that this would be impossible. With this warning and confession, let me turn now to the analysis of the problems involved in the conflict between "realistic" and "utopian" ways of understanding theology and faith.

A realistic way of approaching the problem would be to isolate the issues and to deal with one at a time. I will not do that. Something that Wittgenstein said in his *Tractatus Logico-Philosophicus* came to mind: "the silent agreements needed to understand the common language are extremely complicated." When realists and utopians disagree (as in this case), what is at the root of our disagreements are these "silent agreements," or, as Alvin Gouldner calls them, our "background assumptions." Every language is built upon an unconscious worldview, a hidden unconfessed metaphysics. More important than what is said is the grammar of language that structures both our consciousness and our world.

What are the "silent agreements" behind Christian realism? What are the background assumptions that remain hidden as it criticizes the utopian mentality?

Utopianism Criticized

Christian realists were not the first ones to criticize utopianism. If I am not mistaken, Marx and his followers were the first to scrutinize critically this phenomenon. As you may recall, utopian socialists and left-wing Hegelians claimed that, since men's ideas are the foundation of the social order, to change the social structure you must change consciousness. For Marx this was nonsense.

Society, Marx maintained, is not a product of men's ideas. History is a self-enclosed structure that is determined and made to change by the material, economic relationships between men (classes). Far from being a dynamic force that brings about social change, ideas are nothing more than reflexes of the modes of economic relationships that determine the lives of men. Utopias, no matter how beautiful, are forms of false consciousness, because they ignore the elements that really force society to change: the inner contradictions of reality. Thought and will, thus, are not creative. "It is totally irrelevant what this proletarian or even the whole proletariat directly imagines," remarked Marx. "What matters is *what is* and what one will have to do because of this reality."

Imagination must be displaced by science, dreams by analysis, our wishes by an objective understanding of the historical processes. The essence of Marxist science, accordingly, is "the knowledge of the independence of the forces that actually move history vis-à-vis the psychic consciousness that men might have of them." This is the basic dogma of *all* forms of realism.

Freud did not deal with utopias directly. But on the level of its "silent agreements," psychoanalysis is radically antiutopian also. For Freud the magician and the neurotic are possessed by the same kind of illusion, which makes them fall prey to the utopian consciousness. They all want to abolish reality by the power of imagination. The utopian dreamer ignores the iron determinism of the economic reality. The magician and the neurotic ignore the fact that the reality principle is deaf to the aspirations of the pleasure principle. Since the way out of utopian illusions is science for Marxism, the way out of neurosis is "education for reality." One has to become a realist. And the scientist is the model of the man who has understood and accepted the folly of all utopian dreams.

The antiutopian elements of Marxism and of psychoanalysis are not just a historical coincidence. They agree in their conclusions because they are silently agreed in their starting point. They both emerge out of the positivist spirit of the nineteenth century. They both agree that "imagination has to be subjected to observation" (Comte): thought must be a reflex of what is objectively given. Thus the psychoanalytic ideal of adjustment and the epistemological ideal of objectivity are different forms of the same "silent agreement."

As we start analyzing these common background assumptions, however, we discover that they are expressions of a deeper metaphysical assumption, viz., that social processes have the same autonomy as natural processes and that, therefore, they are independent of our will and imagination. The true spirit of positivism, in Comte's words, "is the general dogma of the invariability of physical laws." This is the starting point for our understanding of social reality. "This will be done," he said, "through the basic interpretation that social movement is necessarily subject to invariant physical laws, instead of being governed by some kind of will." Thus, if one wants to understand society, Durkheim wrote, "the first and most fundamental rule is: Consider social facts as things." This conclusion is necessary. If the social system is autonomous, self-propelling, and independent of will, we may as well ignore as irrelevant all our subjective states. We are entrapped in a philosophical and methodological antihumanism. If the iron determinism of the social reality cannot be broken by men, then for one to understand *reality* it is necessary to suspend man in a sort of parenthesis.

Where do these assumptions lead us? Once one believes in the autonomy of the social system, one is naturally *programmed* to think about the future in futurological, pragmatic terms. *The limits of the future are determined by the structure of the present.* Starting from what is now, one may envisage a better, improved, stronger version of the present. But it will be only *a new model* — just like our cars.

There are no ways out. The system that was once created by men now dead becomes, by means of a magical transformation, a reified reality similar to nature. We are doomed to live the rest of our lives imprisoned in it, although we may eventually reorganize the furniture inside.

Christian realism accepted the basic axioms of positivism, with a slight modification. Drawing on the doctrine of sin, it identified utopian thinking with sinful thinking. Thus, it does not say that utopian thinking is only mistaken or neurotic; it says that it is a projection of man's sinful nature and an expression of his drive for an absolute. Utopias do not lead to liberation as they promise but to worse forms of oppression and slavery. Since all efforts to go beyond the system are doomed to produce results that are far more evil than those found within it, the best thing is to stick to the system and try to improve it by means of pragmatic procedures — checks and balances.

As Mannheim once put it, pragmatism is a way of asking questions:

"How can I do this? How can I solve this concrete problem?" In all these questions we sense the fatalistic undertone: It is useless to worry about the whole because it cannot be abolished anyway. What one totally overlooks, according to Mannheim, is that "whoever criticizes details becomes, by means of this very criticism, a prisoner of the world as it is."

Examining "Silent Agreements"

What are the "silent agreements" found behind utopian thought?

1. Let me say, first, that Christian utopianism (and I use this expression in a positive sense) is not a belief in the possibility of a perfect society but rather the belief in the nonnecessity of *this* imperfect order. It does not claim that it is possible to abolish sin, but it affirms that there is no reason for us to accept the rule of the sinful structures that now control our society.

2. Second, I want to point out that Christian utopianism understands that what we call "reality" is a human construction (see Peter Berger and Thomas Luckmann's *The Social Construction of Reality*). It exists as a reality not because of a divine or demonic necessity but because men and the past built it. And since reality is a human construction, it can be demolished by men in order to build a new one. Whenever we call a provisional social game built by men reality we are involved in idolatry: we are giving ultimacy — demonic or divine — to something that is simply human and not destined to eternity.

3. Mannheim once remarked that it is always the representatives of a certain order of things who despise certain types of transcendent thought as being utopian and impossible to be realized. And indeed, from within their own presupposition, they are correct. As one takes a certain social order for granted, a rather large number of possibilities become impossibilities. Peace is a utopian dream in a society structured in terms of functions. The categories "impossibility" and "utopian," thus, are not absolute but relative to the systems they want to transcend. When a system despises certain ideas as being utopian or incapable of realization, it says very little about the real possibility or impossibility of these ideas, but it definitely makes a confession of its own limitations.

Christian utopianism is based on the vision that all social systems are under God's historical judgment. Sooner or later they will die. If this is the case, it is a serious mistake to take these same systems as the ultimate criteria for what is possible and impossible in history. Why should men's mistakes determine the scope of what the future can bring? Are we prisoners of the past? If God has chosen things that are not to overthrow the existing order (1 Cor. 1:19), and if he "summons things that are not yet in existence as if they already were" (Rom. 4:17), then it seems necessary to think of the real as unreal and the presently unreal as real.

Thus, history — at least from the biblical perspective — can never be seen as self-enclosed. It is open to surprise. It seems to me that what is at stake in the conflict between realism and utopianism is the way we read our Bibles. One alternative is to take the positivistic ideology as the ultimate horizon that provides the perspective for our thought, action, and reading of the Bible. The other alternative is to understand the claims of ultimacy of social reality as against the biblical horizon. Realism's revolt against utopias is a sign that it participates in the revolt against transcendence that characterizes Western civilization. It proceeds, accordingly, to de-utopianize the Bible, with the help of positivistic canons. Utopianism, on the contrary, believes that somehow, somewhere, God is doing his thing: he is overthrowing the existing order. Therefore, it is necessary to debunk our man-made realities.

Let me return to something I mentioned in the beginning. What amazed me as I read this article was that Christian realism, with its special delight in words like "ambiguous" and "ambivalent," should have such an unambiguous and unambivalent certainty about itself. True, utopias very often become illusions, but is realism free, or freer, from this danger? The evidence is contrary. It is not by accident that there is a portrait of John Foster Dulles, the ideologue of the cold war, at Union Theological Seminary, the stronghold of realism.

"Realism" and "pragmatism" are words dear to American ears, hearts, and brains. If this is so, anyone who is involved in social analysis should suspect at once that realism is functional to the system, contributes to its preservation, and gives it ideological and theological justification. This is the source of my irritation. Realism has not yet recognized that it is an American ideology and yet proceeds to pass universal judgment over the other "regional" theologies.

Confronting Bias and Superiority

When I read the *C&C* article with sensitive eyes I was struck by its point of departure: the theology of liberation is a regional, Latin American phenomenon: "The theology of liberation is the most recent and important attempt *by Latin American Christians* to relate current theological perspectives to ethical responsibility for many problems of *their region*." It "is the product of a long evolution in the definition by Catholics of their role *in Latin America*." "The desire of Christians, many of them youthful, to participate in movements of social change was accompanied by efforts at *working out a theological justification for their action*." "A better explanation [for the emergence of such a movement] seems to be that the religious outlook on reality lends itself to a *'moralistic' ideology in utopian form* as a *reaction* to a legalistic and conservative ethic. . . . " (Italics added.) In short: this is an ideological production, with theological pretensions, that has to do with a limited region of our globe.

My friend Gustavo Gutiérrez-Merino told me a few months ago that Anglo-Saxon theologians have always claimed universality for their theologies. And this is true. I do not know of a single theological work from that part of the world that was humble enough to recognize its limitations. But now, as they are pushed against the wall by Latin American thinkers, they are willing to make concessions: "Well, it is true, Latin Americans *also* do theology. But *Latin American theology* . . . it does not have any bearing on our traditional, scholarly and detached ways of thinking about the world." And then Gustavo added: "I will not allow them to get off the hook."

Maybe what we have been saying as Latin Americans has a number of distortions. But we definitely claim that what we say has a number of universal and ecumenical implications, and that you North Americans cannot simply go on "doing your thing" as if our theology were a simple domestic game. We make truth claims for our theology. And when we say this we are saying that the traditional ways of doing theology must recognize their ideological bias, their rather unambiguous relationships with colonialism, racism, and economic exploitation. We believe that your theology to a great degree — although it does not want to recognize this — is part of cultural imperialism.

I find it rather irritating that the author of the *C & C* article, since he was so sure of the ideological functions of Christian utopianism, was not willing to pay attention to its biblical grounds (which obviously need further corrections). And this is coupled with a sort of moral sense of superiority toward the immature and underdeveloped theologians of the South. "Latin American Christianity has passed through these creative but painful experiences during the past decade," says the author. And he adds: *"Just as North American Protestantism underwent them earlier in this century."* (Italics added.)

Yes, you North Americans are mature. You are ahead of us. We Latin Americans are adolescent. You have grown out of utopian illusions. We are, only now, going through the pains of growth. Do we not find here, in the most clear terms, the "silent agreement" on which most of you of the Wealthy World operate? "Only by detaching ourselves from moralistic dichotomies [such as those perpetuated by the theology of liberation] can we see Latin Americans as they are."

It is hard to swallow this. What do you mean? That the only way for us to understand Latin America is to adopt a North American way of looking at things? And after this shameless confession of superiority, *C & C*'s author states in absolute terms: "The church must operate in this framework," i.e., of Christian realism.

In the last instance it is up to the "decision makers" to make their decisions in a pragmatic, realistic way. It is sad — bordering on the ludicrous — to see how one can be so naive about the willingness of the decision makers to make decisions according to morality. Have you not heard of the Pentagon Papers? Of Watergate? Christian realists should read *Moral Man and Immoral Society*. Decision makers make decisions not because of moral sensibilities but because of the "realistic-pragmatic" need to preserve the balance of the system. Business must go on as usual.

What does it mean to be realistic and pragmatic here? It means to operate according to the logic of the system, which totally ignores morality. Realism and pragmatism, on the one hand, and morality, on the other, are self-excluding concepts. The former take as their context the need to preserve the system by means of checks and balances. Morality, meanwhile, ignores all pragmatic issues and is solely concerned with the will of God. This is why the wisdom of God is folly for men. And as we keep this in mind, we gladly accept your critique of Christian utopianism.

Christian Theology and the Afro-American Revolution

June 8, 1970

James H. Cone

James Cone is Briggs Distinguished Professor of Theology at Union Theological Seminary in New York City. His Black Theology and Black Power, *published in 1969, stands as the first systematic presentation of black theology and as a centerpiece of subsequent developments in U.S. liberation theologies.*

HOW IS the theological task related to the Afro-American revolution? It is not easy to answer this question. The difficulty of the task lies not so much in the immensity of the subject but, more importantly, in the seeming discontinuity between "blackness-revolution" and the gospel of Jesus. Black consciousness as experienced in Black Power is by definition revolutionary in white America — if by revolution we mean a sudden, radical, and complete change; or as Jürgen Moltmann puts it: "a transformation in the foundations of a system — whether of economics, of politics, of morality, or of religion."

In America "law and order" means obedience to the law of white people, and stability is nothing but the continuation of the present in the light of the past — defined and limited by George Washington, Abraham Lincoln, and Richard Nixon. Revolution, then, means anything that challenges the "sacredness" of the past, which is tantamount to usurping the rule of white oppressors. That is why J. Edgar Hoover describes the Black Panthers as the most serious internal threat to the American way of life.

For black people revolution means that blacks no longer accept the history of white people as the key to their existence in the future, and they are prepared to do what is necessary in order to assure that their present and future existence will be defined by black visions of reality. We believe, as Ernst Bloch puts it: "Things can be otherwise." That means things can also *become* otherwise: in the direction of evil, which must be avoided, or in the direction of good, which would have to be promoted." The Afro-American revolution involves tension between the actual and the possible, the "white-past" and the "black-future," and the black community accepting the responsibility of defining the world according to its "open possibilities."

The Church Sides with the Structures of Racism

Moltmann is right: "Truth is revolutionary," that is, truth involves "discovering that the world can be changed and that nothing has to remain as it has been." White people cannot share in this future reality as defined by the black revolution. Indeed, we blacks assume that the white position of unauthorized power as expressed in the racist character of every American institution — churches and seminaries not excluded! — renders white oppressors incapable of understanding what black humanity is; and it is thus incumbent upon us as black people to become "revolutionaries for blackness," rebelling against all who enslave us. With Marcus Garvey, we say: "Any sane man, race or nation that desires freedom must first of all think in terms of blood."

In contrast to the revolutionary implications of Black Power, Christianity usually is not thought of as being involved in revolutionary change. Speaking to Italian workers, Pope Pius XII said in 1943:

Salvation and justice are not to be found in revolution but in evolution through concord. Violence has always achieved only destruction, not construction; the kindling of passions, not their pacification; the accumulation of hate and ruin, not the reconciliation of the contending parties. And it has reduced men and parties to the difficult task of rebuilding, after sad experience, on the ruins of discord.

In a similar vein Pope John XXIII wrote: "It must be borne in mind that to proceed gradually is the law of life in all its expressions; therefore in human institutions, too, it is not possible to renovate for the better except by working from within them, gradually...."

Certainly the white churches' (Catholic and Protestant alike) response to the Afro-American revolution, especially the rebellion in the cities, is in character with the pope's comments. It seems that the most "radical" comment coming from the white churches is: "We deplore the violence but sympathize with the reasons for the violence" — which is equivalent to saying, "Of course we raped your women, dehumanized your men, and ghettoized the minds of your children, and you have a right to be upset; but that is no reason for you to burn our buildings. If you people keep acting like that, we will never give you your freedom."

Christians, unfortunately, are not known for their revolutionary actions. For the most part, the chief exponents of the Christian tradition (at least since Constantine) have been identified primarily with the structures of power and only secondarily with the victims of power. This perhaps explains why white Christians in America tend to think of "love" as an absence of power and "reconciliation" as being indifferent to justice. It certainly accounts for the inauspicious distinction made between violence and force: "The state is invested with force; it is an organism instituted and ordained by God, and remains such even when it is unjust; even its harshest acts are not the same thing as the angry or brutal deed of the individual. The individual surrenders his passions, he commits violence." (This is from Jacques Ellul's *Violence* and is the explication of a viewpoint he does not hold personally.)

True, not all Christians have defended this perspective. The Protestant Reformation in the sixteenth century — to a limited degree — was a deviation, especially the so-called left wing tradition. Prominent examples in our century are Reinhold Niebuhr's *Moral Man and Immoral Society*, the Confessing Church in Hitler's Germany, and particularly the noble example of Dietrich Bonhoeffer.

We have already mentioned Moltmann, and we could name other European theologians who are participating in the Marxist-Christian dialogue, relating theology to revolutionary change. (*Openings for Marxist-Christian Dialogue*, edited by Thomas Ogletree, presents an account of this dialogue.) In the United States Richard Shaull and Paul Lehmann have been defining the theological task according to the "politics of God," emphasizing the divine participation in the "messianic movements dedicated to the liberation of man from all that enslaves and dehumanizes him."

Unfortunately, these examples are exceptions and not the rule. In America, at least, the Christian tradition is identified with the structures of racism in their oppression of black people. This was the reason for the white church's compliance with black slavery, its subsequent indifference to oppression generally, and its failure to respond to the authentic demands of black reparations.

No white theologian has taken the oppression of black people as a point of departure for analyzing the meaning of the gospel today. Apparently white theologians see no connection between blackness and the gospel of Jesus Christ. Even the so-called white American "theologians of revolution" did not receive their motivation from an identification with black Americans but from Latin America, Vietnam, and other foreign lands. I do not want to minimize their theological endeavors or question the authenticity of their verbalized identification with the poor, "underdeveloped" nations, but I believe, as Sartre puts it: "The only way of helping the enslaved out there is to take sides with those who are here."

Liberation and the Biblical Tradition

What, then, is the answer to the question: What relevance has theology to the oppressed blacks of America? Since whites have ignored this question, it is necessary to look beyond the white Christian tradition to the biblical tradition, investigating the latter in the light of the past and present manifestation of the black struggle for liberation.

Taking seriously the tradition of the Old and New Testaments and the past and present Afro-American revolution, the *black* theological perspective contends that the content of Christian theology is *liberation*. This means that theology is a rational and passionate study of the revolutionary activity of God in the world in the light of the historical situation of an oppressed community, relating the forces of liberation to the essence of the gospel, which is Jesus Christ. Theology so defined moves us in the direction of the biblical tradition, which focuses on the activity of God in history, liberating people from human bondage.

God, according to the Bible, is known by what he does, and what he does is always related to the liberation of the oppressed. This is the meaning of the Exodus, the Covenant at Sinai, the conquest and settlement of Palestine, the United Kingdom and its division, the rise of the great prophets and the second exodus from Babylon. This is also the reason for God's incarnate appearance in Jesus and his willingness (through the cross) to take upon himself all human oppression and sin.

The resurrection of Jesus means that God is not defeated by oppression but transforms it into possibilities of liberation. People can now be what they are — liberated humans. With liberation as the essence of the Christian gospel, it becomes impossible to speak of the God of Hebrew history, who is the God revealed in Jesus Christ, without recognizing that he is the God *of* and *for* those who labor and are heavy laden.

The emphasis on liberation not only leads us to the heart of the

biblical message, but also enables theology to say something relevant to the black revolution in America. The liberation theme relates
Black Power to the Christian gospel; it renders as an untruth the
unverbalized white assumption that Christ is white, or that being
Christian means that black people ought to turn the other cheek —
as if we blacks have no moral right to defend ourselves from the
encroachments of white people.

New Theological Sources

To explicate the meaning of God's activity as revealed in the liberation
of the oppressed blacks of America means that the theologian must
lose his identity with the white structure and become unqualifiedly
identified with the wretched of this land. It means that there can be no
authentic Christian talk unless it focuses on the empowerment of the
poor — defined and limited by their past, present, and future history.

If God is truly the God of the weak and helpless, then we must
critically reevaluate the history of theology in America, a theology
that owes more to white oppressors than oppressed blacks or Indians. What about Gabriel Prosser, Denmark Vesey, and Nat Turner as
theological sources for assessing the contemporary presence of Christ?
Could it be that American theologians can best understand their task
by studying LeRoi Jones, Malcolm X, or the Black Panthers rather than
merely mouthing the recent rhetoric of German theologians? Hopefully, the rise of black theology will force American religionists to
realize that no theology of the Christian gospel is possible that ignores
the reality of the divine among black people in this country.

Black Theology vs. Feminist Theology

April 15, 1974

Rosemary Ruether

Rosemary Radford Ruether, a contributing editor of C & C, *is Georgia Harkness Professor
of Theology at Garrett-Evangelical Theological Seminary in Evanston. One of the foremost
feminist theologians of the time, she was trained in church history and historical theology
and has published widely on feminism, the Christian roots of anti-Semitism, and the
situation of the Palestinians.*

THE TWO MOST IMPORTANT expressions of liberation theology
to emerge from the American experience in the late 1960s are black
theology and feminist theology. Unfortunately, an undeclared war is
brewing between them. First white male-dominated seminaries across

the country adjusted their self-absolutizing perspective slightly to find a few crumbs for black studies. More recently they divided these crumbs even further to create a parallel corner for women's studies. Thereby these two expressions of criticism of the dominant social context of theological education have been set up to compete with each other.

The black caucuses, appearing a year or two earlier than the women's groups, have generally denied reciprocal solidarity with the women's movement. The second women's movement, like the first, arose as women working for black liberation began to address the issues of their own liberation. Initially women analyzed their own oppression by comparing it to racism. Then, finding their own concern scorned by blacks, they withdrew in hurt alienation.

Are blacks correct in denying solidarity with the women's movement, and are feminists specious in comparing sexism to racism? I would argue that historically racism and sexism have been interrelated but not exactly "parallel." Rather, they have been interstructural elements of oppression within the overarching system of domination by white males.

Moreover, this interstructuring has the effect of alienating white women, black women, and black men from each other. Each group tends to suppress the experience of its racial and/or sexual counterpart. The black movement constantly talks as though "blacks" means black males. The women's movement fails to integrate the experience of poor and nonwhite women. Much of what it means by the "female experience" is in fact class-bound, restricted to the experience of a fairly atypical group of white, usually childless, women who are blocked in their efforts to break into the bastions of white, male, upper-class privilege.

We must understand these oppositions in order to understand the complexity of the interpenetration of racism and sexism in a class society.

Black Theology: Sexist?

James Cone is the most notable of the younger, militant black theologians. He appears to reject any coordination between black theology and women. Cone has declared that women are not a "people" and do not have a "church," implying that they cannot be a liberation movement. Recently he has indicated to this author that he does not negate the women's movement as a legitimate liberation struggle. Nevertheless, he has come to symbolize for the women's movement the pervasive rebuff by black caucuses. Why this tension?

The tension arises not because sexism is irrelevant to black "manhood" but because it is all too uncomfortably relevant. However, this does not make black men male chauvinists in the same way as white men. Rather, the hostility springs from the humiliation of the black male at the hands of white males.

A white southern churchwomen recently sketched for me a model of the racist-sexist system of classical southern society. In this system the white, upper-class male ruled supreme. He dominated a society divided by sex, class, and race. White females and black females were made the opposite sides of each other. The white woman was the dependent ornament in the parlor; the black woman was exploited for sex and work in the kitchen.

The black male was at the bottom, reduced to an asexual beast of burden, denied any self-affirmation through sexual identity. It is this unnameable humiliation that rankles behind the inability of the black (male) movement in America to deal with sexism.

This situation has meant that the black church generally has played a different role in the sexual identity of the black minister than in that of the white minister. The white minister is often thrown into a confused posture toward his maleness. This is because white society considers religion and morality "feminine."

The black church has functioned in the opposite way. It was the one institution run and owned by the black community. It was their one place of public, corporate self-affirmation, the seedbed of whatever training was available for black politics and organizational development. In a society where black maleness was marginalized and placed under constant threat of "castration" (literally as well as figuratively) by the dominant sexist-racist society, the black minister became the one true "man" of the black community, the surrogate patriarch for a scorned manliness.

Functioning as a compensatory patriarchal figure for the whole community, the minister often became superpatriarchal, a symbol of pride for his people to whom they could transfer the privileges denied to them.

Black women have recently tried to challenge the tendency to make them the victims of this development of black manliness. They have tried to suggest that the strength of the black woman under oppression should be regarded with pride, not humiliation, as a part of the black experience. They have suggested that this strength makes possible an alternate paradigm for black male-female relations: They need not be patterned after white male dominance but can be truly reciprocal and mutually enhancing.

In the writings of black women one glimpses their fundamental experience of functioning as the "reality principle" for the entire race. They not only upheld the economic viability of the family unit, giving strength to the new generation, but also bore the ego frustration of the black man. This experience grows the more bitter when the black woman finds herself rejected precisely at the moment when she feels compelled to reject the "feminine" role in order to assert her truthful character as the "reality principle."

The black man, in turn, is constantly pulled after the white woman, who represents the illusionary "feminine" and the forbidden fruits of sexual dominance. No wonder these groups are constantly tempted to turn on each other — the black man blaming the black woman, the black woman blaming the white woman, the white woman reacting in a hurt alienation that could change into a racist reaction — instead of recognizing that despite the outwardly different conditions they share a common victimization under the superstructure of white patriarchy.

Black Theology: Middle Class?

In addition to representing the aspiration of the black community for "manliness," the black church has also been the traditional path toward the *embourgeoisement* of the black community. Consequently, it also has had the tendency to lose contact with the actual condition of the masses and become an enclave of "respectability," alienated and threatened by the chaotic conditions of the impoverished blacks, especially in the northern city. The black masses, therefore, have often turned toward cultic, and even anti-Christian, movements to express their own experience of oppression. They have vilified the black minister — respected as the "proper" spokesman for the black community by whites — as a "crook" and an Uncle Tom.

The lower class has developed its own ways of affirming its different experience of sexuality. It is more comfortable with the non-bourgeois family patterns so deplored by Patrick Moynihan. This pattern is incorrectly described as "matriarchy," since the woman is hardly "dominant" in the usual sense of that word. But there is an autonomy and reciprocity quite different from the standard bourgeois model. Ultimately it is the woman who stands firm. She is the "ground of being" of the people in a way that finds its ambivalent celebration. Even as she is decried for her "lip," it is this toughness and realism that is the foundation of black survival. "Motherfucker" is a constant taunt, because it is also the most serious insult possible.

The tension between black churchmen and the women's movement, then, seems to represent the defensive perspective of the black, middle-class, patriarchal church. It concentrates on confronting the racism of its counterparts in the white church. But it has not yet opened itself up to the disturbing countertrends in the lower-class black community that not only conflict with bourgeois male and female stereotypes but also are alienated from middle-class values and the Christian identity as well.

The Limits of "Black Caucus Theology"

These remarks do not discredit the validity of the theology being done by Cone in a particular context. His theology is an effective and appropriate instrument for its primary task. I would call this "black caucus theology." By this I mean that it is shaped to function in a confrontational fashion within a white power base. It places demands of conscience on white power and seeks to appropriate its advantages for the training of black leadership. But contrary to what Cone himself often declares, I think his kind of theology primarily addresses *white* people. Its content originally was little penetrated by the spirit of the black experience as an alternate source of theological themes. Its substance was taken from German dialectical theology, something Cone has continually defended as appropriate. He has essentially turned white theology upside down in order to reveal its hidden racist ideology.

Cone's prophetic reversal of white theology remains too vaguely "universalist" for the concrete tasks of a radical black church. It may be inadequate for the integral self-development of the black community itself, i.e., as black theology for black people.

The black community needs the transfer of power and skills from white institutions. What is still not evident is whether this power and these skills will really be transferred. One wonders whether black caucuses are not being led in the centrifugal path of the black middle class in militant disguise. The new willingness of white society to promote the skilled black person to full citizenship creates the possibility of disenfranchising this leadership group from the poor black community. We are beguiled into thinking that racism is overcome because a small elite gains new visibility and honor. We are prevented from seeing that the black masses in the ghettos are experiencing a worsening condition that they can no longer tolerate.

A relevant black church must perhaps become far more integrally black if it is to address itself to this situation. It must transform itself to overcome the split between the bourgeois black church and the unchurched black masses. It must become more like the Black Muslims or the Garveyite movements in the sense of focusing on building communal structures of social cooperation by and for blacks within the black community itself. It must take the initiative, in a vast movement of new morale, in transferring resources from white society and building resources from within the black community to transform the "ghetto" from a place of deprivation to a place of positive black communal expression and development.

The symbols that the black church inherited from evangelical Christianity may be too limited for this task. It may have to reach much more toward "soul," toward symbols developed by blacks alienated from the church, and also toward the Caribbean and Africa to find a "blackness" that is not simply antiwhite but can rejoice in itself. Perhaps only Mother Africa can provide some symbols that the uprooted, stolen people cannot derive from the goodness of slavery: symbols for the soul-self, for the goodness of the body-self, for the integration of humankind in nature, the rootedness of peoplehood in the land.

Feminist Theology: Elitist?

The development of women's caucuses in seminaries and feminist theology, parallel to that of the black movement, is a phenomenon of the last few years. However, already there is evidence that women's caucuses may be creating a social encapsulation similar to that of black caucuses. This encapsulation, moreover, has social roots in the history of white feminism in America.

The women's movement in America arose in the 1830s among southern elite and New England Brahmin women turned abolitionists. Its concept of the oppression of women was fueled by its sympathy with the antislavery cause. When the Fourteenth Amendment enfranchised the black male and excluded women, the more militant thought the amendment should be rejected until it included both race and sex. Thereafter they acquiesced in the increasing drift of the women's movement away from equalitarian views toward a racist and class bias.

As the women's movement became a mass movement in the 1880s, it was influenced by the general abandonment of romantic heroic reformism for a racist social Darwinism. Increasingly the movement drifted toward a view that women should be enfranchised in order to double the vote of the white, Protestant middle class and thereby assure the supremacy of this ruling class over the rising tide of blacks and immigrant Catholics and Jews. It thereby also took for granted the de facto reversal of the Fourteenth Amendment in the Jim Crow laws.

At the same time the women's movement backed away from its earlier radical confrontation with the stereotypes of masculinity and femininity and the place of the woman in the home. Instead it accepted the stereotype of the feminine "lady," whose beneficent role in the home should now shine forth into the public arena.

The new women's movement of the 1960s also arose out of an alliance with and, then, a traumatic experience of rejection by the black civil rights and white male radical movements. It has typically sought to go beyond the limits of the old women's movement and to challenge the stereotypes of the feminine and the sexual relations of male and female in home and society. It seems little disposed, therefore, to fall for a new version of the "white lady" myth. Yet its alienation from other radical movements, especially black liberation, and its recourse to a kind of "separatist" ideology — that talks about the oppression of women as more basic than any other form of oppression in a way that makes women a separate cause unrelated to other kinds of oppression — may be working its own kind of subtle social encapsulation.

This separatist concept helps to obscure the way in which the oppression of women is structurally integrated with that of class and race. Sociologically, women are a sexual caste within every class and race. They share a common condition of women: dependency, secondary existence, domestic labor, sexual exploitation, and the projection of their role in procreation into a total definition of their existence.

But this common condition takes profoundly different forms as women are divided against each other by class and race. No woman of an oppressed class and race, therefore, can separate her female struggle from its context in the liberation of her own community.

Women of the elite class and race easily fall into an abstract analysis of women's oppressed status that they believe will unite *all* women. They ignore their own context of class and race privilege. Their movement fails to connect with women of oppressed groups, and it becomes defiled by a demand for "rights" commensurate with the males of their group, oblivious to the unjust racist and class context of these privileges. It may not be wrong to seek such "equality," but it is dangerous to allow the ideology of the women's movement to remain confined to this perspective.

Feminist Theology: Antifemale?

Theology done in the context of women's caucuses in elite universities tends also to be alienated from the experience of most women. Motherhood is a negative trip. The elite woman, who competes with the career pattern of the elite male, is subverted at the point of her capacity to have children. She is usually forced to choose between the two. Absolutized, however, this perspective on motherhood really accepts the "phallic morality" (to use Mary Daly's phrase) that women have decried. It accepts a feminist antifemaleness that loathes women at the point of the specificity of female difference.

Maternity has been the root of female oppression because it represents the one power that men do not have and upon which all men depend for their existence. Not to be able to rescue maternity as a positive symbol for women in a way that can be liberating is really a capitulation to the male false consciousness that tries to convert female potency into the female weakness through which women are subjugated. Sexism cannot be understood, historically or psychologically, unless it is recognized that it rests not on female weakness but on the suppression of female power. Sexism is an elaborate system of handicaps that males erect around women to make female potency appear to be the point of their weakness and dependency, thereby suppressing from cultural consciousness the truth of male dependency. Women who strive for an equality by accepting this male negation of the female remain encapsulated in male false consciousness.

Women's liberation will gain general support from women only when it can be revealed as a necessity that also expresses the mandate of the woman as the foundation of the survival of the race. Male false consciousness has created an antagonistic concept of self and social and ecological relations that is rapidly destroying humankind and the earth. Not only have the personhood and cultural gifts of women been suppressed by this, but males themselves have been allowed to remain in an adolescent form of vainglorious psychology that is no longer compatible with human survival.

Women must reject male chauvinism at the point of the oppression of their own personhood and autonomy. But they must also reject it at the point of motherhood for the sake of the survival of their children. It is at this point that the dialogue between white feminism and black feminism is vital. Black women inevitably ground a militant feminism not only in their liberation as persons but also in the validation of woman as mother, fighting for the survival of her children.

The history of white male chauvinism, with its interstructuring of sexism and racism, is bent on alienating black women and white women and making their contrary experiences incommunicable to each other. When black and white women can penetrate each other's experience and recognize each other as common victims of a total structure of white male domination, this will be the moral victory that will cut the gordian knot of white male dominance. An independent black feminism that can articulate the distinctive character of the black female experience in a way that can reveal this total structure of oppression, then, is the essential element that is needed to cut through the mystifications of white male power that set the three subordinate groups against each other.

Perhaps only black feminism can give us a strong image of womanhood before patriarchy reduced it to shattered fragments. The white patriarchal God has alienated us from our bodies, each other, and the earth. The black patriarchal God is prophetic on the side of the oppressed. He represents the transcendent Almighty who assures the weak that there is a power in heaven stronger than the mighty on earth. But absolutized, he promises more apocalyptic warfare in reverse. The white lady of Mariology always lands woman on her knees before her "divine Son" as the sublimated, and the sexually alienated, servant of the male ego.

One needs to glimpse again the primordial power of the mother-symbol as Ground of Being to restore an ontological foundation to the "wholly other" God of patriarchy. The Christian effort to over-come gnosticism and apocalypticism and to integrate the God of the messianic future with the divine Ground of Being failed because it continued to be based on the patriarchal denigration of the female. Only a regrounding of the power of the future within the power of the primordial matrix can refound the lost covenant with nature and give us a theology for the redemption of the earth.

Womanist Theology: Black Women's Voices

March 2, 1987

Delores S. Williams

Delores Williams is associate professor of theology and culture at Union Theological Seminary in New York City and a contributing editor of C & C. She is known especially for her articulation of womanist theology, a perspective defined in relationship with but differently from feminist and black theologies.

DAUGHTER: Mama, why are we brown, pink, and yellow, and our cousins are white, beige, and black?

MOTHER: Well, you know the colored race is just like a flower garden, with every color flower represented.

DAUGHTER: Mama, I'm walking to Canada and I'm taking you and a bunch of slaves with me.

MOTHER: It wouldn't be the first time.

In these two conversational exchanges, Pulitzer Prize–winning novel-ist Alice Walker begins to show us what she means by the concept "womanist." The concept is presented in Walker's *In Search of Our Mother's Gardens*, and many women in church and society have appropriated it as a way of affirming themselves as *black* while si-multaneously owning their connection with feminism and with the Afro-American community, male and female. The concept of woman-ist allows women to claim their roots in black history, religion, and culture.

What then is a womanist? Her origins are in the black folk expres-sion "You acting womanish," meaning, according to Walker, "wanting to know more and in greater depth than is good for one . . . outrageous, audacious, courageous and willful behavior." A womanist is also "responsible, in charge, serious." She can walk to Canada and take others with her. She loves, she is committed, she is a universalist by temperament.

Her universality includes loving men and woman, sexually or nonsexually. She loves music, dance, the spirit, food and roundness, struggle, and she loves herself. "Regardless."

Walker insists that a womanist is also "committed to survival and wholeness of entire people, male and female." She is no separatist, "except for health." A womanist is a black feminist or feminist of color. Or as Walker says, "Womanist is to feminist as purple to lavender."

Womanist theology, a vision in its infancy, is emerging among Afro-American Christian women. Ultimately many sources — biblical, theological, ecclesiastical, social, anthropological, economic, and material from other religious traditions — will inform the development of this theology. As a contribution to this process, I will demonstrate how Walker's concept of womanist provides some significant clues for the work of womanist theologians. I will then focus on method and God-content in womanist theology. This contribution belongs to the work of prolegomena — prefatory remarks, introductory observations intended to be suggestive and not conclusive.

Codes and Contents

In her definition, Walker provides significant clues for the development of womanist theology. Her concept contains what black feminist scholar Bell Hooks in *From Margin to Center* identifies as cultural codes. These are words, beliefs, and behavioral patterns of a people that must be deciphered before meaningful communication can happen cross-culturally. Walker's codes are female-centered and they point beyond themselves to conditions, events, meanings, and values that have crystallized in the Afro-American community *around women's activity* and formed traditions.

A paramount example is mother-daughter advice: Black mothers have passed on wisdom for survival — in the white world, in the black community, and with men — for as long as anyone can remember. Female slave narratives, folk tales, and some contemporary black poetry and prose reflect this tradition. Some of it is collected in "Old Sister's Advice to Her Daughters," in *The Book of Negro Folklore*, edited by Langston Hughes and Arna Bontemps (Dodd Mead, 1958).

Walker's allusion to skin color points to a historic tradition of tension between black women over the matter of some black men's preference for light-skinned women. Her reference to black women's love of food and roundness points to customs of female care in the black community (including the church) associated with hospitality and nurture.

These cultural codes and their corresponding traditions are valuable resources for indicating and validating the kind of data upon which womanist theologians can reflect as they bring black women's social, religious, and cultural experience into the discourse of theology, ethics, biblical and religious studies. Female slave narratives, imaginative literature by black women, autobiographies, the work by black women in academic disciplines, and the testimonies of black church women will be authoritative sources for womanist theologians.

Walker situates her understanding of a womanist in the context of nonbourgeois black folk culture. The literature of this culture has traditionally reflected more egalitarian relations between men and women, much less rigidity in male-female roles, and more respect for female intelligence and ingenuity than is found in bourgeois culture.

The black folk are poor. Less individualistic than those who are better off, they have, for generations, practiced various forms of economic sharing. For example, immediately after Emancipation mutual aid societies pooled the resources of black folk to help pay for funerals and other daily expenses. *The Book of Negro Folklore* describes the practice of rent parties which flourished during the Depression. The black folk stressed togetherness and a closer connection with nature. They respect knowledge gained through lived experience monitored by elders who differ profoundly in social class and worldview from the teachers and education encountered in American academic institutions. Walker's choice of context suggests that womanist theology can establish its lines of continuity in the black community with nonbourgeois traditions less sexist than the black power and black nationalist traditions.

In this folk context, some of the black female-centered cultural codes in Walker's definition (e.g., "Mama, I'm walking to Canada and I'm taking you and a bunch of slaves with me") point to folk heroines like Harriet Tubman, whose liberation activity earned her the name "Moses" of her people. This allusion to Tubman directs womanist memory to a liberation tradition in black history in which women took the lead, acting as catalysts for the community's revolutionary action and for social change. Retrieving this often hidden or diminished female tradition of catalytic action is an important task for womanist theologians and ethicists. Their research may well reveal that female models of authority have been absolutely essential for every struggle in the black community and for building and maintaining the community's institutions.

Freedom Fighters

The womanist theologian must search for the voices, actions, opinions, experience, and faith of women whose names sometimes slip into the male-centered rendering of black history, but whose actual stories remain remote. This search can lead to such little-known freedom fighters as Milla Granson and her courageous work on a Mississippi plantation. Her liberation method broadens our knowledge of the variety of strategies black people have used to obtain freedom. According to scholar Sylvia Dannett, in *Profiles in Negro Womanhood:*

Milla Granson, a slave, conducted a midnight school for several years. She had been taught to read and write by her former master in Kentucky...and in her little school hundreds of slaves benefited from her learning....After laboring all day for their master, the slaves would creep stealthily to Milla's "schoolroom" (a little cabin in a back alley)....The doors and windows... had to be kept tightly sealed to avoid discovery. Each class was composed of twelve pupils and when Milla had brought them up to the extent of her ability, she "graduated" them and took in a dozen more. Through this means she graduated hundreds of slaves. Many of whom she taught to write a legible hand [forged] their own passes and set out for Canada.

Women like Tubman and Granson used subtle and silent strategies to liberate themselves and large numbers of black people. By uncovering as much as possible about such female liberation, the womanist begins to understand the relation of black history to the contemporary folk expression: "If Rosa Parks had not sat down, Martin King would not have stood up."

While she celebrates and *emphasizes* black women's culture and way of being in the world, Walker simultaneously affirms black women's historic connection with men through love and through a shared struggle for survival and for a productive quality of life (e.g., "wholeness"). This suggests that two of the principal concerns of womanist theology should be survival and community building and maintenance. The goal of this community building is, of course, to establish a positive quality of life — economic, spiritual, educational — for black women, men, and children. Walker's understanding of a womanist as "not a separatist" ("except for health"), however, reminds the Christian womanist theologian that her concern for community building and maintenance must *ultimately* extend to the entire Christian community and beyond that to the larger human community.

Yet womanist consciousness is also informed by women's determination to love themselves. "Regardless." This translates into an admonition to black women to avoid the self-destruction of bearing a disproportionately large burden in the work of community building and maintenance. Walker suggests that women can avoid this trap by connecting with women's communities concerned about women's rights and well-being. Her identification of a womanist as also a feminist joins black women with their feminist heritage extending back into the nineteenth century in the work of black feminists like Sojourner Truth, Frances W. Harper, and Mary Church Terrell.

In making the feminist-womanist connection, however, Walker proceeds with great caution. While affirming an organic relationship between womanists and feminists, she also declares a deep shade of difference between them ("Womanist is to feminist as purple to lavender.") This gives womanist scholars the freedom to explore the particularities of black women's history and culture without being guided by what white feminists have already identified as women's issues.

But womanist consciousness directs black women away from the negative divisions prohibiting community building among women. The womanist loves other women sexually and nonsexually. Therefore, respect for sexual preferences is one of the marks of womanist community. According to Walker, homophobia has no place. Nor does "Colorism" (i.e., "yella" and half-white black people valued more in the black world than black-skinned people), which often separates black women from each other. Rather, Walker's womanist claim is that color variety is the substance of universality. Color, like birth and death, is common to all people. Like the navel, it is a badge of humanity connecting people with people. Two other distinctions are prohibited in Walker's womanist thinking. Class hierarchy does not dwell among women who "... love struggle, love the Folks ... are committed to the survival and wholeness of an entire people." Nor do women compete for male attention when they "... appreciate and prefer female culture ... value ... women's emotional flexibility ... and women's strength."

The intimations about community provided by Walker's definition suggest no genuine community building is possible when men are excluded (except when women's health is at stake). Neither can it occur when black women's self-love, culture, and love for each other are not affirmed and are not considered vital for the community's self-understanding. And it is thwarted if black women are expected to bear "the lion's share" of the work and to sacrifice their well-being for the good of the group.

Yet, for the womanist, mothering and nurturing are vitally important. Walker's womanist reality begins with mothers relating to their children and is characterized by black women (not necessarily bearers of children) nurturing great numbers of black people in the liberation struggle (e.g., Harriet Tubman). Womanist emphasis upon the value of mothering and nurturing is consistent with the testimony of many black women. The poet Carolyn Rogers speaks of her mother as the great black bridge that brought her over. Walker dedicated her novel *The Third Life of Grange Copeland* to her mother "... who made a way out of no way." As a child in the black church, I heard women (and men) give thanks to God for their mothers "... who stayed behind and pulled the wagon over the long haul."

It seems, then, that the clues about community from Walker's definition of a womanist suggest that the mothering and nurturing dimension of Afro-American history can provide resources for shaping criteria to measure the quality of justice in the community. These criteria could be used to assure female-male equity in the presentation of the community's models of authority. They could also gauge the community's division of labor with regard to the survival tasks necessary for building and maintaining community.

Womanist Theology and Method

Womanist theology is already beginning to define the categories and methods needed to develop along lines consistent with the sources of that theology. Christian womanist theological methodology needs to be informed by at least four elements: (1) a multidialogical intent, (2) a liturgical intent, (3) a didactic intent, and (4) a commitment both to reason *and* to the validity of female imagery and metaphorical language in the construction of theological statements.

A multidialogical intent will allow Christian womanist theologians to advocate and participate in dialogue and action with *many* diverse social, political, and religious communities concerned about human survival and productive quality of life for the oppressed. The genocide of cultures and peoples (which has often been instigated and accomplished by Western white Christian groups or governments) and the nuclear threat of omnicide mandates womanist participation in such dialogue/action. But in this dialogue/action the womanist also should keep her speech and action focused upon the slow genocide of poor black women, children, and men by exploitative systems denying them productive jobs, education, health care, and living space. Multidialogical activity may, like a jazz symphony, communicate some of its most important messages in what the harmony-driven conventional ear hears as discord, as disruption of the harmony in both the black American and white American social, political, and religious status quo.

If womanist theological method is informed by a liturgical intent, then womanist theology will be relevant to (and will reflect) the thought, worship, and action of the black church. But a liturgical intent will also allow womanist theology to challenge the thought/worship/

action of the black church with the discordant and prophetic messages emerging from womanist participation in multidialogics. This means that womanist theology will consciously impact *critically* upon the foundations of liturgy, challenging the church to use justice principles to select the sources that will shape the content of liturgy. The question must be asked: "How does this source portray blackness/ darkness, women and economic justice for nonruling-class people?" A negative portrayal will demand omission of the source or its radical reformation by the black church. The Bible, a major source in black church liturgy, must also be subjected to the scrutiny of justice principles.

A didactic intent in womanist theological method assigns a teaching function to theology. Womanist theology should teach Christians new insights about moral life based on ethics supporting justice for women, survival, and a productive quality of life for poor women, children, and men. This means that the womanist theologian must give authoritative status to black folk wisdom (e.g., Brer Rabbit literature) and to black women's moral wisdom (expressed in their literature) when she responds to the question, "How ought the Christian to live in the world?" Certainly tensions may exist between the moral teachings derived from these sources and the moral teachings about obedience, love, and humility that have usually buttressed presuppositions about living the Christian life. Nevertheless, womanist theology, in its didactic intent, must teach the church the different ways God reveals prophetic word and action for Christian living.

These intents, informing theological method, can yield a theological language whose foundation depends as much upon its imagistic content as upon reason. The language can be rich in female imagery, metaphor, and story. For the black church, this kind of theological language may be quite useful, since the language of the black religious experience abounds in images and metaphors. Clifton Johnson's collection of black conversion experiences, *God Struck Me Dead*, illustrates this point.

The appropriateness of womanist theological language will ultimately reside in its ability to bring black women's history, culture, and religious experience into the interpretive circle of Christian theology and into the liturgical life of the church. Womanist theological language must, in this sense, be an instrument for social and theological change in church and society.

Who Do You Say God Is?

Regardless of one's hopes about intentionality and womanist theological method, questions must be raised about the God-content of the theology. Walker's mention of the black womanist's love of the spirit is a true reflection of the great respect Afro-American women have always shown for the presence and work of the spirit. In the black church, women (and men) often judge the effectiveness of the worship service not on the scholarly content of the sermon nor on the ritual nor on orderly process. Rather, worship has been effective if "the spirit was high," i.e., if the spirit was actively and obviously present in a balanced blend of prayer, of cadenced word (the sermon), and of syncopated music ministering to the pain of the people.

The importance of this emphasis upon the spirit is that it allows Christian womanist theologians, in their use of the Bible, to identify and reflect upon those biblical stories in which poor oppressed women had a special encounter with divine emissaries of God, like the spirit. In the Hebrew Testament, Hagar's story is most illustrative and relevant to Afro-American women's experience of bondage, of African heritage, of encounter with God/emissary in the midst of fierce survival struggles. Katie Cannon among a number of black female preachers and ethicists urges black Christian women to regard themselves as Hagar's sisters.

In relation to the Christian or New Testament, the Christian womanist theologian can refocus the salvation story so that it emphasizes the beginning of revelation with the spirit mounting Mary, a woman of the poor: "...the Holy Spirit shall come upon thee, and the power of the Highest shall overshadow thee..." (Luke 1:35). Such an interpretation of revelation has roots in nineteenth-century black abolitionist and feminist Sojourner Truth. Posing an important question and response, she refuted a white preacher's claim that women could not have rights equal to men's because Christ was not a woman. Truth asked, "Whar did your Christ come from?...From God and a woman! Man had nothin' to do wid Him!" This suggests that womanist theology could eventually speak of God in a well-developed theology of the spirit. The sources for this theology are many. Harriet Tubman often "went into the spirit" before her liberation missions and claimed her strength for liberation activity came from this way of meeting God. Womanist theology has grounds for shaping a theology of the spirit informed by black women's political action.

Christian womanist responses to the question "who do you say God is?" will be influenced by these many sources. Walker's way of connecting womanists with the spirit is only one clue. The integrity of black church women's faith, their love of Jesus, their commitment to life, love, family, and politics will also yield vital clues. And other theological voices (black liberation, feminist, Islamic, Asian, Hispanic, African, Jewish, and Western white male traditional) will provide insights relevant for the construction of the God-content of womanist theology.

Each womanist theologian will add her own special accent to the understandings of God emerging from womanist theology. But if one needs a final image to describe women coming together to shape the enterprise, Bess B. Johnson in *God's Fierce Whimsy* offers an appropriate one. Describing the difference between the play of male and female children in the black community where she developed, Johnson says:

the boys in the neighborhood had this game with rope...tug-o'-war...till finally some side would jerk the rope away from the others, who'd fall down.... Girls...weren't allowed to play with them in this tug-o'-war; so we figured out how to make our own rope — out of...little dandelions. You just keep adding them, one to another, and you can go on and on....Anybody, even the boys, could join us....The whole purpose of our game was to create this dandelion chain — that was it. And we'd keep going, creating till our mamas called us home.

Like Johnson's dandelion chain, womanist theological vision will grow as black women come together and connect piece with piece. Between the process of creating and the sense of calling, womanist theology will one day present itself in full array, reflecting the divine spirit that connects us all.

A Platform for Original Voices

June 12, 1989

Ada Maria Isasi-Diaz

Ada Maria Isasi Diaz, a Cuba-born theologian, is coauthor of Hispanic Women: Prophetic Voice in the Church. *She is working on developing mujerista theology — a Hispanic women's liberation theology.*

FOR ME AND MANY OTHERS, Latin American liberation theology has played a key role in what I believe to be the most radical movement of the twentieth century: recognizing and accepting the poor and oppressed as agents of their own history. Those of us for whom Christianity is important have also had to acknowledge the poor and oppressed as privileged by God to be the main bearers of the gospel.

Latin American liberation theology, black theology, feminist theology, womanist theology, and *mujerista* theology all ground themselves in the socio-economic-political situation of a specific group of poor and oppressed people. They are liberation theologies because the lived experience of the marginalized is an intrinsic part of the source for the "doing" of theology, and theologizing is conceptualized as an integral part of the struggle for liberation. Theology is a praxis for liberation — reflective action that contributes to the self-determination of oppressed people.

Latin American liberation theology has helped many other liberation theologies come to these understandings. Other liberation theologies, for their part, have challenged Latin American liberation theology during the last several years to look at two issues that it has neglected: the oppression of women and the oppression of black and indigenous peoples in Latin America. Recently, because Latin American women theologians have made their presence felt, Latin American liberation theology has begun to include the struggle against sexism. Yet to come is any real inclusion of the issue of racism and ethnic prejudice.

Both weaknesses are serious. Women constitute well over 50 percent of the population in Latin America and play key roles in important areas of the "popular church," such as the *comunidades de base* and the promoters and delegates of the Word. Brazil has the second largest black population in the world, while countries such as Peru, Bolivia, and Ecuador have a high percentage of Amerindians. Indeed, even if their negligence is corrected in the near future, male Latin American liberation theologians still have to explain it.

The Centrality of the Poor

Another issue that Latin American liberation theology must face is the way the lived experience of the oppressed is used in the articulation of theological understandings. Usually that experience is distilled through scientific analysis and enunciated in "formal" economic, political, social, and historical categories. The experience of the poor and the oppressed is used as a background against which to do theology and within which to understand the Christian faith. Some liberation theologians, perhaps because they are not fully identified with their own people, have used the experience of the poor and the oppressed as examples of the theological understandings *they* are proposing.

But if the poor and the oppressed are indeed agents of their own history, if indeed liberation theologies make a preferential option for the poor and believe that the experiences and understandings of the poor should be privileged, should be given centrality in the doing of theology, then liberation theologies must reconsider the way they use that experience. In order for the understandings of the poor and the oppressed to be the core of liberation theologies, these theologies must become a platform for their original voices. Methodologically, liberation theologies must start by listening, recording, and transmitting the experience of the poor and the oppressed in their own words, using their own images and explanations.

Liberation theologians, in other words, are able to do theology only insofar as we are integral parts of our communities of struggle. Our task is to organize what our communities are saying about God and our relationship to the divine and one another. The articulation of the community must not be reduced or accommodated to fit into the theological and dogmatic schemas of the different faith traditions. On the contrary, if we are serious about the hermeneutical privilege of the poor and the oppressed, their voices must be allowed to question faith understandings held by the churches and systematized by different theologies, both of which historically have paid no attention to what the oppressed say and believe. For example: In general, Hispanic women relate to and pray much more to the Virgin Mary than to God or Jesus; we relate to the church in ways we find life-giving instead of the way the churches prescribe; our "popular" religious practices are much more important to us than "prescribed" church practices. Does not all of this question established theological understandings? And we who engage in *mujerista* theology, a Hispanic women's liberation theology, are committed to taking all of this seriously when we do Christology, Mariology, systematics, ecclesiology, instead of denouncing it as incorrect.

Once liberation theologians have organized the religious articulation of our communities, we must represent the written "texts" to the community as a tool for analyzing its particular situation of oppression. Strategies for the liberation struggle emerge from that analysis. Liberation theologians also have the responsibility of working to build solidarity among oppressed communities by sharing the understandings of their community with other communities of struggle. Finally, we must make the voices of our community known to the theological community at large and go on to *insist* that this specific voice become an integral part of what is normative. Otherwise our theology will be yet another means of "sanctifying" the established order.

Canaanites, Cowboys, and Indians

September 11, 1989

Robert Allen Warrior

Robert Warrior, a contributing editor of C & C, *is New York correspondent for the* Lakota Times, *a member of the Osage Nation, and a doctoral candidate at Union Theological Seminary in New York City.*

NATIVE AMERICAN THEOLOGY of liberation has a nice ring to it. Politically active Christians in the U.S. have been bandying about the idea of such a theology for several years now, encouraging Indians to develop it. There are theologies of liberation for African Americans, Hispanic Americans, women, Asian Americans, even Jews. Why not Native Americans? Christians recognize that American injustice on this continent began nearly five hundred years ago with the oppression of its indigenous people and that justice for American Indians is a fundamental part of broader social struggle. The churches' complicity in much of the violence perpetrated on Indians makes this realization even clearer. So, there are a lot of well-intentioned Christians looking for some way to include Native Americans in their political action.

For Native Americans involved in political struggle, the participation of church people is often an attractive proposition. Churches have financial, political, and institutional resources that many Indian activists would dearly love to have at their disposal. Since American Indians have a relatively small population base and few financial resources, assistance from churches can be of great help in gaining the attention of the public, the media, and the government.

It sounds like the perfect marriage — Christians with the desire to include Native Americans in their struggle for justice and Indian activists in need of resources and support from non-Indians. Well, speaking as the product of a marriage between an Indian and a white, I can tell you that it is not as easy as it sounds. The inclusion of Native Americans in Christian political praxis is difficult — even dangerous. Christians have a different way of going about the struggle for justice than most Native Americans: different models of leadership, different ways of making decisions, different ways of viewing the relationship between politics and religion. These differences have gone all but unnoticed in the history of church involvement in American Indian affairs. Liberals and conservatives alike have too often surveyed the conditions of Native Americans and decided to come to the rescue, always using *their* methods, *their* ideas, and *their* programs. The idea that Indians might know best how to address their own problems is seemingly lost on these well-meaning folks.

Still, the time does seem ripe to find a new way for Indians and Christians (and Native American Christians) to be partners in the struggle against injustice and economic and racial oppression. This is a new era for both the church and for Native Americans. Christians are breaking away from their liberal moorings and looking for more effective means of social and political engagement. Indians, in this era of "self-determination," have verified for themselves and the government that they are the people best able to address Indian problems as long as they are given the necessary resources and if they can hold the U.S. government accountable to the policy. But an enormous stumbling block immediately presents itself. Most of the liberation theologies that have emerged in the last twenty years are preoccupied with the Exodus story, using it as the fundamental model for liberation. I believe that the story of the Exodus is an inappropriate way for Native Americans to think about liberation.

No doubt, the story is one that has inspired many people in many contexts to struggle against injustice. Israel, in the Exile, then Diaspora, would remember the story and be reminded of God's faithfulness. Enslaved African Americans, given Bibles to read by their masters and mistresses, would begin at the beginning of the book and find in the pages of the Pentateuch a god who was obviously on their side, even if that god was the god of their oppressors. People in Latin American base communities read the story and have been inspired to struggle against injustice. The Exodus, with its picture of a god who takes the side of the oppressed and powerless, has been a beacon of hope for many in despair.

God the Conqueror

Yet, the liberationist picture of Yahweh is not complete. A delivered people is not a free people, nor is it a nation. People who have survived the nightmare of subjugation dream of escape. Once the victims have been delivered, they seek a new dream, a new goal, usually a place of safety away from the oppressors, a place that can be defended against future subjugation. Israel's new dream became the land of Canaan. And Yahweh was still with them: Yahweh promised to go before the people and give them Canaan, with its flowing milk and honey. The land, Yahweh decided, belonged to these former slaves from Egypt and Yahweh planned on giving it to them — using the same power used against the enslaving Egyptians to defeat the indigenous inhabitants of Canaan. Yahweh the deliverer became Yahweh the conqueror.

The obvious characters in the story for Native Americans to identify with are the Canaanites, the people who already lived in the promised land. As a member of the Osage Nation of American Indians who stands in solidarity with other tribal people around the world, I read the Exodus stories with Canaanite eyes. And, it is the Canaanite side of the story that has been overlooked by those seeking to articulate theologies of liberation. Especially ignored are those parts of the story that describe Yahweh's command to mercilessly annihilate the indigenous population.

To be sure, most scholars, of a variety of political and theological stripes, agree that the actual events of Israel's early history are much different than what was commanded in the narrative. The Canaanites were not systematically annihilated, nor were they completely driven from the land. In fact, they made up, to a large extent, the people of the new nation of Israel. Perhaps it was a process of gradual immigration of people from many places and religions who came together to form a new nation. Or maybe, as Norman Gottwald and others have argued, the peasants of Canaan revolted against their feudal masters, a revolt instigated and aided by a vanguard of escaped slaves from Egypt who believed in the liberating god, Yahweh. Whatever happened, scholars agree that the people of Canaan had a lot to do with it.

Nonetheless, scholarly agreement should not allow us to breathe a sigh of relief. For, historical knowledge does not change the status of the indigenes in the *narrative* and the theology that grows out of it. The research of Old Testament scholars, however much it provides an answer to the historical question — the contribution of the indigenous people of Canaan to the formation and emergence of Israel as a nation — does not resolve the narrative problem. People who read the narratives read them as they are, not as scholars and experts would like them to be read and interpreted. History is no longer with us. The narrative remains.

Though the Exodus and Conquest stories are familiar to most readers, I want to highlight some sections that are commonly ignored. The covenant begins when Yahweh comes to Abram saying, "Know of a surety that your descendants will be sojourners in a land that is not theirs, and they will be slaves there, and they will be oppressed for four hundred years; but I will bring judgment on the nation they serve and they shall come out" (Gen. 15:13, 14). Then, Yahweh adds: "To your descendants I give this land, the land of the Kenites, the Kenizzites, the Kadmonites, the Hittites, the Perizzites, the Rephaim, the Amorites, the Canaanites, and the Jebusites" (15:18–21). The next important moment is the commissioning of Moses. Yahweh says to him, "I promise I will bring you out of the affliction of Egypt, to the land of the Canaanites, the Hittites, the Amorites, the Perizzites, the Hivites, and the Jebusites, a land flowing with milk and honey" (Exod.

3:17). The covenant, in other words, has two parts: deliverance and conquest.

After the people have escaped and are headed to the promised land, the covenant is made more complicated, but it still has two parts. If the delivered people remain faithful to Yahweh, they will be blessed in the land Yahweh will conquer for them (Exod. 2:23 and Deut. 7–9). The god who delivered Israel from slavery will lead the people into the land and keep them there as long as they live up to the terms of the covenant. "You shall not wrong a stranger or oppress him [sic], for you were strangers in the land of Egypt. You shall not afflict any widow or orphan. If you do afflict them, and they cry out to me, I will surely hear their cry; and my wrath will burn, and I will kill you with the sword, and your wives shall become widows and your children fatherless" (Exod. 22:21).

Whose Narrative?

Israel's reward for keeping Yahweh's commandments — for building a society where the evils done to them have no place — is the continuation of life in the land. But one of the most important of Yahweh's commands is the prohibition on social relations with Canaanites or participation in their religion. "I will deliver the inhabitants of the land into your hand, and you shall drive them out before you. You shall make no covenant with them or with their gods. They shall not dwell in your land, lest they make you sin against me; for if you serve their gods it will surely be a snare to you" (Exod. 23:31b–33).

In fact, the indigenes are to be destroyed. "When the Lord your God brings you into the land which you are entering to take possession of it, and clears away many nations before you, the Hittites, the Girgashites, the Amorites, the Canaanites, the Perizzites, the Hivites, and the Jebusites, seven nations greater and mightier than yourselves, and when the Lord your God gives them over to you and you defeat them; then you must utterly destroy them; you shall make no covenant with them, and show no mercy to them" (Deut. 7:1, 2). These words are spoken to the people of Israel as they are preparing to go into Canaan. The promises made to Abraham and Moses are ready to be fulfilled. All that remains is for the people to enter into the land and dispossess those who already live there.

Joshua gives an account of the conquest. After ten chapters of stories about Israel's successes and failures to obey Yahweh's commands, the writer states, "So Joshua defeated the whole land, the hill country and the Negeb and the lowland and the slopes, and all their kings, he left none remaining, but utterly destroyed all that breathed, as the Lord God of Israel commanded." In Judges, the writer disagrees with this account of what happened, but the Canaanites are held in no higher esteem. The angel of the Lord says, "I will not drive out [the indigenous people] before you; but they shall become adversaries to you, and their gods shall be a snare to you."

Thus, the narrative tells us that the Canaanites have status only as the people Yahweh removes from the land in order to bring the chosen people in. They are not to be trusted, nor are they to be allowed to enter into social relationships with the people of Israel. They are wicked and their religion is to be avoided at all costs. The laws put forth regarding strangers and sojourners may have stopped the people of Yahweh from wanton oppression, but presumably only after the land was safely in the hands of Israel. The covenant of Yahweh depends on this.

The Exodus narrative is where discussion about Christian involvement in Native American activism must begin. It is these stories of deliverance and conquest that are ready to be picked up and believed by anyone wondering what to do about the people who already live in their promised land. They provide an example of what can happen when powerless people come to power. Historical scholarship may tell a different story; but even if the annihilation did not take place, the narratives tell what happened to those indigenous people who put their hope and faith in ideas and gods that were foreign to their culture. The Canaanites trusted in the god of outsiders and their story of oppression and exploitation was lost. Interreligious praxis became betrayal and the surviving narrative tells us nothing about it.

Confronting the conquest stories as a narrative rather than a historical problem is especially important given the tenor of contemporary theology and criticism. After two hundred years of preoccupation with historical questions, scholars and theologians across a broad spectrum of political and ideological positions have recognized the function of narrative in the development of religious communities. Along with the work of U.S. scholars like Brevard Childs, Stanley Hauerwas, and George Lindbeck, the radical liberation theologies of Latin America are based on empowering believing communities to read scriptural narratives for themselves and make their reading central to theology and political action. The danger is that these communities will read the narratives, not the history behind them.

And, of course, the text itself will never be altered by interpretations of it, though its reception may be. It is part of the canon for both Jews and Christians. It is part of the heritage and thus the consciousness of people in the United States. Whatever dangers we identify in the text and the god represented there will remain as long as the text remains. These dangers only grow as the emphasis upon catechetical (Lindbeck), narrative (Hauerwas), canonical (Childs), and Bible-centered Christian base communities (Gutiérrez) grows. The peasants of Solentiname bring a wisdom and experience previously unknown to Christian theology, but I do not see what mechanism guarantees that they — or any other people who seek to be shaped and molded by reading the text — will differentiate between the liberating god and the god of conquest.

Is There a Spirit?

What is to be done? First, the Canaanites should be at the center of Christian theological reflection and political action. They are the last remaining ignored voice in the text, except perhaps for the land itself. The conquest stories, with all their violence and injustice, must be taken seriously by those who believe in the god of the Old Testament. Commentaries and critical works rarely mention these texts. When they do, they express little concern for the status of the indigenes and their rights as human beings and as nations. The same blindness is evident in theologies that use the Exodus motif as their basis for political action. The leading into the land becomes just one more redemptive moment rather than a violation of innocent peoples' rights to land and self-determination.

Keeping the Canaanites at the center makes it more likely that those who read the Bible will read *all* of it, not just the part that inspires and justifies them. And should anyone be surprised by the brutality, the terror of these texts? It was, after all, a Jewish victim of the Holocaust, Walter Benjamin, who said, "There is no document of civilization which is not at the same time a document of barbarism." People whose theology involves the Bible need to take this insight seriously. It is those who know these texts who must speak the truth about what they contain. It is to those who believe in these texts that the barbarism belongs. It is those who act on the basis of these texts who must take responsibility for the terror and violence they can and have engendered.

Second, we need to be more aware of the way ideas such as those in the conquest narratives have made their way into Americans' consciousness and ideology. And only when we understand this process can those of us who have suffered from it know how to fight back. Many Puritan preachers were fond of referring to Native Americans as Amelkites and Canaanites — in other words, people who, if they would not be converted, were worthy of annihilation. By examining such instances in theological and political writings, in sermons, and elsewhere, we can understand how America's self-image as a "chosen people" has provided a rhetoric to mystify domination.

Finally, we need to decide if we want to accept the model of leadership and social change presented by the entire Exodus story. Is it appropriate to the needs of indigenous people seeking justice and deliverance? If indeed the Canaanites were integral to Israel's early history, the Exodus narratives reflect a situation in which indigenous people put their hope in a god from outside, were liberated from their oppressors, and then saw their story of oppression revised out of the new nation's history of salvation. They were assimilated into another people's identity and the history of their ancestors came to be regarded as suspect and a danger to the safety of Israel. In short, they were betrayed.

Do Native Americans and other indigenous people dare trust the same god in their struggle for justice? I am not asking an easy question and I in no way mean that people who are both Native Americans and Christians cannot work toward justice in the context of their faith in Jesus Christ. Such people have a lot of theological reflection to do, however, to avoid the dangers I have pointed to in the conquest narratives. Christians, whether Native American or not, if they are to be involved, must learn how to participate in the struggle without making their story the whole story. Otherwise the sins of the past will be visited upon us again.

No matter what we do, the conquest narratives will remain. As long as people believe in the Yahweh of deliverance, the world will not be safe from Yahweh the conqueror. But perhaps, if they are true to their struggle, people will be able to achieve what Yahweh's chosen people in the past have not: a society of people delivered from oppression who are not so afraid of becoming victims again that they become oppressors themselves, a society where the original inhabitants can become something other than subjects to be converted to a better way of life or adversaries who provide cannon fodder for a nation's militaristic pride.

With what voice will we, the Canaanites of the world, say, "Let my people go and leave my people alone?" And, with what ears will followers of alien gods who have wooed us (Christians, Jews, Marxists, capitalists), listen to us? The indigenous people of this hemisphere have endured a subjugation now one hundred years longer than the sojourn of Israel in Egypt. Is there a god, a spirit, who will hear us and stand with us in the Amazon, Osage County, and Wounded Knee? Is there a god, a spirit, able to move among the pain and anger of Nablus, Gaza, and Soweto? Perhaps. But we, the wretched of the earth, may be well-advised this time not to listen to outsiders with their promises of liberation and deliverance. We will perhaps do better to look elsewhere for our vision of justice, peace, and political sanity — a vision through which we escape not only our oppressors, but our oppression as well. Maybe, for once, we will just have to listen to ourselves, leaving the gods of this continent's real strangers to do battle among themselves.

Evangelicals' Latin Future

March 18, 1991

Laura O'Shaughnessy

Laura Nuzzi O'Shaughnessy, who has spent considerable time in Central America, teaches government at St. Lawrence University and is co-author of Nicaragua's Other Revolution: Religious Faith and Political Struggle.

> *Tongues of Fire: The Explosion of Protestantism in Latin America*, by David Martin (Cambridge, Mass.: Basil Blackwell, 1990), 368pp.
>
> *Is Latin America Turning Protestant?: The Politics of Growth*, by David Stoll (Berkeley: University of California Press, 1990), 424pp.

EVANGELICAL PROTESTANTISM in Latin America is alive, growing, and shows no signs of abating. It now claims the allegiance of 12 percent of the people of the region, including 10 to 20 percent of the populations of Brazil, Chile, El Salvador, and Guatemala. Both of the books under review attempt to explain this development, each from within a different explanatory framework.

David Martin sets the story in a historical context that emphasizes the "modernizing" influence of Protestantism. He begins with a historical discussion of the rise of Methodism in eighteenth-century England, detailing the serious challenge it mounted to the Church of England by means of its direct spiritual and emotive appeals to the less privileged. In a similar manner, Martin argues, Pentecostalism (Protestantism in its most ecstatic forms) has replaced the now mainline Methodist church in Latin America.

Embedded in Martin's line of reasoning is the question: What future role will Pentecostalism play? In response, Martin can only speculate, but the implicit focus of his discussion suggests that Pentecostalism may become a force for progress as believers are born again, machismo is corrected, family structure becomes more stable, and social mobility becomes a possibility. In this regard his approach is consistent with modernization frameworks that explain the West's progress as a result of innovative values, and Protestantism as an integral part of those values.

Not surprisingly, Martin minimizes twentieth-century national and international political dynamics in Latin America to a startling degree. Nowhere is this lack more telling than in his discussion of General Efraín Ríos Montt, born-again ruler of Guatemala (1982–83). Here is Martin on the impact of the Ríos Montt period: "It may be that Protestantism was now finding an ethos within which Guatemalan nationalism might express itself safely and apolitically. That, if true, is a sure sign of a faith become fully indigenous, whatever the U.S. connections and financial assistance."

David Stoll, on the other hand, engages readers in understanding the political context in which evangelicalism is growing. His portrayal of the Ríos Montt period, therefore, is far more extensive. Stoll illuminates the contradictions between the general's stated policies and the army's destruction of a revolutionary movement supported by part of the Catholic church. He also documents the relationships between Ríos Montt's church, The Word, its North American parent organization, Gospel Outreach, and the part of the North American evangelical community which sought to defend the general's record in the United States.

Tongues of Fire may be the more encyclopedic book, but it relies heavily on secondary sources, and at times its impact can be kaleidoscopic. (At the same time, on a descriptive level, it gives readers an understanding of Pentecostalism's powerful oral and visual appeals.) Stoll's work is based heavily on primary research, and is focused almost exclusively on three case studies: Guatemala, Nicaragua, and Ecuador. Moreover, the focus is not exclusively on Pentecostals, but on evangelical Protestants — those who are "born again," accept the final authority of the Bible, and spread the message of salvation.

Stoll has chosen these case studies because his major purpose in writing this book is to explain why Latin America is becoming Protestant. In so doing, he rejects as incomplete the conspiratorial notion of a U.S.-sponsored effort to further the growth of evangelicalism in order to impede genuine social change in Latin America. At the same time, he strongly warns the evangelical community to beware the dangers inherent in allowing their churches to be manipulated by the North American religious right.

For Stoll, Protestantism generates social change whose direction is not predetermined. Unlike Martin, who sees the growth of evangelicalism as a force for upward social mobility and acculturation, Stoll argues that the debt crisis and governmental austerity programs of the past two decades have worked against the economic betterment of life for Latin America's poor. Most important, economic conditions have caused divisions *within* the evangelical community — divisions between those who want their churches to remain "otherworldly" and those who want to take into consideration the social dimensions of the gospel. Because of its internal dynamics and divisions, evangelicalism is a force to be reckoned with. Even though Stoll admits that the role Protestants played in the European Reformation has passed to radical Catholics in Latin America, he cautions against focusing exclusively on liberation theology, which has been overemphasized as the vanguard of religious reformation in Latin America.

Imagined Encounter

Stoll's case studies purport to accomplish two things: to document the clash between liberation theology and evangelical Protestantism and to speculate about a potential union of these two most powerful forces. Stoll's speculations on an "encounter" between liberation theology and evangelical Protestantism is the most intriguing part of his thesis. He admits that this is hard to imagine at present. If it were to occur, he says, it would result from the attempts of some evangelicals to incorporate the social dimensions of the gospel into the spiritual messages of their churches. This "contextualization" of the gospel runs the risk of dividing evangelical congregations, but it also moves the contextualizers closer to the social positions of liberation theologians.

A meeting ground between evangelicals and liberationists would change both groups dramatically and have profound consequences for Latin America. Ironically, Stoll's case studies do not lend credence to his hopes for rapprochement. Indeed, they serve more to document the tension between progressive Catholicism and evangelical Protestantism, and to demonstrate how difficult a dialogue would be, even if the United States did not play an interventionist role.

Stoll's first case study is Guatemala. The Nicaraguan evangelical community and its relationship to the Sandinista government are the subject of his second case study. While CEPAD (The Evangelical Committee for Aid and Development) worked *with* the Nicaraguan government on many housing and health projects, other more conservative Protestants distrusted the Sandinistas and their embrace of liberation theology. Consequently, the conservatives were caught between the revolutionary government and the U.S. government — which used appeals for freedom of religion and charges of religious persecution as essential parts of its counterrevolutionary strategy.

Stoll's final study examines the controversies over the largest of the evangelical relief agencies, World Vision in Ecuador. With its social programs and generous North American funding, World Vision challenged the efforts of progressive Catholics to organize the Quechua Indians.

In the highland province of Chimborazo, the progressive bishop of the Indians, Monsignor Leonidas Proaño, had divested his church of its land holdings, publicized the official minimum wage (which most landowners were not paying) and trained his priests and catechists to defend Indian rights. The bishop also made a conscious effort to break with traditional "folk" Catholicism, which required payment of fees in exchange for administering the sacraments.

These reform actions did not succeed. The Quechua were in no position to demand a minimum wage; moreover, they believed that without payment the sacraments could not perform their protective functions. Disillusioned with Catholic reformers, they were receptive to the appeals, social projects, and money of World Vision. Ironically, when indigenous empowerment did occur, it worked to the benefit of the evangelical community, not to the benefit of the Catholics who had been organizing at the grassroots for over a decade.

The most surprising weakness of Stoll's work is its lack of serious discussion of liberation theology, especially given the importance Stoll attaches to it as a catalyst for evangelical growth. Stoll's concern is with evangelicals, which may account for the cursory presentation of liberation theology. But, for whatever reasons, he misses seeing that liberation theologies have evolved over the past fifteen years as liberationists, like their evangelical counterparts, have differed on their understandings of the kingdom of God, of salvation, and of the relationship between church and state. This omission is regrettable, given Stoll's thesis on dialogue.

Both these books offer a wealth of information on the internal dynamics of evangelicalism's appeal in Latin America. But, as a Latin Americanist, a believer, and a social scientist, I must conclude that David Stoll is more in touch with Latin America's reality.

New Dynamics in Theology:
Politically Active and Culturally Significant

May 16, 1988

Larry Rasmussen

Larry Rasmussen is Reinhold Niebuhr Professor of Social Ethics at Union Theological Seminary in New York City and a contributing editor of C & C. *He is the author of several books, including the popular* Bible and Ethics in the Christian Life, *written with Bruce Birch.*

FOR BETTER THAN TWO DECADES the consensus in theology and ethics has been that we have no consensus. Roger Shinn announced this fact before most people had noticed it ("The Shattering of the Theological Spectrum," *C & C*, September 30, 1963), but the years since have borne him out. At the American Theological Society's plenary session last year, one panelist described the current landscape as the "Balkanization" of theology — even, in a careless bit of exaggeration, its "Beirutization." If this is the lay of the land in the United States, how much more fractured is the theological terrain of the *world* church!

Yet something is afoot. "Consensus" is premature, and not quite the word, but shared dynamics and converging themes are visible. The themes number a baker's dozen, though only a few can be uncovered here. Even those have to be seen in light of shared dynamics; so we begin there.

A Double Movement. We are on the forward edges of widespread religious renewal that is politically active and culturally significant. It may be happening in Islam with an intensity not yet matched in Christianity, but it is happening in Christian circles, and Jewish, nonetheless. We cannot foresee the outcome, but we can describe the effective forces.

The dynamics are not new. Ernst Troeltsch, writing at the turn of the century, saw them at work in the early church and watched them erupt now and again throughout church history. What is new is their currency for us.

The forces at work are characteristics of two movements that usually go their separate ways. One movement is the development of a dynamic, community-creating religion among lower socioeconomic classes or other marginalized groups. Here an urgent sense of clear, stark, human need is joined to a faith full of feeling and energy. This is an empowering religion with a common home among subjugated and disempowered social groups. It is marked by the exhilarating experience of divine power as the power for "peoplehood," and for making a way where there is no way.

The other movement is the conceptual and ritual revisioning of inherited traditions in times of deep, often bewildering, change. Cultivated criticism, bold theological reflection, and constructive exploration both in thought and in liturgical enactment are its trademarks. It is the ardent search for the new, powerful God-talk that Bonhoeffer yearned for, but thought would be forthcoming only after a period of necessary silence and renewal (at least in those quarters where Christianity was most acculturated and where the experience of the Holocaust and two World Wars shattered the confidence of both Western religious streams and alternative humanisms).

When these two movements come together, new religious vitalities are sometimes loosed upon the world, shaking things up and giving them new direction at the same time. The outcome is never unambiguous; it always caroms between new social unities and strengthened social factions. The political expressions may be revolutionary, reactionary with a vengeance, or reformist. For certain, nothing is the same.

Crossing Over

The movements must join forces, Troeltsch noted, if religious, cultural, and social transformation is to occur. Intellectual and ritual "re-visioning" without the base communities doesn't go further than the addresses of scholars writing books and articles for one another, or small clusters of the faithful engaged in "experimental worship." And community-creating religious movements without bold thinkers and practitioners who come from, or join, their ranks never escape the social backwaters and lagoons long assigned them.

Ours is a moment when these two movements are converging. Many in the U.S. haven't taken full account of this yet, because we've not noticed that Christianity has shifted decisively from the religion of the rich to the faith of the poor. The poor have exercised a preferential option for the church, of all things! And the vitality of Christian faith has passed from the European and North American world to peoples in Africa, Latin America, and Asia, to the women's movement most everywhere, and to the communities in our own midst who are most in touch with these.

More and more, Christianity is a faith of struggling peoples who are recasting it amidst those struggles. The one future trend we can be most sure of — the doubling of the world's population in the next fifty years, with most of the growth happening in poor countries — will intensify this. The most dramatic church growth, the starkest human needs, and the most aggravated social struggle relevant to a rather confident secular and scientific age, will share much the same geography.

If this double movement is the dynamic, what common themes break the surface of theological reflection?

Emergent theologies are all *socio-critical* theologies in which reflection arises from *group experience and identity*. They are by no means identical: left and right evangelical and Pentecostal; Latin American, black, and feminist theologies of liberation; Native American, African, and Asian theologies of creation and culture. But they strike a common profile: shared group experience is the material of critical reflection; and theology is done as a communal process from a self-consciously defined and particular perspective. This process is no longer even within hailing distance of the Enlightenment quest for both universalism and individualism in one rationally coherent world, and for a *nonprovincial* theology and morality. (Who speaks any longer of "the Christian doctrine of man"?) Reflection emerges from shared experience and proceeds with a view to common identity and struggle, trying to grasp existence theologically and socially in the same moment, using it to consolidate and empower the group, and to further efforts at social change. This is a far cry from liberal theology's effort to adapt Christianity to the modern world and make sense of culture on terms relevant to a rather confident secular and scientific age.

Massive, public suffering is the material reality addressed in much theological reflection; and *the suffering and hidden God* comes more and more to the fore. The character of this suffering moves theological attention to the social systems that shape our lives — economic, political, cultural — as well as to public events themselves (the Holocaust, programs and policies of economic austerity, military intervention, terrorism, ethnic nationalist expression, struggles for survival and freedom). Reflection characteristically happens *from* the underside of society itself, or with a view *to* reality as experienced there, thus reinforcing theology's socio-critical character. Attention still includes the common events to which religion has always been party — birth, rites of passage, death, and the cycles of days and seasons which give order and meaning to an otherwise chaotic, or sometimes vacuous, history. But the shift of emphasis to public suffering and to exposing the public dimensions of *private* pain, is decisive.

Politics; Liberation

Two streams of reflection merit special comment. One is political theology in Europe, chiefly Germany, which is best characterized as the voice of the bourgeoisie questioning its own religious and cultural assumptions and its own economic and political systems. It arose from the collective experience of mass public evil and suffering: not only the World Wars, but especially the Holocaust. The Holocaust was theologically even more troubling than the international conflict itself because it was the genocidal effort of one self-proclaimed people of God to extinguish another. Elie Wiesel's comment that "all the victims were Jews, and all the perpetrators Christians" is not factually precise in either clause, but the truth is much too close to deny. In any case, the Holocaust, the single most demonic reality in the single most deadly century to date, together with increased attention to "North/South" economic issues, "East/West" peace issues, and threats to the global environment, have all found a voice in European theology. After the Holocaust any credible God-talk must be able to take account of burning children, and any credible theological ethic has to show it is determined to head off such atrocities at their very beginnings, deep in the habits of hearts and minds and in public policies. The conciliar project of the World Council of Churches — "Justice, Peace, and the

Integrity of Creation" — nicely names the broad *theological* agenda (not simply the moral one).

The second stream of theological reflection is the explosive emergence of liberation theology, whether of class (the poor), race (black), geography and culture (Asian and African), or gender (feminist) and sex (gay-lesbian). While each begins with identifiable group experience and each is a major new voice, none ends there. Any group's experience makes no sense apart from its relationship to others'.

All liberation theologies represent what Michel Foucault has called "the insurrection of subjugated knowledges," and all insist that justice is the moral test of God-claims and spirituality. They are profoundly oriented to public life, and they push for the kind of Christian faith that would help end massive suffering.

The God of much current reflection is the suffering and hidden God. This is not Aristotle's self-sufficient God. Nor is it the great God, immaterial and changeless, of all the "omni's" of centuries of Christian allegiance (omnipotent, omniscient, omnipresent). Nor is it the timeless and impassible divine being who is known through the mind alone, and who was the keystone of Christian apologetics in its most formative encounter of all — with classical culture. Neither is this the God of the mighty acts of intervention in human history, the crashing force from without. This is the agitated, but hushed, God of the cross; a God found, as Luther said, "not in speculative thought but in suffering experience." A God of pathos, compassion, and mercy.

Kosuke Koyama's opening in *Mount Fuji and Mount Sinai* speaks for many. He relates a harrowing childhood experience — the fire-bombing of Tokyo. One of the huge bombs screamed past his head and thudded into the earth just in front of him. The bomb, a dud, disappeared into the earth as Koyama leapt over the crater and continued to run from one shelter to the next in search of his family.

Koyama says of it all:

The slow assimilation of the traumatic events of 1945, which only gradually yielded their theological implications, has moved me toward the emotive region of the cross of Christ. The theology of the cross, as the core of the gospel message, gives me the fundamental orientation in which to engage in theology while living in a world dangerously fragmented by violent militarism, racism, and nuclearism.

Heightened human power and greater public suffering have moved millions into "the emotive region of the cross." God is a suffering God whose power is hidden in weakness. But it is a power for hope and joy there, and sober moral responsibility. It is a power for life.

Grabbing Our Existence

A third theme has already been intimated, *the ethical qualification and intensification of all Christian symbols*. Ours is a time of "ethical theology," rather than ethics as an implication trailing at some distance after a presentation of beliefs established on other grounds. Ethics is *part* of grabbing our existence theologically. Moral problematics precede and accompany dogmatics.

General reasons for ethical intensification are not hard to come by. The great issues of our time are moral: the uses of power; wealth and poverty; human rights; the moral quality and character of society; loss of the sense of the common good in tandem with the pampering of private interests; domestic violence; outrageous legal and medical costs in a system of maldistributed services; unprecedented developments in biotechnologies which portend good but risk evil; the violation of public trust by high elected officials and their appointees; the growing militarization of many societies; continued racism; the persistence of hunger and malnutrition; a still exploding population in societies hard put to increase jobs and resources; abortion; euthanasia; care for the environment; the claims of future generations. The list is endless. With more and more attention necessarily riveted on matters of morality and ethics, it is hardly a surprise that we ask about moral content as a measure of the meaning of any God-talk, and test the potency of faith claims by the difference they make for human well-being and the well-being of the wider creation.

"Ethical" theology has become so commonplace that we easily forget how often it has *not* been so. The function of religion in most times and places has been to render the world meaningful for people who didn't have the power to do much of anything beyond what had been assigned them by fate. Kings and peasants, rich and poor, masters and slaves, would always exist. Men were by nature suited to some tasks, women to others. Plagues and famines were "acts of God." Religion was there to offer some cosmic meaning for the natural order of things, and some cosmic consolation when people suffered because of it. This fatedness is gone for many now. It runs full grain against the ethos of modernity and another legacy of the Enlightenment — human agency for the democratic transformation of society.

Simply put, the world can be different, it ought to be, and we are the agents of its transformation. This fact pushes socio-ethical and political-ethical issues into prominence. That almost all the new voices in theology are voices of emerging peoples who are driven to toss off the heavy layers of fate and circumstance, and who press justice as a matter of faith, only intensifies this theological trend. If the preoccupation of early Christian centuries was to give creedal expression to

Christian faith in a way that would make intellectual and metaphysical sense in a Greek world, and the preoccupation of the Reformation was the status of the guilty sinner before God, the attention in our time has turned to the moral and ethical dimensions of making history.

This includes an ethical qualification for any serious faith claim. *If* the way in which we understand and talk about Jesus Christ permits or fosters anti-Semitism, then that way is rejected. If our interpretation of Scripture perpetuates the oppression of women, or racism, then that exegesis is disqualified. If Christian symbols mask and sanction imperialist relationships, then a nonimperialist rendering must be found, or the meaning of the symbol transformed.

Human power is on the agenda of virtually every creative impulse in theology today. The reasons are two: heightened power in some quarters and the quest for power in others. The former is in keeping with what is perhaps *the* distinctive mark of our age — the quantum leap in human power to affect all of life in truly fundamental and unprecedented ways. Human power, largely through modern technologies, has a novel range of impact, novel objects, and novel consequences. The human capacity to author life and skip all over the genetic alphabet raises theological questions, just as does the human capacity to destroy life on a grand scale and actually put ourselves, for the first time, in a position to be uncreators. Even someone so cautious as James Gustafson says: "The ordering of all life is shifting in a sense from God to humanity and doing so more rapidly in this century than in all the previous centuries of human culture combined" (*Ethics from a Theocentric Perspective*, vol. 1).

Yet the capacity to split genes and atoms, and to effect the environment on a new scale and in grave ways, is only one reason human power — and its relation to divine power — has become a theological preoccupation. The other is the strong theme of *empowerment* in the theologies of subjugated but spirited peoples. The theme of empowerment does not first appear with the question of decisions and strategy. (What now do we *do?*) It is a component of the most fundamental theological notions themselves — power and the presence of God, power and the vocation of humanity, power and the work of Jesus Christ and the Spirit, power and conversion, salvation, transformation, liberation, the life of prayer, the meaning of the Scriptures and of the Sacraments, etc. As with the enhanced human capacities to create and destroy, so too here reflection is about the relationship of human agency to divine agency in a new era. How God's power is imaged in relation to human power is a matter of much present exploration. What is clear is the rejection of monarchical and hierarchical images of power as "power *over.*"

The preoccupation with human power will likely continue, both for reasons of the enhanced impacts of human power in a shrinking world, and growing social conflict. The history of the world is written around emerging peoples' quest for land and other resources, and established populations' defense of them. In a world where it is easier and easier to annihilate people but more and more difficult to conquer and subdue them social conflict will likely increase.

Jesus

A radically theocentric Jesus with a decidedly human face emerges from many, and very different, quarters in present theological scholarship. The volume of attention is itself phenomenal. David Tracy has said that "more has been written about Jesus in the last 20 years than in the previous 2000." That is not a claim anyone would even want to try to verify, but it does point up extraordinary interest.

One would expect interest in Jesus from a pride or two of biblical scholars; they get paid for stalking Jesus and visiting old Christians. Yet their interest is hardly solitary. One of the premier liberation theologians, Juan Luis Segundo, has said that "Latin American theology has been mainly interested in going back to the primitive circumstances where, in the proximity of Jesus of Nazareth, Christians began to do theology."

Segundo wants to start fresh in large part because so many understandings of Jesus Christ have functioned as important elements in the pieties of dominant and exploitive groups. Armed with the fruits of a century of developing biblical scholarship and tools, Segundo expects — and finds — that the historical Jesus *undercuts* many long-held understandings of Christ. He finds a radically theocentric and socially radical Jesus, a Jesus who means major revisions in Christian notions, at least those regnant since Constantine.

Others are newly intrigued by Jesus for other reasons. Christians engaging in inter-religious encounter may seem an unlikely group, since Christianity has long attached a centrality, uniqueness, and exclusivity to Jesus, claiming there is in fact no other name under heaven whereby we might be saved. Yet it turns out that the historical Jesus now haunting the world of scholarship may just be the best thing going in inter-religious dialogue. It is a Jesus who does not well support Christianity's triumphalist claim and a Jesus who keeps nudging a major shift, *from a Christocentric theology to a theocentric Christology.* Which is to say: God, not Jesus, is the power at the center of things, and a God-centered life is precisely what we see in Jesus. A theocentric Christology is far more ecumenical in the religiously plural world than is a Christocentric theology with its exclusivist absorption of all of God into the Jesus of Christianity.

One of the parties to inter-religious dialogue is the community

of Jewish scholars. They have also shown new and extensive interest in Jesus. They share with others the discernment of a theocentric
and radical Jesus who looks very different from later claims about
him. Their contribution is more than the ever-necessary reminder that
Jesus was a Jew and not a Christian, that he lived a Jewish life that
he understood in a Jewish way, and that the movement gathered immediately around him was a Jewish one involved in Jewish renewal.
Jewish scholarship goes on to let us distinguish Jesus the Jew and his
movement from the communication of him and his message in the
non-Jewish and sometimes anti-Jewish ways that are already present
in early Christian writings. In doing so, it reinforces the shift from a
Christocentric theology to a theocentric Christology.

Christian biblical scholars have also shown a vibrant new interest
in the historical Jesus, much of it utilizing an approach to Christology
"from below," i.e., an understanding that begins with the humanity
and ministry of Jesus, who, precisely as a figure embedded in history,
moves toward God and lives as one wholly centered in God. Over and
over again the Jesus found is a compelling disclosure of the suffering
and compassionate God. Since Jesus has now become "the man who
belongs to the world" (Jaroslav Pelikan, *Jesus through the Centuries*),
and since most of the Christian world now lives in the Third World,
we will likely hear more of this radical, theocentric, and suffering Jesus
with a very human face.

These five themes — socio-critical and group-identified theology;
public suffering and a suffering God; the ethical qualification and intensification of faith claims; a preoccupation with human power; and
the unsettling lure of the historical Jesus — are only a few of the converging concerns in current theology. They give witness to a more
cohesive sentiment and promise than "Balkanization" lets on. Most
of these themes, though not all, reflect the dynamics of the double
movement of renewal and revision. Together with the responses they
invoke, they portend the recasting of much of Christian faith. That
recasting will continue.

Part 3

Religion and Politics

The reflections, reviews, responses, and stories that appear in this section are attempts to reflect theologically upon daily events. They range from the experience of homelessness to a church-based community effort to build hundreds of low-income houses; from considerations of euthanasia to an ethical skewering of Ronald Reagan's policy priorities; from the Pittston coal strike to the Sanctuary movement.

These are all about goings on in the United States. They all — in varying ways — deal with issues of justice.

These articles take different forms. Some describe how individuals and groups transcend their own mixed and selfish motives to stand for justice, as they comprehend it. Others analyze and critique efforts at public policy aimed at social problems. The forms are different because the writers employ different ways of shaping their experiences, different ways of communicating truths.

The implications for the churches touch several levels as well. Entering the public debate permits the church to speak of some eternal principles, but it also exposes the church to critical self-discovery, to being judged by standards it might not otherwise have encountered.

Postponing Socialism

December 26, 1977

Robert Lekachman

The late Robert Lekachman, who held the title of Distinguished Professor at the City University of New York and was one of the most widely read economists in the U.S. during the last twenty-five years, first wrote for C&C in 1960 and became a contributing editor in 1974. He was author of Visions and Nightmares: America after Reagan *and a participant in numerous struggles to make government accountable to the poor.*

IF ON NOVEMBER 12, a chilly Saturday in Washington, you had happened to pass the office building that houses the Democratic National Committee a few blocks from the Mayflower Hotel, you might have paused to contemplate the interesting spectacle of several hundred people holding candles, a few alight but most long since extinguished by a sharp wind. The good-humored but shivering crowd, indifferently observed by a few policemen, took turns singing familiar union and civil rights songs out of Pete Seeger handbooks and listened to speakers who exhorted them to go back home and organize pressure upon their Washington representatives to promote full employment, racial and sexual justice, national health insurance, and other desirable objectives.

After an hour or so, letters were read from Secretary of Labor Ray Marshall and Democratic National Committee Chairman Kenneth Curtis. Both gentlemen professed themselves ardent advocates of jobs for all. Soon the crowd of demonstrators, mostly young but plentifully sprinkled with gray heads, dispersed as amiably as they had assembled. Television — from West Germany but from no domestic network — filmed the entire scene.

This was the media event (if only the media had come) of the Democratic Agenda weekend organized by Michael Harrington's Democratic Socialist Organizing Committee (DSOC). In spite of media inattention, the weekend as an organizational event was a howling success. More than a thousand people registered and more than eight hundred of them remained to listen on Sunday morning to the UAW's Doug Fraser and to participate in workshops concerned with follow-up activity among their constituents at home. These enlightened thousand were a mixture of trade unionists, academics, community organizers, radical businessman, and politicians — among the latter were two Democratic National Committeemen and a pair of New York City councilwomen.

Among much else, they heard Mike Harrington urge everybody to hold Carter to his campaign promises and the pledges of the Democratic platform, termed by Carter-the-candidate a contract between him and the voters. Gar Alperovitz of the Exploratory Project for Economic Alternatives and Nat Weinberg, former research director for the United Auto Workers, advocated democratic planning. Hazel Henderson of Environmentalists for Full Employment explained why full employment and environmental protection are complementary rather than competitive objectives. Several economists, including this one, excoriated the Phillips Curve, which embodies the notion of a necessary trade-off between unemployment and inflation. At luncheon, William ("Wimpy") Winpimsinger condemned economists (present company excepted) as barriers to progress. There were panels on practically everything: the cities, the quality of work, energy, the Third World, tax reform, jobs, inflation, and so on.

This Is Victory?

As an early member of DSOC and one of the initiators of this gathering, I took heart from the number and quality of those present and also from the support of three presidents of major unions: Wurf of AFSCME, Fraser of the UAW and Winpimsinger of the Machinists. Their presence gave credibility to Harrington's persistent coalition strategy of alliance among socialists, blacks, church social activists, left liberals and the progressive wing of the labor movement. Any large and enthusiastic gathering of like-minded individuals evokes momentary euphoria. This one was certainly no exception.

Yet, and yet, I came away distressed about the politics of coalition in a conservative, ideologically innocent country bereft of any substantial left-wing party. How can one quarrel then with Harrington's attempt to draw upon the only place where there are substantial troops, the labor movement? Indeed if DSOC is to grow from cult to mass movement, it must enlist ordinary members of unions headed by our three friendly union presidents.

Nevertheless, the exigencies of alliance do produce a distinct sense of anticlimax. During the weekend the prime example was Harrington's reaction to the latest version of the Humphrey-Hawkins Full Employment bill, which has been floating around Congress for three years in a condition of suspended animation. In response to rising black unemployment and the pressure of the Congressional Black Caucus, Carter endorsed a yet weaker version of a bill that had already been watered down several times. The "compromise" negotiated between Carter agents and Congressional sponsors announced a 4 percent unemployment target by 1983(!), but mandated absolutely no new action either by Congress or the White House. Just to rub the point in, the bill empowers the president at the end of three years to modify the employment target (which once was set at 3 percent to be achieved in eighteen months). And it installs inflation as a problem equal to unemployment.

For those of a certain age afflicted by long memories, the outcome
of this haggling was bitterly reminiscent of the 1944 and 1945 struggles over the full employment bill of that era. By the time Congress
had finished with a strong measure, it had become the Employment
Act of 1946, which required nobody to do anything. (It did create two
of the gabbier groups in Washington where there is no shortage: the
Joint Economic Committee of Congress — shorn of power to sponsor
legislation — and the Council of Economic Advisers — which offers
whatever advice a president cares to heed.) As a final insult the late
Senator Robert A. Taft voted for the 1946 statute. Senator Goldwater
should have no trouble voting for this one.

All the same, the Black Caucus announced a famous victory, and
both Fraser and Winpimsinger specifically endorsed the measure. So
did Harrington, although he took care to label it only a tiny step forward. At that he exaggerated. By including inflation as a policy target,
the new bill offers Washington politicians an even stronger excuse for
inaction against unemployment. If in 1980 Carter decides to revise
upward the unemployment target, all he need do is cite the menace
of inflation and his obligation under the bill to alleviate it as well as
unemployment.

To treat this important defeat as even a minor victory amounts
to product mislabeling. It exposes all hands to alternative charges of
disingenuousness or political idiocy. There is the additional danger
that union, black, church, and liberal pressure upon Carter to take
meaningful action against continuing unemployment will relax after
this "triumph."

I said as much in my own remarks to the conclave. Once again
second thoughts intrude. Should one publicly disagree with important allies even when they are badly mistaken? These allies have
taken their own soundings of public, Congressional, and presidential opinion. Perhaps they are right that when the national mood is
conservative, symbolic victories are better than none. As I grope for
a satisfactory political position, I rather think that pragmatic radicals
can err by placing too much emphasis upon the adjective and too
little upon the noun.

After all, the point of coalition with nonsocialists is to raise their
consciousness — not to accept *their* positions so charitably that no
one can tell the socialists from the Democrats. It goes without saying
that the creation of a serious left in the United States is a long labor.
Fraternal compromises on issues like Humphrey-Hawkins are unlikely
to do much for the cause.

Well, it was a nice weekend. There is always the hope, based on
extensive previous evidence, that I am wrong again.

Organizing Mississippi Woodcutters:
The Short End of the Stick

November 24, 1980

Leon Howell

Leon Howell has been editor of Christianity and Crisis *since 1985. From 1966 on he has written continuously for* C&C *about Asia — where he lived for many years — the ecumenical movement, community organizing, and sports, among other things. Twice his work — for editorials and for news — was singled out for Awards of Merit by the Associated Church Press.*

THOMASTOWN, Mississippi — Willie Lee Little is a woodcutter, one of more than ten thousand in Mississippi. Perhaps 75 percent, like Little, are black. Little has disc problems in his back and does not cut every day, as many do. But he is a woodcutter and last month he took me into the Mississippi woods to show me his trade.

He has an old but serviceable truck that will hold two stacks of wood cut to the 5'3" length required for wood pulp. When fully loaded it will hold about 3.5 cords of wood. Bigger and better trucks hold up to five cords and have a loading wench. Little uses mules when he needs help dragging out a log. And he has a chain saw, *the* tool of his trade.

I watch in amazement as this man in his fifties, "playing in pain" as sports pages put it, uses his saw like a magic wand. It knocks a tree down right where he wants it to fall. Then he zips off the branches and quickly divides the trunk, without any measurement other than his practiced eye, into 5'3" lengths. Again and again he repeats the process.

On this day he has had a late start because he had to take his truck into nearby Macon for repairs. He is working without a helper and loads the truck alone. When he is finished, he will drive the load to a nearby woodlot, one of about 250 in Mississippi, where he will be paid $34 a cord because it is pine. He would get $27 for hardwood. He is paying $8 a cord to the landowner for stumpage. Depending on the wood and the difficulty of getting it out, stumpage varies from $3 to $8.

It's at the woodlot that he runs into a problem, one he shares with woodcutters all over the South. Little says: "Last Thursday I takes in a load that may not have been quite full. The scaler gets it at 3.1 cords. So on Friday I bought a load I just knowed was going to be 3.5 because I sho nuff stacked it up. I got 3.35 cords measurement. I *believes* — I just *know* — I had at least 3.5 and probably more."

Like his colleagues, Willie Lee Little has no choice. "We don't get a fair scale at the woodlots. But we don't have nothin' to fight with.

You says, 'Look here, you shorted me.' And the man answers, 'If you don't like it, take it somewhere else.' Where the same thing happen. One thing, you ain't got no protection."

Larry Miller, a white Mennonite who came to Mississippi in 1965 from Indiana to do his alternate service and has stayed on, is a new woodcutter. He is college-educated — many woodcutters are functionally illiterate — and measures his loads with his own stick. He believes that he gets the squeeze on the "stick" on the average of half a cord out of every three he sells. That means a loss of $17 on a load that should bring a gross of $102.

"Some of these guys cut as much as fifty cords a week. That means a loss of $150 to $200. And we really have no choice. The scaler says, 'Are you satisfied with the measurement?' I find it hard to dialogue with them. In hard times like this summer, when they were only taking wood a couple days a week, he may just turn away those who give him a hard time."

If a college-educated white is intimidated, one can only imagine what a poor black experiences when dealing with the man at the lot.

Legally, woodcutters are independent contractors, and they sell their product to the wood lots. The woodlots are ostensibly independent but in fact they purchase for the giant paper and pulp corporations like International Paper, Masonite, and Scott Paper. Unlike an employee, the woodcutter has no workers' compensation or disability insurance. And he furnishes all the equipment needed for the job: trucks, tires, gas, oil, chain saws, and the like. While the cutters' costs (and company income) have risen by several hundred percent, the income of woodcutters has increased only 18 percent in ten years.

They are exploited in a 1980s version of share-cropping. Indeed, many woodcutters buy their products and borrow against their homes through the woodlots, increasing their dependence.

High Risk, Low Gain

The work is dangerous, but the only woodcutters who wear hard hats and protective chaps against chain saw backlash are in one area where the insurance companies got involved. Dr. Michael Jabaley, a boyhood friend of mine, now a surgeon living in Jackson who is nationally known for his expertise on the human hand, tells me that he regularly operates on woodcutters with no medical insurance who have either cut their hands terribly with saws or had them crushed by shifting logs.

Yet a woodcutter can get a truck and chain saw for perhaps $2,000, and most average an income of $5,000 a year. Many, like Willie Lee Little who worked in a foundry in Chicago while his family grew up in

Mississippi, have returned to a Mississippi much changed since they left. Using firewood for heating and living in simple houses with their own gardens, many find the life better in Mississippi poverty "than behind the bars of the city," in Little's words.

More than a decade ago the Gulf Coast Pulpwood Association made an effort to organize woodcutters, beginning in Alabama and spreading into Mississippi. But strikes against woodlots were not effective. As C. C. Miller of Weir said in October, "No matter how unhappy people is, less than half would join a strike against a woodlot here." The demand was for higher prices, an approach now judged in retrospect to be ineffective as long as the lots can "squeeze the stick."

But the United Church of Christ Board for Homeland Ministries, especially staff member John Moyer, continued to show interest in the poverty of this tertiary labor force and funded research into the paper industry and the conditions of the workers. Two years ago several religious denominations met in Mississippi and created a new instrument, the Southern Woodcutters Assistance Project (SWAP). The Rev. Jim Drake, who for fifteen years had worked with the United Farm Workers and Cesar Chavez, was asked to head the project.

Jim and Cris Drake moved to Mississippi and began to feel out the situation. Drake recalls the winter of 1978–79, when they were forced out of one house because of the nature of their work. It was as hard, he says, as any he had with the Farm Workers. One of the first people he met was Little, who had belonged to the UAW in Chicago and remembered "not eatin' lettuce as much as I loves salad."

Little says: "Jim Drake, he's just about the best organizer I ever met. The man just came through out of nowhere with a good idea and now the woodcutters has hope."

Employing organizing methods learned from the Farm Workers, Drake and a small staff concentrated on the forty or so counties in the central and southern part of the state most involved in the timber business. (The Delta region is not part of this.)

In February 1979, they had persuaded sixty families in twelve counties to meet together in Canton, where they started a cooperative. The fee to join is $12.50 and monthly dues are $3. They borrowed $3,000 from Chris Hartmire and the National Farmworkers Ministry to create an inventory. Chain oil, which they sell at $2.50 a gallon rather than the commercial $3.50, was a hot item. A busy woodcutter uses two gallons a week in his saw. He also uses a new chain once every two or three weeks and the co-op sells them for $11.50, against a price of around $25 at woodlots and stores. The co-op takes an 11 percent markup; stores take more than 100 percent. Stocking nine items, the co-op has saved woodcutters an estimated $100,000 in eighteen months.

Once the cooperative was in place, says Drake, "we had something to sell other than organizers' hot air." They moved to house meetings in the Farm Workers' style.

"We located an interested woodcutter and then gave him our rap about what working together and using the co-op could do. 'We can do it here.' We would ask him to arrange a meeting with no more than five other people at his house or church. There we would repeat the rap — it takes about an hour and all organizers use the same approach — and then ask them to invite five more people."

"Only then, with twenty or thirty exposed, did we move to form a local group. We got one member to be the co-op rep, serviced twice a month by Roy Harmon [cousin of Washington Redskins' halfback Clarence Harmon], a woodcutter. And we got another to be the rep for the credit union, which is building slowly as a way to provide the small loans that tie these people to the woodlots."

By August there were three hundred or more members who met to formally establish the United Woodcutters Association. They paid back the $3,000 to Chris Hartmire, who came to the meeting. They elected officers — Willie Lee Little is a vice-president of the association and president of the credit union — and passed three resolutions: (1) to extend the association throughout the state with a $3 monthly dues; (2) to get a federal charter for the credit union; (3) to begin work on the problem of the short stick.

The SWAP staff now numbers fourteen, as income has grown from dues, a strong response to direct mail appeals and contributions from two foundations, the New World Foundation and the Center for Community Change, and from religious groups, including the United Church of Christ, the Northern and Southern Presbyterians, Disciples of Christ, United Methodist Church, the Claretian, Dominican, and Franciscan religious orders and the (Roman Catholic) Campaign for Human Development.

Preventing "Burn-Out"

Each staffmember is paid $55 a week and provided with medical coverage. Housing costs for some are cut by communal arrangements or by living with local families; costs over $35 a month are subsidized by SWAP. Drake says, "We could have twice as many staff if we had more funds. And we are doing this differently from the Farm Workers [who pay $10 a week]. The money is small but the staff is paid, not volunteer, which I hope will cut down on burn-out. No one will make any money, but we don't want people to leave poorer than they came."

Most SWAP staffers are at work organizing more local groups. Margaret Murphy heads the United Woodcutters' Services, sorting through insurance claims, obtaining unemployment compensation in a few cases where woodlots had deducted money without providing policies, and working on educational programs to help woodcutters organize their finances and provide accident insurance for themselves.

Her husband, Jeff Sweetland, directs the new legislative emphasis. This winter a number of seminars are underway to train woodcutters in putting pressure on their legislators and in building community support for legislative proposals.

The past year's legislative effort was directed toward the UWA's first legislative convention, held September 6. The staff had a pool guessing the turnout beforehand; the highest estimate was 450. More than 600 were registered, and as many as 100 more may have attended without registering.

All the convention resolutions had to do with the short stick problem. The UWA is calling for the Mississippi legislature to pass a Fair Pulpwood Scaling and Practices Act. They want the woodlots licensed; those found cheating by a state board would lose their right to do business. Arbitration would be possible in some cases of disagreement.

Sweetland believes it will be very difficult even to get the bill introduced in the 1981 session of the legislature, which runs only from January to March. But the fastgrowing UWA will elicit church and civic group support for meetings with local representatives and senators. "Either way, we'll win," Sweetland believes. "We may not get a law in this session but we'll begin putting pressure on the yards and the state agencies to provide better enforcement of existing laws."

The woodlot operators and the companies behind them have a lot of political clout. But the issue appears ultimately winnable. First, the woodcutters enjoy considerable sympathy from the wider community who knows how little return they get from their hard work. Second, the timber owners are also affected by the "short stick" because their stumpage payments are based on the same measurement. Finally, the state also loses because the same calculation determines its severance tax of 23 cents a cord for pine, 18 cents for hardwood.

The big companies, with headquarters elsewhere, are not favorites in Mississippi because they export much of their lumber and pulp to other parts of the nation to make finished products. Gov. William Winter has been heard to say lately that Mississippi wants to attract businesses that pay more than a minimum wage and are not simply attracted by the cheap labor force.

Signs of Change

The six hundred members of the UWA are all truck owners. On the average, they employ two workers who are not direct members but who, with their families, help make an effective organization of eighteen hundred. And that will grow.

The organization is predominantly black and the black majority is especially evident in the public meetings. But many whites belong to the co-op and this effort of blacks and whites working together for an economic goal is a sign of changes that have taken place in Mississippi. In the late 1960s I visited the state from time to time to report on the Delta Ministry. On this trip a black woman told me, "Things are as different from 1965–68 now as night and day. But they've got a ways to go. Banks still don't loan us money. And when blacks went to the quarry where whites swam, it was posted to keep everybody out."

Jim Drake is confident that the organization will continue to grow and mature. He believes leadership is emerging, although it will not be in the charismatic tradition of the Farm Workers. Eventually, he believes, only a few outside staff people will be needed to provide technical services. He then would consider moving to another state to begin the process again. Mississippi is only one of several states where woodcutters are at the bottom of the pile.

The spirit is moving. There are now thirty-six local groups in thirty counties. E. J. Flowers, a retired woodcutter who organized a new local on his own and brought fifty people to the September convention, sums it up: "You think about it, a woodcutter and what he has to undergo. A man goes to village to tank up. I went and tanked up today and it was twenty-some dollars. And that woodcutter feeds his truck up and it ain't goin' just so far. And when he gets out there with that wood, that man puts that stick on him and he may have a cord or a half a cord more than what it says on the stick. But he can't argue, because if he started, then that man will tell him 'Don't come back.' And you done had it!

"What I'm trying to say in so many words, we have all said through the years. 'The big fish is eatin' up the little fish.' That's saying the same thing. The woodcutters just don't have the chance unless they organize."

The Administration's Social Doctrine: Reaganethics

December 14, 1981

John C. Bennett

John C. Bennett, the dean of American Christian ethicists, has written for C & C *for fifty years. He retired in 1970 as president of Union Theological Seminary, New York.*

IT MAY BE TOO EARLY to judge the effects of the administration's economic plan, but it is not too early to examine and debate the already revealed doctrines and assumptions of the administration because they are of great ethical and social significance. I am going to lift up for examination four such doctrines or assumptions. I believe that they are all in conflict with the teachings of both ecumenical Protestantism and Roman Catholicism.

1. The rights of property are generally seen as obstacles to any serious correction of the current distribution of wealth and income for the sake of justice and social health. One often articulated doctrine is that taxation should be used only for revenue and not to bring about social changes, including changes in the distribution of wealth. This goes directly against the experience of many decades during which progressive taxation has been essential to make American capitalism morally tolerable. To reduce the upper limit of taxation for the rich from 70 percent to 50 percent and to remove most inheritance taxes is to take long steps away from progressive taxation as a correction of the inequities of capitalism. (David Stockman says that the supply side people were most interested in this 70 to 50 percent reduction. It was indiscreet for him, given his responsibilities, to feed materials for the article to a journalist, but his revelation of his own ideas about Reaganomics is a service to the public.)

We hear much talk these days of the right of people to keep what they earn. The administration would acknowledge that this right has to be abridged for the sake of taxation for essential revenues, especially for national defense, but we need to look at the whole conception of "earning" and of property that underlies its approach. Earning is a social process. Society as a whole provides the protections and the economic environment that make earning possible. Many people and factors contribute to this process, which enables those most favorably placed to earn large incomes. Population growth in a particular area increases the value of property that lucky people can skim off for themselves. Earning is greatly increased by those with monopolistic advantages that have been created as much by cunning and

luck as by exceptional economic creativity. These gains are made at
the expense of competitive correctives in the system.

How much do speculative increases of wealth have to do with
"earning"? Speculative increases of earned wealth and speculative increases of inherited wealth are protected by changes in the tax laws. Is
it not just and necessary for the health of the system to use taxation to
give back to the public much of what it has contributed to conditions
that make the earning of large wealth possible? Both ecumenical Protestant and Catholic teaching have greatly emphasized the relativity of
all property rights. Pope Paul VI spoke for a remarkable consensus of
Christian teaching when he said: "Private property does not constitute
for anyone an absolute and unconditioned right. No one is justified in
keeping for his exclusive use what he does not need, when others lack
necessities" (*Populorum Progressio*, par. 23).

2. Another doctrine implicit in the administration's assumptions
and policies is that private enterprise is inherently good, but that public enterprise is inherently open to suspicion and in most cases no
better than a necessary evil. National defense, of course, is an exception to this; it is not only gladly accepted as a public enterprise, but
it is made as unaccountable to the people as possible. Even serious
debate as to the reasons for it is discouraged.

Should we be so suspicious of efforts of the community as a whole
to deal with problems that are so large that only the strength of the
national community can match them? Why must it be assumed that
it is in principle better for solutions of national economic problems
to come as byproducts of the search for private profit? I recognize
that this method often has advantages in terms of dynamism and efficiency. The market does create moments of truth for private enterprise
that public enterprise may often evade. It is also true that serious conflicts of interest develop between the public and large concentrations
of private economic power.

The Burden of Proof

There are clearly two sides to this question. I am not questioning the
value of private initiatives, of the extensive economic pluralism that
they make possible or their capacity for innovation. I recognize the importance of private incentives for productivity. But criticism is in order
when incentives lead to great concentrations of wealth and power.
What I question is the current dogma that puts so great a burden of
proof on public enterprise as compared with private enterprise.

One central issue in this context is the relative virtue or innocence
of private and public economic power. When the units are checked
by competitors, private power has much to be said for it. But especially when it takes the form of enormous conglomerates or of

multinational corporations that operate in countries with weak governments, it needs to be questioned. Private power is less visible than public power. It is less accountable to the people most affected by it. Public power is made accountable by various balancing processes and by the fact that those who manage government at every level can be changed by the votes of the people.

In 1931 Pope Pius XI, who was more conservative than his recent successors, laid down an important principle. In the midst of an attack on socialism in his encyclical *Quadragesimo Anno,* he says: "It is rightly contended that certain forms of property must be reserved to the state, since they carry with them an opportunity of domination too great to be left to private individuals without injury to the community at large" (par. 114).

In our society it is always an open question as to what political unit — federal or local or the "state" in our special sense — should have control. We should avoid a priori dogmas about this, but we must not forget that the national state has been responsible for most of the reforms in the interest of poor and exploited people; this was most dramatically evident in the case of racial minorities in recent years. Larger conceptions of the welfare of the people have seemed to reverberate better and to get a better hearing on the national level than on the local or regional level. The needs of neglected and deprived people seem to be cumulatively felt on the national level.

We should approach the choice between private and public forms of power with minds that are open to the claims of both. I wonder if what is at stake is not covered up by the slogan about giving back the power to the people. What people? George Gilder's book *Wealth and Poverty* is almost a bible for those who have recently come to make absolute claims for private enterprise. Michael Walzer points out that "of capitalism as a system of power Gilder has nothing to say" (*New York Review of Books,* April 2, 1981). For him it is an idealized system of service.

This is an area of experiment and debate in which the church — as a watchtower that knows the nation as a whole and is aware of the needs and the hurt of all social groups — can contribute insights available to no other institution. Its pastoral experience and its insights concerning the self-deceptions that go with power, whether public or private, can be sources of wisdom.

3. One assumption that is not celebrated as a doctrine but which seems generally to be taken for granted is that it is more appropriate for the most vulnerable people — the poor, the handicapped, the sick, the young people who are unemployed, and many of the elderly — to make greater sacrifices and take greater risks with their own lives, even in regard to their health, for the sake of the well-being of the

economy as a whole than it would be for the more favored people. We are told that this is justified because if they make these sacrifices, there will be more jobs and more productivity, and as a result benefits will come to all classes. This is no different from the old "trickle-down" argument. (I wrote this before I knew of Stockman's use of "trickle-down"!) There has often been much trickling down, and the poor are not one-third of the population anymore but nearer to one-eighth. But today they number about twenty-nine million more than the population of either California or Canada, and present policies could easily for a time push many millions more into poverty as a sacrifice for the health of the economy.

The Burden of Sacrifice

Quite apart from the question as to whether Reaganomics will work in the long run and have some of the results that are hoped for, we know that in the short run there will be tens of millions of victims of this sacrifice. There are promises for the future but their fulfillment is going to be delayed, if it ever comes. The president is calling for even more budget cuts in social programs, but Congress is resisting this because it is less ideological. Even if one were to grant the claims of those who make promises for the future based on these policies, should there not be in addition to the much emphasized "safety net" a transitional safety net to protect these many victims during the now inevitable delay in the fulfillment of the promises? It is morally intolerable to ask so many unfortunate people to take much greater risks to their health and to their essential well-being than the rest of the population when they have less margin of security against such risks. And it is not only unjust but indecent to give at the same time great tax advantages to those already rich and comfortable.

Those who are victims of these policies are sacrificed in part to the enormous military build-up. This is related to the great desire to make our country great in the eyes of the world. But it is a poor sign of greatness to treat so many of our people in this way. This will give us a bad image not only in the eyes of poorer nations but also in the eyes of the other industrialized democracies, which do not sacrifice their own people in this way. We like to think of ourselves as the leader of the "free world," but we undermine this role when we demonstrate the human cost of our free institutions.

4. A favorite idea of President Reagan seems to be that when there are budget cuts at the expense of people, voluntary action should be stimulated to compensate for the losses they suffer. This appeal to private generosity may seem to fit well the message of the church. What is provided by the society as a whole for its members, both in the best of times and in the worst of times, must as a matter of justice

be supplemented by private gifts to meet special needs of individuals and families. Still I find two things wrong with this dependence on private giving.

The most obvious is that there is reason to doubt that such voluntary aid would ever be enough in volume to provide substitutes for what may be cut in food stamps, school lunches, Medicaid payments, additional weeks of unemployment compensation — to name a few of the losses people will suffer. Is it not ironic that at the very moment when we have this new appeal for private generosity we are told that the tax cuts, especially those for the very wealthy whose taxes are cut from 70 percent to 50 percent, will actually reduce the incentives for giving that have been operative? Institutions that have depended on such large gifts are now expecting to have great difficulty in keeping up what they are already doing. We can hardly expect to find large new sources of philanthropy to meet new needs.

There is yet a deeper problem. Even if these exhortations for more voluntary efforts and for more private generosity were able to go far in meeting these new needs, this whole approach would be unjust. It is unjust when large groups of people, except in emergencies, must depend for the necessities of life on the unstable and passing impulses of generosity of private persons rather than upon the sense of responsibility of the community to which they belong.

I have always been impressed by the words of the great Russian Orthodox religious philosopher, Nicolai Berdyaev: "A person's fate cannot be made to rest solely upon other people's spiritual condition. This is where the significance of law comes in. No one can be made to depend upon his neighbors' moral qualities and inward perfection" (*The Destiny of Man*, p. 120). At least that should not happen in a just and decent society that respects all its members and recognizes that they have rights as human beings. Laws cannot take the place of personal virtues, but one personal virtue is to will to be taxed for the sake of the common good.

Equality and Justice

One general consideration underlies all of these doctrines and assumptions having to do with the status of the idea of equality in relation to what we believe about social justice. It is evident that those who espouse the administration's doctrines and assumptions have no place for the claims of equality as a source of judgment upon economic structures and policies. I doubt if many of our readers would equate justice with equality or would call for the use of law to create or preserve complete economic equality in our population. This would require oppressive regimentation, and evading the law would become a way of life for most people. Society would become too static as incentives to make innovations involving risk would be reduced. I have already said that there is good in the incentives to improve one's condition that capitalism provides.

This should not mean, however, that there are no limits either to the accumulation of wealth or to the development of aggregates of private economic power. Up to a point there is truth in the contention that protection of private property helps protect against total control by the state. This is especially true when such property becomes embodied in private institutions such as universities, churches, and even labor unions. However, when accumulations of property reach a certain point those who control them may too readily control the state itself in their own interests.

There are degrees of economic inequality that destroy fellowship, that are incompatible with equal dignity, that increase pride and arrogance in the rich and either servility or alienation among the poor. Justice is not identical with equality, but systems of justice should be under the criticism and pressure of ideas of equality. Christians should know well that most of the arguments for inequalities by those who benefit from them, arguments which are now so popular in this country, stem from self-interest and are supported by callousness.

Jacques Maritain, the great Catholic philosopher of the last generation, provides the following beautiful quotation from Thomas Aquinas, who is expounding and improving on Aristotle:

It is up to friendship to put to work, in an equal manner, the equality that already exists among men. But it is up to justice to draw to equality those who are unequal: The work of justice is fulfilled when this equality is achieved. Thus equality comes at the terminus of justice, and lies at the base and origin of friendship" (*The Rights of Man and Natural Law*, p. 37).

In his most influential book, *A Theory of Justice*, John Rawls emphasizes the principle that social and economic inequalities "are just only if they result in compensating benefits for everyone, and in particular for the least advantaged members of society" (pp. 14–15).

This general idea — that structures and policies that aim at justice should be under the criticism of the idea of equality — should be tested by the common American affirmation of belief in equal opportunity for all. The public school system is a symbol and embodiment of this belief. The usual statement of this belief distinguished between equality of opportunity and equality of results. But regularly there is omission of what should be a central part of the belief in equality of opportunity: Inequality of the economic conditions under which children live may be so great that equality of opportunity is an illusion.

Equality of opportunity is nonexistent if some children go to school malnourished and others go well fed. Equality of opportunity is nonexistent when we compare the schools in the most deprived sections of many cities with those in prosperous suburbs. Obviously there are handicapping conditions that cannot be overcome by law or by the most just public policies and structures. The morale of families may be so bad in either inner city or suburb that equal opportunity for development is threatened or undercut. However, these situations provide no excuse to tolerate the kinds of inequality of condition that public policies and structures can prevent.

The surest test of the justice in a society is the effect of its policies on its children, and especially on those children who are most likely to be neglected or injured: the deserving children of those who are regarded by authorities as the "undeserving poor." There are other persons who need attention, persons of all ages, but a society that is sensitive enough to combine both justice and loving compassion at this point is likely to pass other tests. Guided by the doctrines and assumptions that I have described, this administration is not putting itself into the position to pass this test.

I fear that the words of James Tobin, the Yale economics professor who recently received the Nobel Prize, may prove to be correct: "The message is clear enough: Inequality of opportunity is no longer a concern of the Federal Government" (*New York Review of Books*, November 19, 1981). There was no mandate for this.

A Theological Reflection on Sanctuary

February 21, 1983

Eric Jorstad

Eric Jorstad is a graduate of both Yale Divinity School and Yale Law School. He is a law clerk to U.S. District Judge Diana Murphy in Minneapolis.

AS MASKED REFUGEES with pseudonyms travel the new Underground Railroad from fear to at least relative safety and American church people break the law by "harboring an illegal alien," the drama of sanctuary makes for good press. But deeper issues that don't get to the mass media need exploring. The sanctuary movement is more than humanitarian aid, more than a "publicity stunt," as U.S. Immigration and Naturalization Service officials have charged. It is a challenge to the church to reexamine its self-understanding as the one, holy, catholic, and apostolic people of God. I believe that public sanctuary for

Central American refugees poses a fundamental question to the North American church: Is our practice in accord with our basic mission?

It has been suggested that by the year 2000 there will be two political parties in this country, the Christian Fascists and the Christian Socialists. Being a devout pluralist and believer in the power of what John Naisbitt, author of *Megatrends*, calls the "radical center," I do not believe this to be the whole truth nor inevitable. Yet the distinction points to an important and divisive question for Christians. As U.S. churches become increasingly self-conscious about the social and political dimensions of their message and mission, what direction should that growing awareness take?

Social ministry becomes of increasing concern, and certainly includes the individual and institutional acts of compassion and caring through hospitals, emergency food pantries, nursing homes, shelters for the homeless, support groups for those in distress, mental illness, family violence, and so on. But I refer here especially to social ministry as advocacy for justice, addressing public issues of economic, foreign, and military policy. Even as some sectors of the churches raise their voices ever more loudly in quest of peace-with-justice, an increasingly vocal opposition questions the legitimacy of the church dealing with these issues. Largely because of the criticisms of the Institute for Religion and Democracy (IRD), national media have focused on the advocacy and justice programs of the National Council of Churches and World Council of Churches. The question they ask is: Has the church betrayed its mission by becoming an organ of partisan, and sometimes revolutionary, politics? The counter question is: Can the church be faithful to its mission if it does not speak out and address specific public issues in the political arena?

The movement to provide public church sanctuary for Central American refugees casts these questions into a distinctively new light. It does so in three ways: by raising a church which transcends the boundaries of nation-states, by raising a church with a clear commitment to the poor and powerless, and by raising a church of an empowering solidarity between the peoples of Central and North America. Together, these three call the American church to a conversion, a return to its first and fundamental sense of itself: In other words, the sanctuary movement calls the church to be catholic (universal), holy (in love seeking justice), one (in solidarity), and apostolic (faithful to the message of the Cross).

Sanctuary is a powerful symbol of the limits of the authority of the state. Under medieval English law, a fugitive in an officially recognized sanctuary could "abjure the realm" and move from the sanctuary out of the country in safety. The sanctuary of the church stood at the boundary of the nation-state, as a kind of door. The sanctuary represented an order which transcended the sovereignty of the nation-state. In this century, the Lutheran theologian Dietrich Bonhoeffer declared the church sanctuary to be a place of sanctuary from political idolatry. He denounced the placing of German swastika flags around the altar of God, as if Christians should kneel before the flag as well as before God.

Transcending the Nation-State

Sanctuary represents the church's ultimate allegiance to God alone. It thus relativizes the claims of any particular nation-state. Further, sanctuary represents an order which cannot be encompassed by *any* nation-state, and transcends all their boundaries. This has traditionally been expressed by saying the church is catholic. Sanctuary symbolizes the universality of the church.

Whether or not public sanctuary for Central American refugees can be justified in any particular congregation, the sanctuary movement has reawakened the consciousness of the church to this sense of the *whole*, to this sense of a transcendent order which stands over all human orders. It thus emphasizes the secularity of politics and is a critique of all "divine empires," whether created in the name of "communism" or "democracy." The sanctuary movement calls the church to hold the state accountable to God's justice.

The three ways that the New Testament understands the mission of the church as sanctuary also define its commitment to the poor and powerless — as an inclusive community, as an advocate for the powerless, and as an agent of reconciliation. This was clearly put to the unjust king Jehoiakim by the prophet Jeremiah:

> Woe to him who builds his house by unrighteousness,
> and his upper rooms by injustice;
> who makes his neighbor serve him for nothing,
> and does not give him his wages....
> Do you think you are a king
> because you compete in cedar?
> Did not your father eat and drink
> and do justice and righteousness?
> Then it was well with him.
> He judged the cause of the poor and needy;
> then it was well.
> Is not this to know me?
> says the Lord. (Jer. 22:13, 15–16)

The distinguishing characteristic of those who know the Lord, the prophet says, is to act on behalf of the poor and needy. Jesus reaffirms this when he says, "As you did it to one of the least of these my brethren, you did it to me" (Mt. 25:40). God identifies in a special

way with the poor. Isaiah describes the cessation of oppression and
the pursuit of justice for the powerless as an act of holiness, more
holy than "vain offerings," "the calling of assemblies," the "appointed
feasts," or even the making of "many prayers."

> Wash yourselves; make yourselves clean;
>   remove the evil of your doings from before my eyes;
> cease to do evil;
>   learn to do good;
> seek justice;
>   correct oppression;
> defend the fatherless;
>   plead for the widow. (Is. 1:12–17)

Public sanctuary for Central American refugees takes a stand on
behalf of a particularly powerless and vulnerable group of people,
who have fled persecution in their own country only to face possible
prosecution in ours. Whether or not public sanctuary can be justified in
any particular congregation, the sanctuary movement calls the church
to reexamine its fundamental commitment to the poor and powerless.
Is practice in accord with mission? Sanctuary asks the church to seek
to be *holy*, not only in the ritual within the "sanctuary" of worship,
but also in its faithfulness to its mission. Worship and social ministry
are united in the concept of sanctuary.

Empowering Solidarity

One of the most important aspects of public sanctuary for Central
American refugees is its goal of empowering the refugees themselves
in their struggle for peace with justice in their native country. Sanctuary offers not only protection, but also a platform. While underground,
the refugees cannot but be passive before the events in our country
and their own. But as they share their story, a bond of solidarity is
forged with their host congregation, and indeed with all who would
hear and enter into a relationship.

The sanctuary movement calls the church to be one. It brings the
voice of the Latin American church into the heart of the North American church. The North American church has historically been more
active in speaking than in listening, when it comes to the rest of the
world, especially the Third World. This ecclesiastical and cultural imperialism is clearly expressed in the following hymn, to the tune of
the "Missionary Hymn":

> From Greenland's icy mountains,
> From India's coral strand,
> Where Africa's sunny fountains
> Roll down their golden sand,

From many an ancient river,
From many a palmy plain,
They call us to deliver
Their land from error's chain.
Can we whose souls are lighted,
With wisdom from on high,
Can we to men benighted,
The lamp of life deny?

My purpose here is not to argue for or against the world missions movement, but to suggest an attitude common in the North American church. We have tended, with western Europe, to see ourselves as the center of world Christendom. Like it or not, that is changing. The unity of the church can no longer be maintained by Third World theologians studying at first world seminaries. The voice of the Latin American church, for one, is rising out of the experience of their people and their understanding of how God is at work in their history. Sanctuary for Central American refugees brings this voice into our midst. It asks us not only to be *benefactors* of the powerless, but also to be *beneficiaries* of their witness of faith. Sanctuary makes possible an empowering partnership between North and Central American peoples. Sanctuary thus calls the church to be truly *one*. The widely ecumenical character of the sanctuary movement further exemplifies this.

In these three ways — in transcending the nation-state, in a clear commitment to the poor and powerless, and in empowering solidarity — the church is called to reexamine its mission as catholic, holy, and one. Is its practice in accord with its mission?

The whole mission of the church cannot be subsumed under social ministry; that view is patently and obviously untrue. But it is true that social ministry — in this case sanctuary for Central American refugees — challenges the whole church in *all* its aspects to be faithful to its mission. There is no church without social ministry. There is no church without faith active in love seeking justice. The North American church is being challenged to grow in its understanding of and actions based on the social and political dimensions of the gospel. The current sanctuary movement poses this challenge in a distinctive and potent way. It is not a question, as some would argue, of "mixing politics and religion." Rather, it is a question of faithfulness to the mission of the church in history. How can the church embody its witness to the promise of liberation in its present time and space? Sanctuary sanctifies present time and space as a place where God's New Creation is breaking in upon a recalcitrant world.

...and Apostolic

This call to be one, holy, and catholic leads to the fourth and final challenge which the sanctuary movement poses to the church: to be *apostolic*, that is, to be faithful to the message of the Crucified One. The impoverished and brutalized people of El Salvador, which means "the Savior," has been pierced in the side. Out flows water and blood — the tears of years of suffering and terror, the blood of tens of thousands of Good Fridays in unending succession. The Savior is stretched and nailed between sky and soil, between heaven and earth, a silent witness to the dream of God's justice and the reality of human cruelty. In El Salvador, Christians who try to help the poor are labelled "subversives" and become targets for death squads. Many priests and lay workers have been killed; Archbishop Oscar Romero was assassinated at the altar saying Mass. Jesus, too, found that an act of compassion could be seen as subversion (Mt. 12:9–14). There are wall signs throughout El Salvador which read: "Be a patriot, shoot a priest." Yet even as the Good Fridays continue, there are glimpses of an Easter dawn. Before his murder, Archbishop Romero said, "If they kill me, I will rise in the struggle of the Salvadoran people." The people still believe that life, through God, can overcome death.

The North American church must face a difficult question: Is our country helping pound the nails into the suffering body of El Salvador? The sanctuary movement gives our church a chance to hear this question, as if spoken right from the cross. It thus draws us into a deep inner wrestling with the meaning of our Christian faith in relation to the policies of our government. It draws us into the suffering of the Latin American church, with hard questions about our church and our role there. But it draws us even further than that. Jesus said, "And I, when I am lifted up from the earth [i.e., crucified], will draw all persons to myself" (Jn. 12:32). The Savior draws us to know and experience his resurrection. To experience the crucifixion of the people of El Salvador is not the last word, for we can also be drawn to experience their resurrection. The victim becomes the healer. That is the deepest message of the sanctuary movement. When we choose to stand by the Cross, by the victims, by the refugees, we are also choosing to stand with ourselves. There is really no border between us. Our own liberation is bound inextricably with the liberation of our brothers and sisters in Central America. We are freed to experience their hope and to struggle with them to make it real. In church sanctuary, the victims of the violence carried out in our name can touch and heal us.

On Christian Intellectuals

March 19, 1984

Cornel West

Cornel West directs the Afro-American Studies Program and teaches religion at Princeton University. A C&C *contributing editor, he is the author of* Prophesy Deliverance: An Afro-American Revolutionary Christianity *and* The American Evasion of Philosophy.

IN HIS INFLUENTIAL *Prison Notebooks*, the Italian Marxist Antonio Gramsci makes an important distinction between "organic" and "traditional" intellectuals. To put it crudely, the former are those who, because they are organically linked to prophetic movements or priestly institutions, take the life of the mind seriously enough to relate ideas to the everyday life of ordinary folk. Traditional intellectuals, in contrast, are those who revel in the world of ideas while nesting in comfortable places far removed from the realities of the common life. Organic intellectuals are activistic and engaged; traditional intellectuals are academic and detached.

Like most such constructs, Gramsci's distinction is too broad and vague to do full justice to the complexity of intellectual activity. Yet it is useful. Prior to the emergence of modernity, intellectuals primarily were organically linked with either the church or rich patrons. Contrary to popular opinion, medieval intellectuals were organic intellectuals, often involved in public turmoil. Today most intellectuals are employed by educational institutions. They are traditional intellectuals preoccupied with academic affairs.

A distinctive feature of religious traditions in the modern world — represented in seminaries, ecclesiastical agencies, and especially churches — is that, at least ideally, serious intellectual activity is understood as inseparable from moral and political practice. In contrast to predominant modern conceptions of knowledge, which subordinate ideas to technical control and manipulation, religious notions of knowledge accent ethical accountability and political fruition. This is especially so for the Christian tradition in which the principal form of intellectual activity consists of making clear and plain the content and character of Christian living.

Christian intellectuals should differ from others by refusing either to exalt or to denigrate the life of the mind. They should raise questions about the modern "objective" search for truth and the enthusiasm for social engineering. The ideal Christian intellectual is neither a detached seminary professor teaching potential elites of the church nor an engaged layperson in solidarity with the downtrodden, but rather the dedicated and devoted Christian member of a group or community informed by the best available systemic social analysis of self and society and guided by the most insightful interpretation of the Scriptures and tradition. This ideal Christian intellectual is an organic intellectual, simultaneously immersed in the tortuous realities of the day and enticed by the felicities of the mind.

What Is the Task?

Contemporary circumstances make it difficult for such Christian intellectuals to emerge. First, the professional ethos of the secular academy continues to seduce many seminaries and divinity schools. Principled and fruitful interaction with the academy is indispensable; yet the academy cannot serve as either model or paradigm for Christian cultivation. Second, increased denominational concerns breed parochial modes of intellectual activity that are narrowly defensive and obsessed with internal operations. This reversion to premodern sentiments — aided by modern capital — is nostalgic and escapist. Third, the world of highbrow journalism offers stimulation but it does not lend itself to the kind of intellectual depth requisite for profound Christian vision, analysis, and practice.

The tasks of Christian intellectuals are to uphold the centrality of prophetic preaching of the Word, preserve the richness of the Christian past, and put forward informed Christian ways of life and struggle. These tasks include traditional and organic types of intellectual work, — but their aim should be the production of sermons and texts which become potent within the lives of everyday people. This does not mean that sermons and texts should simply cater to parishioners, but rather that they should be directed to the pertinent issues that fundamentally affect the lives of church people.

The critical function of Christian intellectuals remains a crucial item on the theological agenda. And none of the schools of thought and action on the scene contains acceptable perspectives on this issue. This is so primary because theologians and preachers are reluctant to engage in what Gramsci calls a "self-inventory" — a critical examination of their own middle-class status, academic setting, or social privilege. Yet a more self-critical viewpoint is imperative if the body of Christ is to function in a more Christian manner.

Churches in Communities: A Place to Stand

February 2, 1987

Jim Gittings

Jim Gittings is a veteran church journalist who lived in Asia for a number of years, served as an editor of AD, *owned and published* Seventh Angel, *and is now based in Greenville, S.C., where he serves as communications director of ALM International.*

WALK WEST, if purse-snatchers and crack-crazies permit, along Blake Street in Brooklyn's Brownsville section. A few shattered buildings remain standing among the rubble-strewn lots; all else is a desolation.

Yet the outlook changes when one rounds a corner onto Mother Gaston Boulevard. First, small shops appear. They are not much to look at, but they are obviously conducting a vigorous trade. Next come nests of public housing: These multistoried units have been up for two or three decades; the trees in their courtyards are grown to third-floor height, and somebody is keeping graffiti under considerable though not total control. And finally, abruptly, a stroller enters a neighborhood of new and attractive two-story row homes, more than eight hundred of them on this early November day, with an additional two hundred or so scheduled for completion by April 1.

The houses — erected by something called the Nehemiah Project — are the only low-income mass housing to be erected in New York City since Congress and Ronald Reagan's administration pulled the plug more than five years ago on public housing funds. The brick two- and three-bedroom dwellings cost $53,000 each to build, and are sold for $43,000 (a $10,000 second mortgage, interest-free, is payable to New York City upon resale). As completed, each house has been occupied immediately — has *had* to be occupied immediately, given the ubiquity of thieves prepared to strip plumbing and fixtures from vacant structures — by a family whose name has been drawn from a waiting list exceeding four thousand. Purchasers usually, though not always, are members of the black or Hispanic majority communities in the Brownsville area. They earn between $15,000 and $25,000 per household, and have managed to accumulate or borrow $5,000 for a down payment (the monthly mortgage payment averages $325 to $345). Departure of these people from public housing accommodations or from "Section VIII" apartments (the Nixon era's version of federally subsidized housing) has freed up space there for even poorer families.

Because the Nehemiah Project has succeeded in erecting homes quickly and at low cost, because its sponsors have put together a smoothly functioning web of available mortgage credit for would-be purchasers, and because the project is such an obvious success in terms of infusing a neighborhood with new life, a lot of people want to copy it.

Five days of wandering the Brownsville, Ocean Hill, and East New York sections of Brooklyn convince me, however, that the Nehemiah effort *for so long as it is conceived of as a "project" or a "program"* cannot be duplicated. The politicians miss the point entirely: The new homes and their proud owners, attractive as they are, constitute only an episode, a single achievement, in a still unfolding process by which a hitherto powerless people has entered into politics, into what Aristotle defined as "public discourse," and thereby has won the capacity, as George Todd points out, to become "the subject of its own story."

Against a background of decay and change, a Lutheran pastor, the Reverend John Heinemeier, convened a group of Catholic and Protestant clergy and laypersons on April 6, 1978, to discuss ways churches and their members could address area problems. The handful of people who attended listened to a description of the work being done by an organization in the adjacent Borough of Queens that was also centered upon the churches. Encouraged by what was learned, the East Brooklyn group agreed to meet again. By the third meeting, June 8, members of the group, now swollen to forty clergy and laypersons, were led in discussion by Edward T. Chambers, from the Industrial Areas Foundation (IAF).

The encounter between Chambers and the Brooklyn group was portentous for both interests. This is not the place to trace in depth the history of Industrial Areas Foundation — its beginnings under "radical community organizer" Saul Alinsky in the Chicago of the 1940s, its entry into national prominence (and a certain notoriety) in the 1960s and 1970s as a result of its organizing role in The Woodlawn Organization (Chicago), the Kodak FIGHT controversy in Rochester, and similar community-industry and community-urban government struggles elsewhere. Chambers, once a Catholic seminarian who later spent two years in a Catholic interracial house in Harlem under Dorothy Day's tutelage, was hired by Alinsky in 1957. He went on with Alinsky to lead in organization of Southwest Chicago (1959), take part in 1962 in the Woodlawn–University of Chicago struggle, organize the FIGHT forces in the Kodak wars (1965–67), and cofound with Alinsky the IAF Training Institute in 1968. Chambers is, in fact, Alinsky's heir, and he has continued since his teacher's death to expand and adapt the Alinsky *pratique* by establishing eighteen IAF-affiliated community organizations in California, New York, Maryland, and Texas.

The utility of the Brownsville meeting for Chambers was this: He had recently removed the Industrial Areas Foundation from Chicago to its present headquarters location in Garden City, on Long Island, and needed an extra client (in addition to the Queens group) in the New York area. The utility of Chambers for the Brownsville group was equally related to self-interest. "We didn't know anything except that nothing was to be expected in solving our problems from anybody but ourselves," one who was present remembers, "and Chambers was just the man to tell us how much it was going to cost."

What Ed Chambers told the East New York–Brownsville church people was that their community was "a bunch of rubble," and their problem was one that "I won't touch unless you raise $200,000 to get started." He pointed the church men and women toward the upper echelons of their denominations as places to begin their funding drive, at the same time insisting that they also set up a dues-paying system for area congregations that would cost each, depending upon size, from $500 to $3,000 a year.

"I agreed to help them a little in raising the money," Chambers reports, adding that "the United Church of Christ's Board of Homeland Ministries took the first risk, putting up $45,000. I guess I'd better get that on the record since both the UCC and the Presbyterians did not respond when we needed really big money."

Growth and Action

The new organization — called East Brooklyn Churches (EBC) — raised its needed $200,000 of "front" money from denominations and from their own members (local contributions, mostly from congregations, totalled $13,000). But in many ways, know-how about money raising was the least of what the fledgling group drew from Ed Chambers. "The man kept us in touch with reality," Lutheran pastor Dave Benke remembers, "and with our anger. He insisted that our people, pastors included, should be training in organizing skills. He demanded that we *research* every project or issue to be addressed. And he made us practice ahead of time for every important meeting or 'action.'"

Despite Chambers's constant reminders that the East Brooklyn pastors and church members look at their condition directly and soberly, the numbers grew at each meeting. At first only seven congregations found it possible to come up with the necessary dues: Our Lady of Mercy, Our Lady of Presentation, St. John Cantius, Risen Christ Lutheran, St. James Holiness, Our Lady of Loretto, and East New York Christian Fellowship. Within ten months — all this in 1979 — six more joined. They were St. Peter's Lutheran (the church of Pastor David Benke), St. Rita's, St. Malachi, Our Lady of Lourdes, Christ Community Reformed Church, and the Church of the Divine Metaphysic. Somehow this little group managed to send thirteen people away for ten days of training at Industrial Areas Foundation Training Center, then in Baltimore.

By the beginning of 1980 the group was clearly on its way *somewhere*. In January of that year eighty-five people of the neighborhood completed a twelve-hour training session in communication, research into community needs, and delegation of responsibilities. Later in the year the group began its now close relationship with Bishop Francis Mugavero, Roman Catholic bishop of Brooklyn, and received his endorsement. It examined its membership, too, and proudly reported — as the minutes note — "We are Protestant and Catholic, clergy and laity, black, white, Hispanic, poor and middle-class, old and young, and all residents of the community."

Empowerment

Readers whose last contact with organized community action groups occurred in the 1960s and '70s may miss two important characteristics of the IAF-related new-style outfits. In the first place, IAF-related groups do not organize around issues; they organize around churches and other solid organizations for the benefit of people in the neighborhoods. Issues, by the new style, become occasions and opportunities for people to gain experience in empowering themselves; when an issue passes, or changes, the organization remains.

A second difference between such groups as EBC and predecessor organizations is to be found in the absolute, cold, crisp insistence of the new outfits upon competence as a *first* requirement to be met in the hiring of staff. Though the majority communities in the Brownsville area are black and Hispanic, EBC's first paid organizer was a white man, Mike Gecan, who gained his experience with Industrial Areas Foundation. Gecan's administrative hand was upon the new organization's first steps, and its first actions. In 1981, however, Gecan and EBC took on board an associate, former United Farm Worker organizer Stephen Roberson, who is black. Roberson is today the most visible EBC staff person on a day-to-day basis, and has developed mature inner-city organizing skills of the highest order. He is, in particular, the originator of the network of house meetings across the area at which basic training and recruitment are done, and at which people are encouraged to accept and fulfill basic assignments on committees and in research. During these meetings, leaders emerge. Says Roberson, "You can only demonstrate that you are a leader here; you can't just talk about it. And a leader is one whose efforts lead to residual benefits for others."

Against a background of these events and actions, in which more than fifty congregations are now involved and in which hundreds of people have gained experience in dealing with elected and appointed authorities, the story of the Nehemiah Project can be understood. As Saul Alinsky said: "The relevant skill in modern urban life is that of knowing how to hold public officials accountable" — and that, as we shall see, is what EBC and the Nehemiah Project have been all about.

Finding the Money

Through August, September, and October of 1981 the work of planning went on. Mike Gecan, Chambers, I. D. Robbins, and the EBC pastors came up with a scheme: The churches would raise $7.5 million; then approaches could be made to government. The pastors got busy. The Missouri Synod Lutherans, an unexpected source, expressed interest and later made a $1 million commitment to the undertaking that the Rev. Johnny Ray Youngblood, of St. Paul's Community Baptist Church, had baptized the "Nehemiah Project" (after the Old Testament story of the rebuilding of Jerusalem).

Mike, meantime, ran a training session for priests who were to make an all-important collective approach to Bishop Mugavero. Nine of the priests, led by Father John Powis of Our Lady of Presentation, made the trip together with representative lay persons. They told the bishop of their plans to build two- and three-bedroom houses; he immediately offered $250,000. A woman exulted: "That's an excellent beginning," and they went away. Soon the bishop got back to them: "I think I can get a million." Again the response: "That's great. Now why not go to the Orders for more?" Eventually, the Roman Catholics of Brooklyn would produce $2.5 million for Nehemiah, and the Episcopalians of Long Island Diocese would come up with $1 million more.

Bishop Mugavero gave more than money to East Brooklyn Churches; he became the members' companion-in-arms, the co-conspirator of them all. It was Mugavero who, as spokesperson, led the first EBC visit to Ed Koch, mayor of New York. In the square outside City Hall, Pastor Heinemeier led the group in prayer, and then they filed in to His Honor's office. Mugavero began the conversation with a mistake: "We have raised $12 million to build homes; now we'd like $12 million from you" (actually the bishop had commitments of only $7.5 million). Koch, in a familiar gesture, spread his hands: "We haven't got it, Bishop; our funds are all committed." Then, as though making a great sacrifice, "We'll give you land, though." This gesture, of course, was expected; the City had title to vast stretches of vacant land in the East Brooklyn area, and no idea in the world of what to do with it.

Again the bishop returned to the subject of money. He was at that moment not only the representative of the Roman Catholic Diocese of Brooklyn, but in some measure of one million New York voters of Italian origin. He said, "Ed, this is so important. There's got to be some way for you to find that money. If necessary, why don't you steal it for us?"

KOCH (*Laughing to his aides*): The bishop is telling me to steal it!

MUGAVERO: If necessary, I'll give you absolution.

For three weeks there was no response from Koch. Then the glad news came from the mayor. At a press conference EBC announced its intention to build five thousand single-family row houses, and there were two bishops, one Lutheran treasurer, and a top representative of the mayor of the City of New York to lend credence to the promise.

The Nehemiah home-owning process became more complicated than the above, of course. The City of New York provides land and a $10,000 no-interest loan. Mortgages come via the New York State Mortgage Agency. Removal of landfill for excavations is done at city expense, and soft costs, already described, run about a third of normal. For the Nehemiah plan a single sewer hookup serves multiple homes: The cost savings have run more than $3,000 per house.

Despite these arrangements, not everything has run smoothly for Nehemiah Homes. Delays in demolition have held up construction; owners of isolated lots have sometimes delayed acquisition of property, thus destroying the block-long construction possibilities that earn for Nehemiah's builders their maximum construction savings. Still, construction has proceeded faster by far than the average for housing built in New York. The rejuvenated Mother Gaston neighborhood keeps people expectant of further success. And Nehemiah did not forget to say thank you to Mayor Koch and to (now) Governor Cuomo, too. The two men were hailed by ten thousand EBC members at a huge rally last year.

Who? What?

Sooner or later it occurs to every observer of the Nehemiah Project and of the East Brooklyn Churches to ask two questions:

Who really runs things?
What do the churches get out of it?

The answer to the leadership question fits the presumptions of neither old-style liberals nor radicals. In plain: The churches run both the Nehemiah Project and EBC, and specifically the pastors of churches run things, together with three or four persons from each congregation who meet with pastoral approval. EBC has no president, for example, because it is a cooperative of congregations, an organization of organizations. EBC does possess, however, an informal executive committee — a clergy caucus of member pastors and women religious.

Only one predisposed to either spiritualize or denigrate the reality of relational patterns within a congregation will be surprised at the continuing role of the clergy in direction of the Nehemiah Project and of EBC. In an area bereft of banks, civic clubs, industry, and professionals, the churches were the only organizations — apart from the rackets — that remained alive amid the wreckage of community. Pastors of these churches *of course* became managers and stewards of whatever cohesive, unifying forces remained (apart from the racketeers' brass knuckles and the policeman's stun-gun), and therefore they *of course* held the key to whatever latent legitimate popular power remained in the burgeoning slum.

Equally important, and again with the exception of the rackets, churches have been the only place in the area, in recent years, where marginal wage-earners and even unemployed persons could nevertheless watch capital accumulation occur and discover, in the end, that sums accumulated would be held at least partly for their collective disposal. Even in Brownsville of this decade, the money placed in the collection plate in a large parish on Sunday can be substantial even when it comes from the pockets of the poor. The point is not entirely lost in a small congregation either: Almost every church can allocate at least some money for causes that honest residents cannot afford, by reason of poverty, to fund themselves. Such money, used as EBC has employed it, became leverage for more money from denominations themselves. And *that* money, in turn, became leverage for city and state money. The process is indeed one of power: a power that is nonetheless real for the fact that it develops from small gifts that proceed from the simple piety of the working or hope-to-be-working poor.

The churches get another thing from EBC and its Nehemiah Project: a viable, functioning community in which to grow. Recently Pastor Johnny Ray Youngblood and his St. Paul Community Baptist Church gave EBC an interest-free $100,000 loan. St. Paul's can afford the gesture: Youngblood preaches to three thousand and more persons every Sunday, in part because new people have found new homes nearby.

Eleven of twelve Roman Catholic parishes that approached Brooklyn Bishop Mugavero for help in getting Nehemiah started were aid-receiving churches. The priests of these churches promised their bishop that they would get their churches off subsidy if he would help them with Nehemiah. All but one of the parishes has already succeeded in fulfilling the vow, in part because of the new optimism of the area in which they exist, in part because members of black Baptist congregations agreed through EBC to come to Catholic churches to teach stewardship. These "tithe training sessions," as Baptists call them, are astonishing encounters that, in one observer's words, "get as theological as hell."

Even Benke's little Lutheran church has flourished. "In absolute terms we have increased our membership by only 50," the pastor says, "but deaths in our congregation, and the continued flight of some families, made it necessary to get 250 new members to increase by that number. We really have 250 people here that we didn't have before. What's more, our little church of white, black, and Hispanic people is famous all across the Missouri Synod as "*our* Brooklyn church." That feels good to the members, and it feels good to me."

But the biggest advantage that has come to the churches as a result of their work with East Brooklyn Churches and the Nehemiah Project is the growth in the self-consciousness of strength in pastors and people. I. D. Robbins expressed it best of all. Said he, "This church organization is powerful. It can put four thousand people on the streets to confront a problem, and ten thousand to deal with a mayor. The group has related itself closely to powerful city and national figures — to people like Bishop Mugavero and Governor Cuomo, for example. While doing these things members of EBC have related to each other in a way that is incredible. You can say about them that, far from being balked by political factors, they have made over political conditions to fit the needs of the community. They sense this, are proud of themselves, and hence are happy — and unquarrelsome."

Riding home, I think about one thing I was told: "In almost three years at Nehemiah, there has not been one single default on a mortgage."

That points up the other thing that churches and their pastors get from involvement in the Nehemiah Project: a sense of deep respect for the hard-pressed people, earners of extremely modest wages, whom they seek to serve.

A Room without a View

March 16, 1987

Tom Kelly

Tom Kelly is C&C's associate editor and a Ph.D. in history. He has been a college professor, news vendor, social worker, actor/director, translator, speech writer, and messenger in addition to a journalist with C&C.

THE UNION HOTEL was the top of the line, the social worker told me: the best of the Bowery hotels where the city placed homeless men from its shelters, and by implication, where the best (most stable) of the homeless men were placed. He gave me the little white card that confirmed New York City would be responsible for my rent for one month at the Union, and off I went, down the half-mile length of the Bowery, to check into my new home.

It was a few days after Christmas, 1981. I had spent the last two homeless weeks (I had been unemployed for some months) getting bed and board day by day from the Men's Shelter. Now at a stroke my most immediate anxieties — where, and in what conditions, I would spend each succeeding night — seemed lifted from my shoulders. With that elation driving me, plus a touch of panic lest I be too late to get into the hotel that same night, I sped down the icy sidewalks.

It seemed I'd gotten the straight scoop. Most of the hotels where homeless men are stashed cluster around the northern end of the Bowery, along with the Men's Shelter and several missions — Salvation Army, Catholic, Volunteers of America — adding a definite lack of class and a surplus of panhandlers and drunks to the neighborhood. But my directions led me past the hotels and missions, through several commercial blocks (wholesale and retail lighting fixtures), and into the beginnings of Chinatown before the Union Hotel sign popped up. And even then — a token of exquisite discretion, I thought — the entrance wasn't even on the Bowery, but halfway down the block on Hester Street, next to a (Chinese) hairdresser's.

Through the street-level double doors a broad flight of steps, rubber-covered and steel-banded, led up to the second floor. There stood the hotel clerk's cage — a real one, with wire mesh — guarding a narrow passage to the lobby, actually a bare, loft-like space with some used school chairs and a TV. The head clerk, burly, bearish, red-haired, and red-faced, took my card, and my career as a "ticket man" had begun. John, the head clerk, hastened to make it clear that being a ticket man was not the same as being a self-supporting tenant; he had some doubt as to whether ticket men qualified for the human species. Certain house rules insured against contamination: Ticket men must be out of the building from 8 A.M. to 4 P.M. daily (8:00 to 1:00 week-

ends); can use the hotel's single shower stall 6 to 7 A.M. and 10 to 11
P.M. only; cannot use the lobby or watch the TV at any time.

Cerberus

But just as there are ranks among the angels, at the Union some ticket
men were more equal than others: Put simply, there was a black floor
(the second) and a white one (the third). I don't really know how
long this had been going on, but I'll tell you this: John had an ancient
dog — lame, mangy, nearly blind, had to be carried down the steps to
reach the street, but one thing that dog could still do: smell a black
man, and mount the remnants of an attack should a black man attempt
to cross into the sacred precincts of the lobby.

Not that there was any material difference between the floors; it
was just the principle of the thing. Each floor held three parallel cor-
ridors, two with facing cubicles down each side, and a third whose
"rooms" faced the outside wall. This last row was chiefly for paying
guests, since the facing wall boasted several windows — and light and
air, in season — along its length. The rooms were all the same, though:
Wooden, gray-painted walls reached to about seven feet above the
floor; the (lockable!) door swung inward to reveal a cot affixed to the
front, side, and back walls and something under three feet wide —
half the width of the room; next to the foot of the cot was a wooden
locker (also lockable). A rubber mat ran from the foot of the locker to
the door, the bottom of which ended short of the floor, so the swamper
could mop at least half the floor of each cubicle without unlocking the
door. A couple of clothes hooks and a light bulb (40 watts, not surprisingly) were affixed to the walls. And across the tops of all the
rooms stretched a heavy wire mesh, resembling a horizontal chain
link fence, to discourage the temptation to break-and-enter. Be it ever
so humble.... You can believe that I luxuriated in the awareness that I
could — and had — closed and locked a door between me and everybody else, and it would (probably) stay closed until I chose to open
it again. Home at last.

At one end of the floor was a large washroom in ancient tile and
ruined marble, with a row of mirrors over basins (some of which
worked) facing a row of doorless toilet stalls (ditto) and urinals (also
ditto). This was about the only place you ever saw any of the nearly
one hundred men you shared the floor with. What made that so peculiar was that, because of the eight-ply walls and the shared overhead
space, you quickly became aurally intimate with neighbors you could
go for weeks without seeing, or not recognize when you did see
them.

Some folks have nothing to say, of course, whether you see them
or not; some you can recognize only by the rhythm of their snoring,

or of their self-abuse. But I did come to know a few of my neighbors, even if I no longer remember their names, and probably never knew more than one for each. There were two young men a few doors up and across my corridor, who came from the Shelter about the same time I did; the room only belonged to one of them, of course, but they had found a small TV in a trash bin and would watch it together long into the night, the one fixated on the screen sitting on the floor while the sleeper used the cot. When both were awake they often played cards — Fish and Double Solitaire — and talked about selling pot (or oregano dressed up as pot) in Washington Square Park. Occasionally an old Shelter customer would come calling, and shed a few bucks for a baggie of greenish stuff or on the turn of a card.

A few doors in the other direction on my side was another young kid who had himself figured for a big breakthrough in the TV repair field any time now. He usually kept his door open when he was there and awake, not least to ventilate the place, which was crammed with electronic stuff — well, TV, radio, cassette player; you will gather it didn't take much to "cram" one of those rooms — some of which he had taken in to repair, other bits of junk he had bought or found and sought to salvage.

An older, white-haired guy used to come around the corner and talk to this kid about how he had a relative in New Jersey in the TV repair business he was sure would give the kid a break any time, except right now there were some family fights and the business had maybe gone belly-up but maybe he would sell it.... A very Shelter kind of conversation, this relatives stuff (Tom Waits gets it down well in a song called "Cemetery Polka" on his *Rain Dogs* album, which you could do worse than listen to).

Anyway, this thing between the old guy and the kid came to a bad end when the old guy picked up a dead TV from somebody else down his row for nothing, and promised it to someone else for $15 after he got it fixed, which of course he intended for the kid to do. Well, it turned out the kid couldn't fix it; he talked transistors and stuff, and read those catalogs people like that read, but I don't think he understood much of it, because he seemed never to finish working on the things he was working on. He also used to go out for "job interviews" which he would talk about for several days in advance, and then come back from and never mention again. So in the end the old guy figured he was out $15 because the kid was dumb and that was that.

The kid was not a ticket man, by the way; I think he got some kind of disability payments — he sometimes claimed he had been in the army. You could always tell what part of the cycle his morale was in by how many doohickeys he had plugged in and lit up, and how

often he blew the fuses, sinking the whole floor into darkness and
silence.

The Great Ziegfeld

I shared a wall with the man I became most familiar with at the Union,
though it was weeks before I ever saw him, and we hardly ever con-
versed. He had a habit of addressing the world at large when in his
cups, which is to say once a week or so, at about 2 A.M. On such occasions he would raise his mellow and obviously actor-trained voice to
pursue a narrow range of themes, including his own general unwor-
thiness — as illustrated by his having broken his vow to abstain from
strong drink, or at least from more than one after work on a cold (or
warm) night — and the perfidy of restaurant managers and the restaurant business in general (he worked as a waiter, though I was never
able to determine whether it was for a series of places and bosses, or
for the same ones). The former theme elicited by far the more emotional response from speaker and (involuntary) listeners alike; the one
ending in tears and mighty sobs, the latter in shouts of "Shut up!," or
more frequently, "Shut up, faggot!," and ultimately the rousting out
of the night manager to come pound on the drunken waiter's door to
threaten eviction.

But on a quiet weekend afternoon my neighbor, though still em-
inently audible, could be quite a different sort. It was his habit on
such occasions to invite one of the older residents to his cubicle and
display some sort of scrapbook or volume illustrating the history of
the American musical theater, and spin elaborate plans for a revival
of some long-forgotten musical of the 1920s, of which he was to be
sole producer and one of his restauranteur-employers the angel.

The few occasions when I actually saw him, it was in the row of
shaving mirrors, and most often about to leave for work, dressed in
something approaching a tuxedo. He was mid-forties, thin and grey-
haired, with pale, almost transparent skin like paper, as though he had
sought to shave himself away. The broken blood vessels in his nose
and cheeks showed at once the alcoholic and the fresh-faced child.
The glancing fear in his eyes measured the secret chasm between his
days and nights.

Enterprise Zone

Shortly after I moved into the Union Hotel, a friend touted me onto a
part-time job (this would be January, 1982). At first it was a few hours
a week, later a few days, and after a couple of months I began working
full time. With my second full paycheck I began paying my own rent,
and ceased to be a ticket man; that also meant I no longer took any
meals at the Shelter cafeteria on Third Street. But for those first three

months I continued to eat at least one meal a day, and often two, at the Shelter. And that meant a lot of walks from Hester Street to Third and back. For the sake of variety on these walks, and to avoid the panhandler assemblies that are a feature of the Bowery, I sometimes went by way of Chrystie Street.

Chrystie Street is actually the western lane of a parkway that marks the west edge of the old Lower East Side, where so many of the European immigrants of past generations made their first homes. The trees in its central island now tower above most of the (three- and four-story) buildings that face them; most of the grass has been paved over for swings, jungle-gyms, basketball courts, and benches, but in the bitter winter of 1982, the parkway island was gray and deserted. There was life on the Chrystie Street sidewalks, though — in several varieties.

The first few blocks north of Hester Street held several Chinese warehouses, which meant mounds of fresh vegetables and fish on the snow-piled walk. Then came Delancey Street, in Rodgers and Hart's day the home of "sweet pushcarts gently gliding by," now mainly a broad on/off ramp for the Williamsburg Bridge to Brooklyn. But the southwest corner of Chrystie and Delancey had a life of its own, in the form of a crew of young black hookers who apparently worked out of the hotel halfway up the block, and for sure ducked into the corner laundromat now and then to warm up. The two or three on post when I passed (these were not peak business hours) were usually in the midst of vivid conversation, and always had a more-than-civil word for me. (I always declined their kind offers, explaining I could not currently afford the pleasure, but promised faithfully to return to their corner when my fortunes improved — a promise I must confess I have not kept.) Most impressive of them all was the young woman who stuck to her evidently trademark hot-pants in 20-degree weather. What her secret was, other than determination and layers of panty-hose, I cannot imagine. But whatever it was, it was a constant inspiration, I can tell you.

A few blocks further up, south from Houston Street, it was a different story — or a different part of the same story. On an irregular schedule I never figured out (but which the customers seemed to know somehow) a string of prostitutes would arrange themselves about ten yards apart down the street, outside the row of parked cars. Potential buyers would slow their cars to about 10 mph as they made their judgments; occasionally one would pull to a stop and signal the hooker of their choice to get in; some went around the block more than once before deciding yes or no; more often than not, it was no. No raucous laughter here, no chatter as on Delancey Street. For one thing it was damn cold standing in the wind and the slush. For another, nearly all the girls (and boys dressed as girls), up close, looked in terrible shape — from sickness, pimps' bruises, junk, or just plain hard times. Maybe the heavy makeup covered it from the buyers in their passing cars. Maybe not. What was on offer here was fellatio-as-U-drive, cheap. The hope was to be dropped off a few blocks and a few minutes away, a few bucks richer. But there were no guarantees, no protection. A dangerous game, and no game.

Just a block from here, at Houston and Bowery, the winter of '82 witnessed the advent of street-corner windshield-washing in lower Manhattan. A very mixed bag of down-and-out males took up this enterprise, which soon came to have its own semipermanent oil-drum of burning trash to keep the crews warm. One of two basic techniques was employed: The customer's windshield (or at least the driver's side) was washed clean during the red light, before any remuneration was requested; or the slush and dirt on the driver's side was stirred into an opaque mess, and payment then demanded before it was wiped off again. The choice of technique seemed originally a matter of temperament, but as the dark drew down, the cold set in, the window spray was depleted, the cleaning rags grew filthier, and the preventive consumption of Night Train increased, the distinction between the two techniques tended to blur. Sooner or later some suburban type would complain to a cop, and business would disperse for the day. (That was five years ago, of course; today, when the weather is right, the business is ubiquitous.)

I Guess You Had to Be There

While at the Union I took to attending 11:30 Mass at St. Joseph's Church in Greenwich Village. This was partly a habit acquired during my ticket-man period, when I had to be out of the hotel on Sunday mornings anyway, and was attracted by the baroque music at St. Joe's and the free coffee and donuts after in the church basement. St. Joe's also served as a sort of liberal "magnet church" for those in New York's outer boroughs, where Catholic practice still seemed modeled on the classic rural Irish parish — the rough-hewn curate striding the country lanes with a heavy stick, thrashing the courting couples out of the hedges, driving them to exile and/or marriage (the boys tended to do both; the girls, neither). Not only were the sermons liberal, but St. Joe's took in homeless (about a dozen, sent from the City shelters on a night-by-night basis) at a time when few metropolitan churches did — as a matter of fact, it is still that time.

Anyway, one Sunday, after the donuts and conversation, I attended a slide-show on homelessness given in the church hall, intending to put in my own two-cents worth on my pet peeve — that *daytime* provision for the homeless in winter was given no significant consideration. Imagine my surprise when the slides showed "homeless" persons' rooms with plaster walls that went all the way to the ceiling, about six times the area of my own cubicle, and even windows of their very own. (What they were actually showing were SROs, which is another, though of course not unrelated, crisis.) That's when it began to dawn on me that homelessness looks different from the outside. And that while the problem/issue/crisis of homelessness is defined by others than the homeless themselves, it will always to some extent be misconceived.

This is not to say that homelessness is impossible for the homed to understand; the people Eugene O'Neill wrote about as sitting "in the back room of Harry Hope's saloon on an early morning in summer, 1912" are still sitting — mutatis mutandis — in the lobby of the Union Hotel today. The thing is, you have to pay attention. At last, a national union of the homeless is struggling to form itself. It began by focusing on conditions within public shelters and the right to meet and organize in those spaces, but already organizers have undertaken outreach from the shelters to the surrounding communities. Meanwhile, I have never talked to a homeless man who didn't say a job would be a better solution to his problem than a shelter bed.

Outside, governments throughout the 1980s have wavered between denial, resentment, and grudging acceptance of the homeless in their charge — the parallels with the Kubler-Ross stages of reaction to death are enticing: the homeless as ghost at the Reaganaut feast. Churches and other community voluntary organizations have had to fight out the conflict between fear and duty within their own bodies, and those struggles continue. Homelessness "policy" is a formless chaos, but we must believe in times like these that in chaos lies possibility. If we do not isolate homelessness as a "problem" all its own — as if it were unrelated to decent employment opportunities, the "warehousing" of affordable apartments, public and private urban development and real estate scams, and even mental health policy — we will have less grounds for treating the homeless as an alien species. If we allow our actions in community to be informed by the voices and needs of those we have marginalized from that community, all will benefit — the community itself most of all.

Going Back

When I set out to write this piece, several months ago, I had blocked out of my memory a number of the details of the story — street names, distances, the name of the Union Hotel itself. I might say that I left the hotel under somewhat painful circumstances: I had determined to stay while I built up enough cash reserve to get a decent apartment. That brought me to midsummer, which brought the bugs out of the bedding, or walls, or wherever, and my hasty and sore-bitten departure from the Union Hotel.

Finally, after several fudged attempts, on a sunny autumn day I retraced my steps, noting the old names and old places. As I approached Hester Street from the Bowery, it seemed to me the brick outside walls of the old hotel had been newly painted. In one open window on the Bowery side, facing the Chinese movie-houses, a young black man sat (the window was on what I knew as the black floor) staring out over the roofs. The name, Union Hotel, when I finally saw the sign, didn't seem familiar, only a little ironic.

I paced off the distance from the corner to the hotel door and, opening it, counted the steps rising up into the dark.

A Dissent on Dissent

October 26, 1987

Robert McAfee Brown

Robert McAfee Brown, whose name is symbolic for engaged theologian and ethicist, is a contributing editor of C&C, *and author of* Theology in a New Key: Responding to Liberation Theology, *and* Saying Yes and Saying No: On Rendering to God and Caesar.

IT WAS IN Los Angeles (and to a lesser degree in San Francisco) that the real John Paul II stood up. Importuned in both cities by bishops and lesser breeds within the law to be open to the possibility of change within the church, particularly in regard to the status of women, he dashed whatever hopes American Catholics might have had at the beginning of the trip that he was going to listen — in the sense of taking proposals seriously rather than simply rebutting them — and closed the Vatican doors imperiously against pleas for fresh insight.

The location where this was first made plain is ironically appropriate, since Los Angeles has been one of the most conservative archdioceses in the Roman Catholic world, a vast bastion against Vatican II in the days of Cardinal McIntyre. The pope's response to all pleas for change was direct and blunt: The Catholic church has no room for dissent, and those who believe otherwise are guilty of disloyalty. The net result of this aspect of the papal visit is that the church, rather than now presenting an image of being open to the future, comes across as more locked in the past than ever, television age or no. (A laicized priest remarked in radio commentary in San

Francisco that he had heard the theme forty years ago when he first entered the minor seminary of his order. It was as though Vatican II had never taken place.)

This, I fear, is what will remain strongest in people's minds after the hype, the fawning radio and TV anchors. the feature articles in all the newspapers, and the television shots of adoring Catholics being manifestly (and understandably) thrilled by seeing, touching, and receiving communion from the one they revere as the Vicar of Christ on earth, the closest embodiment of the immediate presence of God they will ever encounter. When all that has receded in the collective American memory — such things have a habit of receding very rapidly — one almost fears that in the aftermath of the sternness of the papal admonitions to the faithful to hold the line and foreswear all possibility of change, there will soon come a new "Syllabus of Errors" from Rome, enumerating all the achievements of modern civilization, such as the struggle for equal rights for women, and placing them under papal anathema.

Faithful Dissent

So why should a Protestant get exercised by all of this? After all, he's not our pope, and we are not beholden to him. Why can't we just let go of the papal visit and get back to business as usual, whether it is supporting the Arias Peace Plan in Central America, or criticizing George Steinbrenner, or trying to put our own ecclesiastical houses in order? Without downgrading any of those worthy activities, we can't settle for them as an all-inclusive agenda. What, then, *do* we do with the papal visit?

In addition to being listening posts and supplying Kleenex for our aggrieved Catholic friends, who have to take all this much more personally than we do, and helping them find the staying power not to quit but to carry on their own battles within their own church, I think we have an obligation to recultivate — as creatively and winsomely and powerfully as we can — the importance for ourselves not only of the right, but of the *obligation*, of dissent, dissent against all things that threaten the integrity of the gospel to which we are committed. Dissent then becomes not gloomily negative, but gloriously positive.

Our very name, Protestant, from *pro-testari*, meaning "to testify on behalf of," stands for a positive posture we embody and seek to spread. If the Catholic position is now to stifle dissent, and insist that dissent is disloyal, our position should encourage dissent, and insist that dissent is our act of loyalty, lest we enthrone as God given absolutes, ideas, and points of view that are human and fallible.

To take the clearest example from the papal visit, let us dissent within our own communions from the notion the pope has restated for *his* communion, that women are forever to be second-class citizens, denied the right of ordination. Let us dissent from the possibility of asserting that we are committed to the full dignity of women while simultaneously asserting that they are not worthy of participating in our governance processes. Most of us do, of course, ordain women, but that is still tokenism until women are sharing fully in positions of authority in our denominational life.

Our way of dissenting should be not to waste time attacking Rome's position, but to seek to exemplify more fully our own. Let us also, to take one other example, dissent from the papal ruling that divorced people cannot receive the sacraments, by witnessing that in our communions they can, and that we pledge to God and to them to preside over a Lord's Table that is under the governance of grace and forgiveness rather than legalism.

Our task is not to try to "change" Roman Catholicism; it is to find ways to be increasingly faithful to our own understanding of the gospel, and to give special witness to those parts of the gospel that other churches seek to negate. We have to make certain judgments about the world, of course, but if we are to do that with integrity, we must take seriously the scriptural reminder that "the time has come for judgment to begin with the household of God" (1 Peter 4:17), which is *our* house.

That's what faithful dissent is all about.

The Pittston Strike: Being There

February 19, 1990

Andrew McThenia

Andrew McThenia is a professor of law at Washington and Lee University in Virginia. An Episcopal layman, he went on leave during 1989 in order to work as a Jubilee Intern for the church in the coalfields of southwest Virginia during the United Mine Workers strike against the Pittston Company.

IN THE EARLY MONTHS of the United Mine Workers (UMW) strike against the Pittston Company, I was arrested on two occasions, together with coal miners, their spouses, and members of various religious communities. We were apprehended for sitting in the road and blocking coal trucks trying to enter Pittston's largest coal preparation plant. The charge was obstructing traffic.

In 1987 the Pittston Company, Virginia's leading coal producer, terminated its membership in the Bituminous Coal Operators' Association (BCOA), and declined to accept the agreement the BCOA negotiated with the mine workers. The UMW, which historically has taken the position "no contract, no work," as a gesture of good faith continued to work for sixteen months without a contract. Pittston was not impressed. At the end of January 1988, the day the old BCOA agreement expired, the company cut off medical benefits to some fifteen hundred retirees, widows, and disabled miners. William J. Byrne, Pittston's director of financial public relations, offered the following explanation: "It's like a credit card that expires. Theirs expired." Negotiations got nowhere; in April 1989 the strike began, and with it the active campaign of civil resistance in which I participated.

The Force of Law

Many of my colleagues at the bar and within the academy have expressed serious concern about my activities. I have been asked on more than one occasion how I as a lawyer, sworn to uphold the law, can willfully violate it?

I am unwilling to concede that my resistance to the enforcement of the law of the Commonwealth of Virginia — my witness, if you will — was a violation of law. I resisted to bring attention and give support to an equally important set of values which have the force of law to so many coal-mining families. It is not an exaggeration to say that these working-class mountain families have forged, through generations of suffering, norms of community and solidarity more important than any statist definition of law.

What are those norms and how do they come to gain the status of "unofficial" law? And even if there is some law of the community, what moral criteria can we use to judge that law? Those are difficult questions, and I have anguished over them. I do not have an answer that will satisfy everyone, but then I don't have to live with everyone — only myself. What follows is my attempt to address some of those questions.

Individualistic and mobile mainstream America does not understand much about the people who live and work and have their being in the hollows and on the ridges of the Appalachian region. They are a people of memory, and memory is the glue that holds them together.

Pastor Joe Johnson remembers. He is a preacher in the Free Will Baptist Church and a retired union miner who spent some forty years working for the Clinchfield Coal Company, now owned by Pittston. Pastor Joe recalls the organizing days of the 1920s and 1930s — the bitter cold and constant fear of violence on the picket lines, a machine gun mounted on the roof of the company store in Clinchco, the early deaths of so many fellow workers and family members in the mines.

Gay Martin also remembers. Gay, the wife of a retired Pittston miner, operates a food bank from her home in Dickenson County. She recalls those early organizing years when mothers would take their small children to the picket lines and organizing rallies — the smallest in their mothers' arms, the toddlers pulled along in wagons by their older brothers and sisters, and those who were old enough carrying food to their fathers manning the picket lines. Her father and one of her brothers were killed in the mines. Her husband, Gilmer, who has first-stage black lung disease and a bad back from his thirty-nine years underground, lost a brother in a mine accident. These memories are part of what the strike against the Pittston Company is all about.

Shortly after the strike began I saw a young boy at a rally with a hand-lettered message on his sweatshirt declaring proudly: "I am the son of a coal miner's daughter." Families with *four* generations of union miners living in the same hollow in southwest Virginia are not uncommon. Pound, Virginia, is a small community, population approximately 1,500, in Wise County. Under the letter "M" in the Pound telephone directory, there are 270 entries. Nearly two-thirds of those, 164, are for people with the last name of Mullins. Importantly, only 19 names are *not* repeated. Kinship is also a large part of what this strike is all about.

For those families the union is a way of life and they see Pittston's stance as designed to break the UMW and turn back all those strides toward human dignity won with the blood of their forebears — a deconstruction of their history. They see the termination of health benefits not as a legitimate bargaining strategy but as a crude attempt to pit working miners against their own fathers and mothers — a destruction of family. It took a half-century for the workers in the Appalachian coal fields to achieve any justice and equity with the outside interests owning so much of their land, and they know just how vulnerable those gains are. They have only to look to the national regression of the last decade, beginning with the air traffic controllers' strike in 1981.

An Outsider Transformed

But those memories are not my memories and those stories are not my stories. I am not from a coal mining family. I left the Appalachian region thirty years ago and I am solidly entrenched in the middle class — some would say at its pinnacle as a lawyer and member of the academy. Where do I connect and why did I sit in the road?

As an outsider, I hold at least one story in common with so many of those families who see their existence threatened by the systemic violence of the Pittston Company. That is the story of faith. The most neglected aspect of this struggle is the powerful religious strain which undergirds it. Yet it was the backbone of the peaceful resistance movement throughout most of the summer of 1989.

The Bible, Taylor Branch's Martin Luther King biography *Parting the Waters*, and King's own writings have been the texts of the strike captains and many of the picketers. Both times when I was arrested prayers were offered for the strikers *and* for the Pittston Company.

Many of the planning sessions for civil resistance took place in mountain churches. (Last summer CBS featured the strike on its *Forty-Eight Hours* program. Yet they failed to mention the religious aspect of the strike at all. That in spite of the fact that prayer and hymn singing were always integral parts of the picket line activity — including those days when CBS camera crews were filming for the show.) It has been said, with only slight exaggeration, that every fourth UMW miner is either a Free Will Baptist pastor or church-school superintendent.

It was through the common faith that those stories of solidarity and kinship became in a sense my stories as well. I went to the coalfields as a mainline church worker and lawyer — very much a stranger in a strange land. But in the months preceding the strike, people like Gay and Gilmer Martin opened their hearths and more important their hearts to me. As we worked, played, prayed, and broke bread together, we did what people have always done when they gather. We told stories. And what happened is that the barriers of class and professionalism began to crumble. People on the other side of those barriers took seriously Our Lord's admonition in Matthew 25: "I was a stranger and you welcomed me" — and in that reaching out transformed me from stranger to friend.

I had gone to the coalfields as an advocate — always safe in my detached posture as a professional. But I came to accept another notion of advocacy: Probably the most important thing advocates can do is to be with their client as a friend when there is nothing that can be done. To be an advocate is to be open to transformation, to take on the stories and suffering of one's clients.

That is why I sat in the road. That is why I resisted enforcement of the state's law. Because I did not know what else to do. All existing "legal" means of change were foreclosed. Not very theoretical, not very elegant. It is simple. It was not easy, however, because the one thing a lawyer is trained to do is to be in control, to know what to do. But when I figured out that there was nothing I could do, then I was free to be. Free to be with my friends in their suffering.

Living Out a Vision

I was not certain then nor am I certain now that civil resistance was the proper course to follow. No criteria can ensure that the claim to superiority of a community's norms is moral. To ask that question is, I think, to succumb to the statist temptation to define a system as just only if it conforms to the state's law. All one can do is to urge an alternative interpretation of what is "legal." And that act of interpretation begins to assume validity only if one is prepared to live by it — to accept the consequences of living out the vision. The stories that resisting communities tell, the lives they lead, and how they act when it is most likely that they will lose in a confrontation with the state, tell a good deal about the moral strength of their claims.

The only certainly for me is that as a Christian and a lawyer my obligation is to work for God's justice. What justice means comes not from the state but from God, and the call to justice is generally given definition in stories of suffering. The Hebrew prophets make it abundantly clear that there can be no peace without justice, nor can there be justice without peace.

So I listened to those stories and I prayed for discernment. Even then I knew that I was acting in the shadow of error. But life always gives us contingent choices. No ground is safe, no place is neutral. Finally we must act. I can pray only that the life I lead and the actions I take will be consistent with the story that I believe to be true before all others. And that story is one of the life, death, and resurrection of a radical Jew who resisted both common sense and the powers and principalities, and who in the act of resisting absorbed the violence of the world. For me sitting in the road was an act of witness to that story. It was also a time of prayer.

The Cruzan Case

February 19, 1990

John C. Bennett

John C. Bennett, the dean of American Christian ethicists, has written for C & C for fifty years. He retired in 1970 as president of Union Theological Seminary, New York.

IN THE NANCY CRUZAN CASE the U.S. Supreme Court will make a decision that will have profound implications and may be fateful for thousands of people, perhaps for decades. The facts of the case are now well known. After an accident in her twenties, Nancy Cruzan has been in an irreversible vegetative condition for six years. She is kept alive by a tube for artificial feeding in her stomach. Her parents have asked a court to allow the removal of the tube. A lower court agreed to this, but by a 4–3 decision the Missouri Supreme Court refused permission for the removal of the tube.

Its basic assumption was that the state has an interest in protecting all life and cannot be influenced by preference for any quality of life. Fear of having the state make distinctions between qualities of life is understandable. But is not the capacity for consciousness, the ability to respond to other persons and to the environment, the one quality of life on which other desired qualities depend? When that quality is absent, I do not believe the state should protect life. My community is made up of persons not decades from their terminal illnesses. I can testify that most of us fear not death itself but that our bodies may survive our minds. It is sometimes said that Nancy Cruzan does not have a terminal illness — she could live thirty years in this condition — and what may be favored in the case of those late in life does not apply to her. In her case the key word is not *terminal* but *irreversible*, and the prospect of a much longer life makes it all the more important to save her from such a fate.

Judging from what some justices have said, another issue may be decisive: No written proof exists that Cruzan would not wish to live under these conditions; there are only verbal reports of what she has said to a sister and friends. People in their twenties cannot be expected now to leave such written reports; those come later. It was only after hearing about this case that I added to my legally based California "Durable Power of Attorney for Health Care" the statement to have food withheld if I should be in an irreversible vegetative or comatose condition. I hope that the justices will base their opinion on what they believe to be best for the patient and on the reliability of the family's judgment. This family had the unusual experience of having a two-hour public television program devoted to their story. It revealed to everyone concerned, including the lawyers on the other side, their sincerity and loving motives.

Withholding food — starvation — presents a special problem. In this case starvation is not believed to cause suffering. Still, some say that feeding is such an elemental form of caring that withdrawing a feeding tube should not be regarded as a medical choice. Surely such artificial feeding involves a medical decision; its continuance for six years is an *extraordinary* measure which should be regarded as morally optional by those who regard feeding as having a special moral claim. Extraordinary measures do become *ordinary*; but here I am thinking of the length of time combined with the fact that the patient receives no improvement.

To be forced by the state to keep alive indefinitely a body that has no other signs of life than physical existence is an affront to the person; it creates years of tragic and unconstructive grief for loved ones who must keep observing the contrast between that living body with a beloved name in contrast to the person remembered and loved.

Professor Paul Ramsey, a key interpreter of Christian ethics in our time, who was generally conservative about matters of life and death, wrote in his great book *The Patient as Person* (1970) that euthanasia should be permitted in two situations: "deep and irreversible coma" and a prolonged dying in which it is "medically impossible to keep severe pain at bay." Actually he wondered out loud if such control of pain was not medically possible, though the means of control are likely to shorten life. But he had no question about the irreversible coma. After a certain period much less than six years a vegetative condition is as irreversible as a comatose condition.

Threatening Signal

If the Supreme Court does not annul the essence of the judgment of the highest court of Missouri, it will be giving more of a signal to other states than it did in the Webster abortion ruling. In that case it allowed particular legislation in Missouri to stand and at least by implication invited other states to enact their own legislation. In this case support of a state by the judgment of the Supreme Court would limit legislation in that state on that subject for a long time. This would be a new and threatening constitutional signal to all states. It would also be bad news to all who are struggling to find ways to deliver people from the fear that their bodies may survive their minds. This is the more important because of the continuous advances in medical technology to keep bodies alive.

The Central Park Jogger

October 22, 1990

Susan Brooks Thistlethwaite

Susan Brooks Thistlethwaite, United Church of Christ minister and professor of theology and culture at Chicago Theological Seminary, is a C & C *contributing editor, and the author of* Sex, Race and God: Christian Feminism in Black and White.

IN THE SUMMER OF 1989, shortly after the rape in New York's Central Park of a woman jogging alone in the evening, I was called by several news publications for a quote. I gave the same statement to several reporters, none of whom used it: "This week a black woman was brutally assaulted and thrown off a roof in New York. A white woman was brutally beaten and raped in Central Park. All women's lives are valuable, and the news media should pay equal attention to them."

The skein of issues knotted up in what has come to be called, simply, The Central Park Jogger, illustrates the incredible difficulties and dangers of fully separating sex from race from class in our society. It also illustrates the pernicious role of the media as they hunt for a "good quote," one that is controversial enough to make a story.

Now that the trial is over, as we talk about the Central Park Jogger — and talk we must, in sermon, article, conversation, or interview — we should be on guard to hold together the threads so shredded by the public display of TV and newspaper headline. And, as a new horror replaces this one in the two-minute attention span of public reporting, we must refuse to drop these threads of insight, but instead try to connect them.

The Central Park Jogger is an issue of gender because a woman was brutally raped. Often the fact of the rape has risked being forgotten in the media hype.

It is a gender and class issue because the female jogger has an income that nets her media sympathy. The accused, some of whom have now been convicted, are males without economic clout.

It is a race and gender issue because the jogger is a white woman and the assailants are racial-ethnic minority males. Where males from these minority communities have experienced less than equal justice, they will march and rally with their families and communities to force the public to pay attention to them. Ironically, women who have been raped have also received less than justice from the court system, and so women have resorted to marching and public rhetoric to redress this legitimate grievance. And so we have the scenes outside the courthouse of demonstration and counterdemonstration so carefully photographed and so poorly explained.

It is a class, race, gender, and age issue. "Wilding" (if it exists at all) is scarcely the practice of racial-ethnic males over thirty. Undereducated, underemployed, young minority males live in a subculture of despair that crumbles into violence at the slightest touch.

Drawing the attention of the media practitioners to the ways in which they keep these issues hermetically sealed from one another and diametrically opposed to one another is a task we in the religious community can take on.

Yes, we'll get quoted less. But as H. Richard Niebuhr is reported to have said when asked why he had not published as much as his brother Reinhold, "I think about it first." Before we open our mouths to congregation or news reporter, I suggest we follow H. Richard's advice.

The S&L Crisis: Time to Strike Back

November 26, 1990

Ellen Teninty

Ellen Teninty grew up in Baltimore during the civil rights era, was one of the founding organizers of the Plant Closures Project in Oakland, Calif., and now works at the Center for Ethics and Economic Policy in Berkeley. As director of training, she trains people to provide values-based economic education to a wide range of grassroots organizations.

THE DEREGULATION OF the national system of savings and loan associations (S&Ls) in the early 1980s was an engraved invitation to the S&L disaster. True to form, the Bush administration advocates the same deregulation philosophy today, embodied in the S&L "bailout" plan — for which the American people are expected to cough up the certain-to-be-astronomical price — and in efforts to deregulate the fourteen thousand federally insured banks.

Of the S&L failures, less than 10 percent were due to external economic factors such as higher oil prices. The vast majority resulted from the fraud, embezzlement, money laundering, and junk-bond financing that became standard business practice in an uncontrolled market. And the proposal to have middle- and lower-income citizens foot the bill is morally outrageous and economically unsound. That such a plan has advanced as far as it has reflects the degree to which people are "tuned out"; the bill for the damage does not have to come anywhere near the $500 billion projection. The Bush proposal, in fact, is based on the premise that Americans do not learn from their mistakes.

The first Savings & Loans or "Thrifts" were created in the 1800s. People pooled their money to give each other low-interest loans. Thrifts were "mutuals," meaning they were owned by the *depositors*, rather than by shareholders who invested for personal profit. In 1932, Herbert Hoover institutionalized this tradition by setting up a national system, regulated by the Federal Home Loan Bank Board (FHLBB) in Washington, with twelve regional Federal Home Loan Banks related to the local S&L institutions. A few years later Congress created the FSLIC (Federal Savings and Loan Insurance Corporation, a fund to insure S&L deposits) to calm the anxieties of post-Depression depositors and attract funds to the Thrifts. Limits were placed on the amount of interest Thrifts could pay to depositors, and lending was restricted to residential mortgages in the Thrift's home community. S&Ls were reliable, conservative, and unglamorous.

The system worked well for several decades, helping ever-increasing numbers of working Americans realize the dream of a family home. The regulatory cap on interest was designed to keep the charge for home loans low.

Then came the rising costs of the Vietnam War and oil throughout the 1970s, which created inflation. Inflation devalues money. If you are a depositor, and thus a lender, inflation hurts you. If you are a debtor, inflation helps you. Depositors demanded higher interest rates to make up for the decreased value of their wealth due to inflation. They got their way. Interest rates increased throughout the 1970s, and when Paul Volcker took over at the Federal Reserve in 1979 the prime rate soared to 21 percent. The Thrifts paid a measly 5.5 percent and money poured out of them into more profitable investments. By the 1980s, 85 percent of the nation's S&Ls were losing money.

Deregulation and "Bustout"

Ronald Reagan, the emperor of voodoo economics, had by then moved into the White House with the philosophy that profit maximization is the best way to organize the economy. Deregulation of the S&Ls would throw them out into the real world of the competitive "level playing field," where capitalism would weed out the weaklings. The incentive of high profit would attract investors to fire up the economic engine, and housing, jobs, and growth would trickle down. But, as George Will said, "This was not buccaneer capitalism by rugged individualists, but welfare capitalism of well-represented speculators. It was no-fault entrepreneurship, wherein profits are private and losses are socialized."

Two major pieces of federal S&L deregulation were complemented by further deregulation at the state level. In 1980, the Depository Institutions Deregulation and Monetary Control Act ended the cap on interest rates S&Ls could pay to depositors *and* increased the federal insurance guarantee from $40,000 to $100,000 per account. In 1982, the Garn-St. Germain Act allowed the Thrifts to loan to or even directly invest in nonresidential ventures. And it cut the budget for the regulatory FHLBB, leaving only 750 examiners (each paid under $20,000 a year) to watch over 5,500 S&Ls. The results are well described by Steven Pizzo and other staffers of the *Russian River News* in their book *Inside Job: The Looting of the Savings and Loans* (McGraw, 1989): "Deregulation plus the FSLIC created a machine that sucked deposits from across the nation and channeled them into a network of excess, fraud, and corruption."

The timing couldn't have been better. The Justice Department had just taken over the Teamsters' Central States Pension Fund to prevent its further use by the businessmen known as Organized Crime. The S&L doors swung open as a guaranteed and unrestricted source of capital. Business from Las Vegas to Wall Street moved in for the kill.

Money from large investors such as pension funds and insurance companies was broken into $100,000 chunks by Wall Street firms to fall under the FSLIC federal guarantee, thus eliminating any risk. The money was then farmed out to the highest bidder for short-term profit taking. These brokered deposits are called "hot money" because they move so quickly in search of a greater return. The Thrifts showed tremendous growth on the books by attracting hot money with high-interest, short-term Certificates of Deposit (CDs).

"Bustout" is the mob term for taking over a business and relieving it of its assets. An example from Lincoln Savings and Loan is typical. Lincoln buys desert land and arranges to sell it to an associate for a much higher price. Lincoln loans its friend the money, charging a 5 percent origination fee, or $5 million on a $100 million loan, plus another 1 or 2 percent every six months for renewing it. Lincoln shows a profit on the sale of land and on the fees for the loan. Of course the loan will eventually go bad because the desert land wasn't worth a nickel in the first place, but don't worry, it's guaranteed by "the full faith and credit of the U.S. Treasury." By the time a regulator comes around, the schemers are long gone.

A mere two years after the Garn-St. Germain Act, the FSLIC had backed so many fraudulent loans that the insurance fund was almost bankrupt. Ed Gray, who had been brought in by Ronald Reagan as a good ol' boy to head the FHLBB, surprised his friends and actually tried to protect the public interest. His attempts to expose and address the crisis were blocked by both Democrats and Republicans, and he was ridiculed as "Mr. Ed" (the talking horse) and isolated as "off the reservation" by Donald Regan. Then-Attorney General Ed Meese hogtied Gray's attempts to investigate the mess by transferring $1 million out of Gray's already inadequate budget to the war on obscenity.

In 1986, Gray tried to get more money from Congress for the FSLIC so it could pay off the guaranteed deposits and close the hemorrhaging Thrifts. He was chased out of Washington and replaced by a former aide to Sen. Jake Garn (R-Utah), M. Danny Wall. Wall claimed that there was no problem, smothering the crisis until after Bush's election. Eventually a bail-out bill was passed in 1989, but not until the cost to the public of insolvent Thrifts had reached $35 million a day.

"This is not just a financial crisis but a moral crisis," according to Mort Zuckerman, editor-in-chief of *U.S. News & World Report*. The fault is widespread. A political system open to the influence of the highest bidder was, and still is, skewed by the powerful S&L lobby. The regulators are understaffed and underpaid and also susceptible to bribes. The Justice Department doesn't have enough prosecutors trained to conduct financial paperchase investigations and doesn't offer salaries that come near those of the private sector. The court system reflects the racism and classism of the culture and always shows sympathy to the white-collar criminal. Real-estate appraisers have justified hundreds of thousands of phony loans. And auditors from the most reputable accounting firms in the nation have claimed everything was hunkydory while the con men walked out the back door with the goods. And certainly the bankers and Wall Street brokerage houses have known exactly what they were doing.

Until enough of us wake up, smell the garbage, and demand some justice, the same philosophy that created the problem will guide the "clean-up." The public has been left holding a bag of empty office buildings and half-built malls. We now own $100 billion of real estate, including tons of condos — and a piece of the Dallas Cowboys. The "bail-out" allows the most profitable assets to be cherry-picked by the private sector at a discount, leaving the public holding the dogs, such as sites contaminated by toxic pollution. To add insult to injury, the same folks that looted the Thrifts are coming back to buy them again for 40 to 60 cents on the dollar.

The present plan still doesn't give the FSLIC the funds to shut down the insolvent S&Ls. Instead, we are selling these assets as a way of raising money to pay back the guaranteed deposits. Prospective buyers are being offered tax breaks and special long-term financing deals. This "fire-sale" method is calculated to cost us 40 percent more than simply closing the failed S&Ls, paying off insured depositors, and selling the institutions' assets over time at a reasonable price.

The immediate cost of making good on insured deposits is now $160 billion. The estimates of the Bush bail-out plan range from $500 billion to $1.4 trillion. The higher price tag on the Bush plan reflects interest payments to bondholders, the additional cost of stretching the bail-out over thirty years. It represents another supply-side transfer payment from the average citizen to the wealthier, another step in building an economy based on the wheeling and dealing of high rollers, rather than infrastructure, jobs, and production.

Without S&L deregulation, the rich already enjoyed higher interest rates and lower taxes. Wall Street could see financial deregulation as nothing less than a bonanza with juicy fees for accountants and investment banks. On the other end of our economy, wages were down and taxes were up. And there was no longer a source of low-interest, long-term money for home buyers. The concept of a family home went the way of the tooth fairy for most working Americans. Dramatic increases in new beachfront homes and luxury condos were met with almost no new moderate and low-income housing built for the swelling ranks of families in search of affordable shelter.

The Financial Democracy Campaign (FDC), an alliance of community, farm, labor, and church people, is putting forth a rational and moral alternative to the Bush proposal. Its statement of principles says, "Common sense suggests the bail-out should be paid for now with direct appropriation. Simple justice demands that the costs be borne mainly by those who have profited." Representative Joe Kennedy (D-Mass.) has proposed HR 5499, the Savings and Loan Fair Financing and Anti-Fraud Enforcement Act of 1990. It would place an additional 7.5 percent tax on interest on dividends and capital gains above $7,500 *for individuals with annual incomes exceeding $100,000.* Profitable corporations also would have to chip in an additional 5 to 7 percent. The Bush bail-out, if allowed to continue, will cost every family $2,000 to $14,000.

The FDC points the way to financial reforms our country and our economy desperately need. "Public values and national priorities" should guide us to responsibly shape our economy. The campaign urges reforms that would allow our active and direct involvement in setting financial policies, such as interest rates and the direction of investment of our pension funds. It has additional proposals to establish a Home Opportunities Fund. [FDC can be reached at 604 W. Chapel Hill St., Durham NC 27701.]

The philosophy of deregulation for the benefit of the private sector is still very much in vogue. Our pension funds are in a vulnerable situation with the combination of slackened regulation and government guarantees. The 14,000 federally insured banks are being deregulated now. The economy is not a neutral zone. It is where real people make decisions about national priorities. It is where the value system we see on *Dynasty* and *Dallas* gets played out in our communities. It is not too late to learn the needed lessons and speak out. Information and organization are available. Let's shake our cynicism and end this era of economic corruption.

Part 4

Faith and Empire

Unavoidable questions about the systematic official use of torture in Latin America — and about U.S. complicity in such denials of human rights — were raised in 1970 by a dossier smuggled out of Brazil and submitted to the Vatican.

William Wipfler, then with the Latin America Department of the National Council of Churches, used that dossier to write "The Price of Progress in Brazil," the first full-length treatment of torture in Brazil to be published in the United States (Christianity and Crisis, March 16, 1970).

That was one of several events that led in the early 1970s to a decade in which human rights would become a key phrase in U.S. foreign policy — honored more in theory than in practice.

For significant numbers of U.S. Christians, the 1970s brought together earlier struggles against South African apartheid with testimonies coming from Latin America, the Middle East, Korea, the Philippines, and, later, Central America to fashion a distinctive approach to U.S. foreign policy.

This approach continued well through the 1980s — flowering in the U.S. based Sanctuary movement — and was evident in the 1991 Gulf war resistance. It was marked by the centrality of love — concern for human rights and the liberation of oppressed peoples — and by the insistence on justice — on an analysis of the social and political structures of injustice and the forces that could effectively be marshalled against them.

The Palestinian Time Bomb

October 5, 1970

Wayne H. Cowan

Wayne Cowan, who edited Christianity and Crisis *from 1954 until 1986 and now serves as editor-at-large, is Director of Interpretive Services for the General Board of Global Ministries of the United Methodist Church. He is editor of* Witness to a Generation: Significant Writings from Christianity and Crisis, 1941–1966.

Piracy, terror, and blackmail (in the air or anywhere else) are, of course, wrong. The Arab guerrillas should not make the innocent suffer for the faults of others.

But the condition of the Palestinian Arabs has been a time bomb ticking away for 22 years. Everyone concerned has known that someday it would go off. No one, in 22 years, had the will to do what was necessary to defuse that time bomb.

— Joseph C. Harsch, *Christian Science Monitor*, September 17, 1970

Yet the United States Government knows next to nothing about them [the guerrillas] or their leaders. It does not know how to reach them, politically or physically, and it concedes that it sees no means of giving them a place in the negotiations or a stake in the outcome.

— Max Frankel, *New York Times*, September 15, 1970

The commandos...running around in their clown suits [camouflage uniforms]...are the last dying breath of a lost cause.

— A key American diplomat in an Arab country, November 1969

AS THIS EDITORIAL is written the world sits in stunned suspense: Will Jordan fall to the Palestinians...the Syrians...the Israelis...the U.S.? What is to be the fate of the fifty hostages taken by the radical PFLP (Popular Front for the Liberation of Palestine) guerrillas? Where will this tragic bloodletting end, and what purpose does it serve? Will this upheaval cease before the superpowers become involved in the ultimate struggle?

Questions proliferate. Answers are easy to come by only for queries that hardly matter. One thing, however, is clear: For the first time since the creation of Israel the world has been made aware that the Palestinian Arabs have ceased to wait passively and to leave their fate in the hands of others.

Three times in the last quarter-century (1948, 1956, 1967) large numbers of Palestinians fled their homeland. Almost half of the two-and-a-half million Palestinian Arabs now live outside Palestine, forming what has been called "a nation in exile." (It is estimated that two-thirds of the people of Jordan are Palestinian refugees.) Numerous United Nations resolutions intended to compensate the refugees for "lost property rights" and/or repatriate them have produced nothing, and they have lost faith in the will of the big powers and of their Arab brothers to take their cause seriously. Finally they took their fate into their own hands by creating the guerrilla movement, which was described in these pages ("The Elusive Peace," May 11 issue) as "the major new factor in the Middle East mix."

It is no accident that those having the hardest time accepting the most constructive diplomatic initiative of the Nixon administration should be the two groups with the most at stake: Israel and the Palestinians. Both Egypt and Jordan accepted the truce with some relish. The Israelis were mightily pressured by the U.S. to come along because they felt they had much to lose; the Palestinians were, as usual, left out since no one — Arab or non-Arab — has taken their plight seriously enough to devise a way to include them in negotiations, although they are the key Arab group with whom Israel must do business. They are the one group with a legitimate complaint.

Having been left out once more, it should have come as no surprise that their more radically inclined members took such extreme actions as the hijackings. "If some of them now act like the desperadoes," the *Observer* (London) noted in mid-September, "it is partly because for many years they have been offered no constructive role in determining their own fate and, therefore, feel like outlaws."

The sky-jackings have led to a further loss of Arab prestige, and are not to be condoned. Yet we dare not lose sight of the fact that hijacking has been the only way the Palestinians have been able to draw attention to their plight. Those of us who grew up on the Saturday night movie fare of watching the swashbuckling Errol Flynn and his gallant English pirate mates doing in the Spanish galleons should be able to recognize that one man's piracy is another man's guerrilla warfare, however new and uncomfortable the recognition. Besides, the *Fedayeen* learned a lot about their job from Menachem Beigin, the Irgun, and the Stern Gang.

As for the movement of the missiles within Egypt there is widespread disagreement on the effect such movement could possibly have. There are those who hold that much of the furor over the ceasefire violations was related to the negotiations over the price to be paid to Israel for her coming to the peace table — which at this point apparently amounts to $500 million in modern weaponry and record economic aid, both on good terms. Egypt is also undoubtedly using the cease fire to bring as much pressure on Russia as possible. It seems unlikely that the Israeli position has deteriorated (the missiles are defensive weapons), especially since Washington is apparently prepared to offset the impact of whatever gains Egypt may make. Furthermore, the missiles are a response to the humiliation caused by Israeli air raids deep into Egypt early this year.

The one thing that is clear here is, in the words of the *Observer*, that "...a Middle East peace which cannot command the support of the majority of Palestinians and which they have had no responsibility for making will not last long." It is less clear what constructive role they can play, but we had better take Mr. Frankel's assessment seriously and seek to remedy the current absurd situation.

To do so is not to bring into question the State of Israel nor its right to exist but rather to affirm it. At the same time we must face the fact that the rights and needs of *two* peoples — and not just one — are to be weighed and balanced. The time bomb is still ticking.

"El pueblo unido jamás será vencido"

May 12, 1980

Jorge Lara-Braud

Jorge Lara-Braud, a native of Mexico, has served as an assistant general secretary for the U.S. National Council of Churches and as director of the Council on Theology and Culture for the Presbyterian Church (U.S.). He currently teaches at San Francisco Theological Seminary.

THERE WERE about fifty of us church "dignitaries" from about twenty countries, including representatives from Latin America, Europe, and the U.S., flying into San Salvador on Palm Sunday weekend to honor our friend and mentor, Archbishop Oscar A. Romero, assassinated the previous Monday while saying Mass.

Despite the nature of the occasion, there was something of a nervous joviality as we greeted one another in the processional lineup. No one was unaware that the funeral posed its own dangers. There would be more than a hundred thousand people attending. The government, we knew, was not in control of its own military and security forces. The manner of the archbishop's dying had shown once more that assassins were on the loose, professional killers for whom nothing was sacred.

Why go to such a country, to such a funeral, at such a time? I assume that as with others, many of whom, like myself, had become close friends of the archbishop during the three brief years of his leadership, the call to honor his memory was stronger than the hovering sense of possible mass violence. Perhaps some were simply "assigned" by a higher-up who chose not to go. In any case I had learned to treasure this gentle prophet who had brought faith and hope to millions in a country where resignation and despair had become a way of life.

And so, on a radiantly brilliant day, the Mass began in a bit of disarray. An altar was improvised at the top of the stairs leading to the main entrance of the old, unfinished cathedral adjacent to the National Palace, headquarters of the government. Archbishop Romero's coffin had been placed at the foot of the stairs, protected by a six-foot metal fence. I stood at the altar beside the pope's representative, Cardinal Ernesto Corripio Ahumada, archbishop of Mexico City.

The plaza was jammed with the archbishop's flock — mostly poor people on whose behalf his voice had been so compelling. They were there, I presume, for the same reason as we friends from abroad: The call to honor his memory was greater than the danger they perceived. Fifteen minutes after the Mass began, I saw an orderly column of some five hundred enter the plaza, marching eight abreast behind banners that identified them as representatives of the huge coalition of popular organizations called "La Coordinadora Revolucionaria de Masas." These were the famous "leftists" one reads about, whom the archbishop loved and sometimes rebuked. The crowds in the plaza cheered and made way for the marchers as they filed by and laid a wreath at the coffin. Then, still calm and orderly, the column withdrew.

As the Mass continued, Cardinal Corripio paid tribute to the martyred archbishop. Just as he was paraphrasing an oft-heard teaching of Archbishop Romero — "Neither truth nor justice can be killed by violence" — he was stunned speechless, as were we all, by the thunderous detonation of a bomb.

The explosion occurred at the far corner of the National Palace. I stared open-mouthed at the palace and saw leaping fire and thick fuming smoke as if the pavement were aflame. The crowd stampeded away from the palace. There was the immediate sound of some return gunfire. Like a massive wave, thousands headed for the only possible shelter, the empty cathedral behind us. Some trying to climb the fence were killed as others in panic trampled over them. The chief liturgist grabbed Cardinal Corripio and me by the arms and hurried us into the safety of the cathedral as waves of people thronged behind us.

Moment of Crisis

What does one think in such a situation? My first thought was of a radio or television news bulletin in the U.S. which my wife would hear in horror before I could phone her myself. I did, however, get hold of myself. I was going to need all the serenity I could muster. Because I was wearing a doctoral gown and a hood, I knew people might mistake me for a prelate as they searched to be consoled.

People continued to pour into the cathedral. It is relatively small; perhaps half the size of Riverside Church in New York. It cannot comfortably hold three thousand, standing, and by the end of a half-hour's warfare outside, more than five thousand had packed into it, with more still pressing their way in. People were standing on every available surface, including the main altar. There was no room to bend; eventually, there was barely room to breathe. The building shuddered with bomb blasts. Its awful, reverberating acoustics magnified the sound of gunfire; and all of this was heard above a din of cries and prayers from every direction. The smell of war wafted in. I kept panic away by looking after my neighbors, praying with them and speaking calm words of comfort (some learned from the archbishop).

All my life I have been a pathetic "claustrophobic." Being trapped in a small space has been my private nightmare. And yet, in the cathedral of San Salvador at the funeral of the archbishop, though people were dying of asphyxiation, I was strangely calm. My lifelong dread had come true, and I was going through it feeling only a numb rage at the perpetrators of this violence.

Cardinal Corripio, at the right of me, and I were in the second row of humans from the side wall. To my left, in the row behind me, was a woman who had been pleading with God. She had also begun to die. I could just turn my head, but nothing else; there was simply no way to bring her relief. As a Presbyterian layman I improvised what I thought was the Catholic church's rite for the dying. "Your sins are forgiven, go in the peace of God," I prayed. She did die, but there was no room for her to fall down. In some cases, people could manage to inch up the body of a person who had fainted or died and carry it on their hands overhead, but to where, one could not know.

All the dead in the cathedral, I later saw, were women: shorter, slighter women. Trampled or asphyxiated. I trust all of us in the U.S., especially the feminist, will not forget this group of San Salvadoran martyrs.

Then, suddenly, astonishingly, over the bombs and guns and prayers, we heard the sound of cheering. Something else was being carried by hands over heads. It took a while for this object to come into my view, but a chant that was joined by everyone in the cathedral announced its coming: "*El pueblo unido jamás será vencido. El pueblo unido jamás será vencido.*" ("The people united never shall be vanquished. The people united never shall be vanquished.") What the chant was announcing, I eventually could see, was the coffin of the archbishop, held aloft by fingertips, making its perilous way into this sanctuary of faith and terror, to its final resting place. Despite the violence outside, a group from the cathedral had gone out and down the steps to retrieve the coffin.

Even in death, the archbishop transformed despair to courage. How he was honored! People died to give his body, his memory, his faith, room where there was no room. Indeed: *"El pueblo unido jamás será vencido."*

At long last the violence outside ended. It had lasted about an hour and a half. We waited long after the ending to venture out.

We dispersed, but not before pausing to honor the lineup of our cathedral dead. All women. Many other corpses were picked up off the plaza by the Red Cross. As I left with my hands over my head and a sick feeling, I looked at a terrified boy sobbing. His mother was one of the dead women.

Eyewitnesses Confer

That night, we church representatives from around the world met again at the chancery building of the archdiocese to talk over what we had seen. About thirty of us were still in the city. We all had a chance to describe what we had seen. Since we had been scattered throughout the cathedral and outside, among us we were able to piece out to our satisfaction what had happened. This was indispensable. Beginning at 4:30 P.M. the government had begun broadcasting its version of events over a radio network. According to the government the "leftists" of the Coordinadora Revolucionaria had begun the shooting upon arriving, with the intention of stealing the archbishop's coffin and holding the dignitaries hostage in the cathedral. That official version also asserted that since the night before all military and security forces personnel had been confined to quarters.

Our own evidence pieced together as eyewitnesses was a total contradiction of the government's falsehoods. We agreed to put that in writing. All still present signed the statement. Then, as we were about to adjourn, we received a request for an interview with the five top leaders of the "leftists" on whom the violence was being blamed. We agreed. We asked them to describe what they had seen. They did. I asked them if they had carried weapons to the funeral.

"Yes, some of us did," they answered, and named the kinds and numbers of guns they had carried and the kinds of bags of kerosene they used for firebombing. "We are the most sought-out targets now," they said, "and we do not go anywhere any more without being prepared. We will not willingly be killed without a fight." They also described a strategy they use of overturning cars and burning them by throwing their bags of kerosene, to set up smoke screens against oncoming attacks.

What was remarkable about all of this is that their account — both what they volunteered and what they said in response to our questions — differed in no way from what we had pieced together among ourselves previously.

Official Version Prevails

The next day we were to find a radically different account given in newspapers: Salvadoran and U.S. newspapers. Sadly, the Salvadoran junta's account was evidently appropriated by U.S. Ambassador Robert White. Even more sadly, major U.S. newspapers apparently got much of their version from the same sources used by the ambassador, who was not present at the funeral.

One of the last things the archbishop did was to write President Carter pleading that no U.S. military assistance be granted to the Salvadoran Junta. I have just learned of the vote of the House Subcommittee on International Operations. By a vote of 6 to 3 it is recommending an appropriation of $5.7 million.

Can I be forgiven if I regard the majority vote as blasphemy? I hope other Americans will agree. Archbishop Romero literally gave his life for peace. A Mexican bishop said to me as we left the cathedral, "Christ has been killed again. But he will rise again." I believe that. If I didn't I would despair.

The Bishops Blink

August 9, 1982

Robert G. Hoyt

Robert G. Hoyt, a contributing editor of C & C, *was the founding editor of the* National Catholic Reporter *and editor of* C & C *from 1977 to 1985. He is currently senior writer at* Commonweal *magazine.*

BY MEANS I don't wholly understand and won't inquire into, a document marked CONFIDENTIAL has appeared on my desk: the first draft of a pastoral letter on peace and war — "God's Hope in a Time of Fear" — drawn up over a period of many months by a committee of the National Conference of Catholic Bishops.

I wish I could pretend to an exclusive, but the truth is that this particular secret paper seems to be popping up on all sorts of non-episcopal desks. One suspects a purpose. The draft is subject to revision before being voted on at the November meeting of the bishops. Somebody, or maybe everybody, on the committee or elsewhere in the bishops' conference, wants some critical feedback. Here comes some.

First, the key subject addressed in the draft is the morality or immorality of U.S. policy on nuclear weapons and nuclear war. The bishops have never addressed a more urgent question.

Second, the draft fails. That is, of course, my opinion. It means that I don't think the committee has yet arrived at a coherent, intellectually responsible position that takes account of the readily available facts and fits them into the framework of Catholic teaching.

The failure is not for want of effort. The draft is seventy pages long, and one senses blood, sweat, and contention in every paragraph. Two and a quarter pages are needed to list the thirty-seven "witnesses" who appeared before the committee, ranging from Cap Weinberger of the Defense Department to Molly Rush of the Plowshares Eight, from Paul Ramsey through Alan Geyer to Gordon Zahn, from Tom Cornell of the Catholic Peace Fellowship to Edward Rowny, chief U.S. negotiator in the START talks.

The committee did other kinds of homework as well. Their draft quotes or cites not only the New Testament, the Psalms, Isaiah, and Genesis, not only papal and conciliar statements and theological/ethical works, but also *Foreign Affairs* and *Foreign Policy*, Congressional testimony, publications of the International Institute for Strategic Studies, the reports of high-level conferences.

The letter is not *purely* a failure. It says interesting, true, and urgent things about the world's need, in the interests of the world's survival, to create institutional means for resolving conflict without war. It gives evidence of a long episcopal stride toward understanding of nonviolent resistance. And, though it repeats and ably defends the church's official "just war" teaching, it scores another advance by granting orthodoxy and a place in the intramural Catholic debate to dissidents — people like Dorothy Day, Molly Rush, Cornell, Zahn, and the Berrigans. (For a Catholic of my generation and my bias, it is a delight to see the name of Dorothy Day mentioned along with those of Mohandas Gandhi, Martin Luther King, Jr., and the sainted Francis of Assisi.)

It is not the bishops' basic stance on war that gives me trouble. I think there *can* be "just wars," and there may even have been some. The *conduct* of World War II (the firebombings of Dresden and Tokyo, the atomic bombing of Japan, the refusal of any terms but unconditional surrender) eroded its ethical rationale long before it ended. But it began as a just war and might have stayed that way had bishops, pastors, and journalists evidenced less worldly prudence and more prophetic fire.

Measuring the Risk

Nor do I find the drafters of the letter innocent about what nuclear weapons are and do. After reiterating the familiar requirements of proportionality and discrimination in the conduct of war, they ask informed, pointed, almost self-answering questions:

Can nuclear weapons be directed so accurately to their targets, and be so limited in their effects, as really to cause minimal harm to nearby civilians? Would not even a "limited" use of nuclear arms against military targets result in millions or tens of millions of civilian deaths?... What about the long-term effects of radiation, or of famine, disease, social fragmentation, economic collapse, and environmental injury to be expected from any large-scale use of nuclear weapons?

Reflecting on nuclear deterrence, the authors acknowledge that it "may have helped avoid war over the past thirty-seven years." But today:

Each superpower now has so many nuclear warheads and bombs aimed at the other that a failure of deterrence would be catastrophic. Can deterrence prevail under conditions of international crisis, when leaders are fearful, see great issues at stake, imagine the worst about each other's intentions, and must make life and death decisions within a matter of hours or even minutes? Is it likely that this can continue for decades or centuries?

Excellent questions. In my reading of the draft, it seems clear that its authors would answer every one of them in the negative. Assuming that is so, it will appear to many that the bishops would now go beyond saying (as they do) that Catholic morality forbids any but the most restricted use of nuclear arms. The argument seems to march inexorably toward condemnation also of the manufacture and possession of nuclear weapons for deterrent purposes.

Not so. The bishops introduce a distinction between *approval* of deterrence as a morally good thing (which they withhold) and *toleration* of it as the lesser of two evils (which they grant):

Toleration is a technical term in Catholic moral theology; in the case of deterrence toleration is based on two judgments. First,... if nuclear weapons had never been made, we could not condone their creation; second, the role of the nuclear deterrent in preserving "peace of a sort" gives it a certain utility. Hence, the mixed nature of deterrence produces the moral judgment of toleration, a judgment that to deny the deterrent any moral legitimacy may bring about worse consequences than we presently live with under conditions of deterrence. The deterrence relationship which now prevails between the United States, the Soviet Union and other powers is objectively a sinful situation.... Yet movement out of this objectively evil situation must be controlled lest we cause by accident what we would neither deliberately choose nor morally condone.

Some will find this an example of the tortuous reasoning that gives church leaders and ethics itself a bad name. Out of Catholic roots and Niebuhrian nurturing, I think it makes sense, as far as it goes. Unilateral abandonment of nuclear deterrence by the U.S. would give the Soviet Union an immense preponderance in possession of nuclear arms. When we had such a preponderance (a monopoly), we used the God-damned things. Deterrence is terribly risky; yes. Hence sinful; yes. But abandoning deterrence is still more risky, therefore still more sinful; yes.

But this is where the problem rises. Toleration of the logic of deterrence is one thing. Toleration of the actual nuclear policies of the United States and the Soviet Union is another. Neither of the superpowers, in practice, is following a policy of deterrence alone. And (as many passages in this draft letter show) *the bishops know it*. So does everybody who reads the papers. The evidence for that judgement is overwhelming, and you don't need to know a meson from a quark, a Clausewitz from a Kissinger, to understand it. Here's some of it, taken from a *New York Times* piece by Jerome B. Wiesner, president emeritus of MIT, science adviser to John Kennedy and Lyndon Johnson:

Every large city of any country not only is the shelter for its people but is a nodal point for every network in the life-support systems of its area (communications, electric power, fuel supply, medicine, roads, trains, planes, food)....It is easy to count these focal points in the United States and Soviet Union. An automobile road atlas shows that there are fewer than 200 in North America. And since there is no known defense against incoming ballistic missiles, 200 large nuclear bombs...would destroy the recuperative power of either continent....The death count — a total made up of those killed by the initial attack plus the victims of the subhuman conditions that would follow — could be as much as 200 million.

The United States possesses not mere hundreds of deliverable nuclear warheads but tens of thousands, and is manufacturing more every day. They are not needed for deterrence. Whatever the Soviet Union does, the U.S. now possesses dozens of times enough nuclear weaponry — deployed in so many places and modes as to be invulnerable — to deter a Soviet nuclear attack. Those surplus weapons do not merely increase but *multiply* the risks we are running — the risk that nuclear war will happen, the risk that, if it happens, it will create a dead or dying planet.

The point is this. As Theodore Draper has made clear in *New York Review of Books* for July 15, 1982 (and as Lord Solly Zuckerman has argued in *Nuclear Illusions and Realities*), a deterrence policy is shaped by the question, "How much is enough?" It will deliberately and contentedly ignore the question, "Who's ahead?" By keeping the debate centered on the second question, policymakers on both sides have reached for other aims besides deterrence — at least political domination, at most (and worst) the power to "prevail" in nuclear war. In doing so they have put aside the ethical questions raised by the power of nuclear weapons. And the bishops, so far, have fallen into this trap.

Two other matters must be mentioned.

First, nuclear strategy: This draft of the pastoral letter formally and solemnly condemns any first use of nuclear weapons, any targeting of cities, any *threat* to use nuclear arms against population centers. Declared U.S. policy blatantly violates all these requirements.

Second, the evolution of nuclear policy: Three years ago Cardinal John Krol, speaking for the Catholic hierarchy, told the United States Senate that the bishops could continue to condone deterrence only as long as hope remained for a reversal of the arms race and movement in the direction of disarmament. Despite a softening of Reaganite rhetoric, there has been no such movement in *policy:* The stockpiles grow, new weapons and weapons systems, some of them seriously destabilizing, are invented, produced, and either deployed or prepared for deployment, and the Pentagon has drawn up a strategy for the fighting of a protracted nuclear war.

In one passage of the draft, the authors acknowledge their obligation as teachers of morality to go beyond general moral principles, to do more than issue pious pleas for peace: "We must look at the nature of existing and planned weapons systems, the doctrines and plans that would govern their use in time of war, and the consequences of use under various conditions." These acknowledged obligations are never adequately fulfilled. A Catholic (or, anyone else) who accepts the classical just war doctrine, and who looks to the bishops for help in applying it to the here and now, won't get that help from this document in its present form. After arguing the case for toleration of deterrence with proper rigor, it passes by in silence, or with mild expressions of "dissatisfaction," a posture and program that starkly violate the bishops' own criteria for a moral (or morally tolerable) nuclear policy.

What do the bishops need? World War III? One hopes for a clearing of heads and a stiffening of spines among them before November.

South Africa's Blacks: Aliens in Their Own Land

November 26, 1984

Desmond Tutu

Desmond Tutu, archbishop of Cape Town, is internationally known and respected for his continuing role in the antiapartheid struggle in South Africa.

I FIRST DISCOVERED that there are black people in the United States when I was a small boy of about eight years of age and I picked up a battered copy of *Ebony* magazine. I didn't know that there could be literature of that kind, with such subversive qualities, because up to that point I had come to begin to believe what white people said about us. And, picking up *Ebony* magazine, I grew inches....I read about one Jackie Robinson breaking into major league baseball and that did wonders for me as a person.

Now, only those who have been victims of oppression and injustice and discrimination know what I am talking about when I say that the ultimate evil is not the suffering, excruciating as that may be, which is meted out to those who are God's children. The ultimate evil of oppression, and certainly of that policy of South Africa called apartheid, is when it succeeds in making a child of God begin to doubt that he or she is a child of God. That is the ultimate blasphemy....

I recall, too, seeing our first all-black film, *Stormy Weather.* I don't know whether it was a very good film. I don't know what the critics would say. But I don't care. Because for us it was making a political statement, it was making a theological statement. They were just putting together a piece of entertainment, a movie — Fats Waller, Cab Calloway, Lena Horne. Yet it was making a theological statement. It was saying that these whom you see depicted there have the *imago dei*. That these too are created in the image of God and if they are created in the image of God they too are God's representatives, and if they are God's representatives then we too, in spite of all that was happening and still happens to us, we too are children of God. We too are those whom God has honored by asking us to be his partners. Partners in upsetting the powers and principalities. Partners in helping God to establish his kingdom. And God was saying: "Hey, don't go around trying to apologize for your existence, man. I didn't make a mistake creating you as who you are. You are not a faint copy, carbon copy of somebody else; you are an original." That was seeping through into our consciousness in ways that we were not always aware of, and the subversion had begun.

You see, as you very well know, one of the ways of helping to destroy a people is to tell them that they don't have a history, that they have no roots. They did it in many ways. One of them was writing history from the perspective of white people. Now we weren't over-bright, but this history of South Africa began to strike us as odd. We read about white colonists coming to our country in the seventeenth century. Whenever the Dutch or English colonists went over into black territory and got the blacks' cattle, the word used was that the colonists "captured" the cattle. But almost always when they wrote about a similar expedition

on the part of the Xhosas, the Xhosas always "stole" the cattle.
And we were very young, but I mean we began to scratch our
heads....

But you see, if you tell something sufficiently often you come to
believe it and those who listen to you perhaps also believe it. And
you begin to gnaw away at their self-image and they begin to see
themselves as you depict them, when you call them, as we used to be
called "non-whites," "non-Europeans."

Words into Things

Those people who say that language is not important don't know
what they are talking about. Those people who think that language is
merely descriptive of reality don't know what they are talking about.
We who have been victims of a process of denigration know that language is also creative: It brings about what it describes. If you say
to people for long enough that they are non-this, non-the-other, it
doesn't take very long before they begin to believe and speak of themselves also in negative terms. So that it becomes almost a kind of
self-fulfilling prophecy.

It is actually quite wonderful, the kind of things that used to happen at home. Back in the old days they used to call us Natives,
with a capital N. Now, that applied only to people with our color of
skin. If you went to a white South African, born in the country, and
you said innocently, "Excuse me, Ma'am, are you a native of these
parts?" you would know very soon that you had committed the most
awful *faux pas*, and you would wish that the earth would open up
and swallow you. Because she certainly was not a "Native" of those
parts.

They used to have extraordinary road signs which read, "Drive
carefully, Natives cross here." Somebody changed the sign to read,
rather hair-raisingly, "Drive carefully, Natives very cross here." ...

Now, my dear brothers and sisters, I come from a land where they
ban all kinds of literature as being subversive. You are not allowed
to read this and that and the other because it would put ideas in
your heads. Our children are prevented from reading histories that
will tell them about the French Revolution. It would put ideas into
their heads — liberty, fraternity, equality — how can you speak about
those things? The histories that our children have to study have been
expurgated so that you don't see any references to the American War
of Independence. But, we said to the government, you know, you are
late. The book that you should have banned a long time ago is the
Bible....

Land in Flames

I came to this country three weeks ago. We should have come much earlier to the United States. We had to postpone our departure because of the upheaval in our land. We called an emergency meeting of our executive committee [of the South African Council of Churches] because we thought that our land was going up in flames....

So on this occasion, our committee said, let us visit the areas of unrest. We went to a black township called Wattville and we went into the home of an old lady and we said, "Can you tell us what happened?"

She said, "Yes, Bishop. My grandchildren were playing in the front of the house, in the yard.... The police went past here chasing school children. They didn't find them. There was no riot happening at the time, and the police came down the street and swept past my house and they stopped. Bishop, I was sitting in the kitchen which is at the back of my house when one of my children rushed into the kitchen and said. 'Mommy, please come.' I rushed out. My grandson of six was lying just inside the front door. Shot in the back. Dead. Only six years old." Now, even if there was a riot, what in the name of everything that is good could you say a six-year-old would do to police armed to the teeth? How do you manage to shoot a six-year-old in the back?...

South Africa says, "Our economy is going to be based on cheap black labor and we can insure that that labor is cheap by separating off the men from their families and having them live in single-sex hostels for eleven months of the year. Therefore we can pay them as if they were single and the cost of production is decreased accordingly." So those who invest in South Africa, invest in a system which we have described as being as evil, as un-Christian, as immoral as Communism ever was, as Nazism ever was. They invest in a system that depends on black misery and suffering. When some people suggest to them — I don't because I can't; if I stood up here and said that I support disinvestment it would be five years in jail so I am not talking about it — if someone else says to those who invest in South Africa, "Hey, why don't you pull out?" they will be the first to say, "You know, the people who will suffer the most if we pull out are blacks."

Baloney! For all these many years they have depended on black misery and suffering. What makes them suddenly become these wonderful altruists who care about black suffering? I am not a cynic. I am merely asking a question.

Perhaps you have read about the KTC squatter camps in Cape Town, or you may have heard of Crossroads. Let me tell you why there are these squatter camps. They exist because of the South African desire for cheap labor. What happens is that the women folk say, "You know, when we went to church we were told by the minister, when we took our vows, 'What God has joined together let no man put asunder.' And so, we want to fulfill our marriage vows. We want to be with our men."

In South Africa, it is a crime. In a Christian country that has a public holiday dedicated to the family, it is a crime. Isn't it marvelous: "Family Day" in a country which deliberately, systematically, by design of government policy, destroys black family life.

But those women said, "We have had enough. We are going to be with our men folk, come hell or high water." Well, they have been getting hell. These women, because there is no housing available, build squatter camps, with homes constructed of flimsy plastic coverings.... I am glad, you know, that I am not Western; I'm glad that I am not white. I am glad that maybe I am also not civilized — because those who uphold these wonderful standards every day ... go out and they destroy those plastic shelters that the women have put up. You don't read about it anymore because it doesn't make the news....

I carry a strange document for traveling around. It is not even a passport. Now, I am a South African of the golden sunshine, the gold, and the Krugerrand. My father was born in South Africa. My mother was born in South Africa, my mother's mother — you go right back. We belong here. Well then, there are some people who don't understand that. I carry this document for travel purposes. Inside here, where there is a place for nationality, you would think it would say "South Africa." This thing here says of my nationality, "Undeterminable at present." You might think I am making it up. "Undeterminable at present." They don't know where to slot me because they say South Africa is made up of several nations. The Xhosas are one nation; the Tswanas and so forth and so forth....

Among the whites there are French, English, German, you name it. Now we say, "Please just tell us how is it possible for whites of these disparate groups to come together and coalesce and be one nation? And we who are Africans are split up into all these different nations?"

The purpose, obviously, is to turn us into aliens in the land of our birth. Because, you see, when you are an alien, one thing you cannot claim is political rights.

So, when we stand up and say that this is evil, this is un-Christian, they say, "Hey, you are mixing politics with religion." They tell us. "You are a Communist." Now maybe that sounds familiar. And then we ask, "Hey, which Bible do you read? Would you kindly tell us which Bible you read which would enable you to have this dichotomy?"

We don't read the same Bible. When did the people of Israel experience God for the first time as God? Did they experience God in worship? That is not what the Bible says. The Bible says the people of Israel experienced God when God performed a political act, helping rebel slaves escape out of bondage. And from that time on people said, "Ah, this is the kind of God we have. A liberating God. A God who takes the side of the oppressed, of the hungry, of the exploited, of the weak."

Which Bible do you read? Have you read Matthew, chapter 25? Jesus tells a strange parable there. He says, "How is it going to be determined how you go to heaven or to the warmer place? Did you feed the hungry? Did you clothe the naked? Did you visit the sick? Did you visit those who are in prison?" Jesus says, "Inasmuch as you have done it to these you would have done it to me." So if you want to know where I am in South Africa, you go to the KTC squatter camp. That is where I am.

A Strange Country

And so, let me finish, my friends, and say your country is a strange country. Let me be careful. I am a visitor here. Your country: When the Polish leader General Jaruzelski did something to Solidarity, your country, before you could say Jackie Robinson, applied sanctions against Poland.

And then the same kind of thing is done to black trade unionists in South Africa and you say Hey, what are you doing about that situation? They say, no, no, no. Sanctions don't work. Sanctions don't work. We must have a policy of constructive engagement. We must talk to these people and try to persuade them.

And so I end by saying, How come you allow the kinds of things that happen in South Africa to happen with the aid of your government?

We depend on you. We depend on you because our liberation is your liberation. As long as we are unfree — to that extent you are going to be unfree in this country. And let me say to you, there is no doubt we are going to be free. Whether you help us or not. For the God whom we worship is the Exodus God, the God who leads his people always out of bondage into freedom....

Under Construction:
Nicaragua's New Polity

July 22, 1985

Andrew Reding

Andrew Reding is a journalist whose reports for C & C during the 1980s provided distin-
guished coverage of Nicaragua. His article on the Nicaraguan elections of 1984 received a
Project Censored Award. The following is excerpted from his coverage of the Nicaraguan
National Constituent Assembly.

A RHETORICAL BATTLE is being waged in the U.S. over whether
the Nicaraguan revolution is keeping or betraying its promises, but
without the ammunition of facts. During the days I observed the National Assembly at work, no other foreign correspondent was on hand,
with the exception of reporters who were representatives of the (U.S.)
Socialist Workers party. I have seen no coverage in mainstream media since my return, even though yards of space have been given to
Nicaragua-related stories emanating from the White House and Capi-
tol Hill. It's because of the vacuum of reportage that this account will
provide an unusual amount of detail.

A Set of Goals

The assembly is in fact functioning, .working both on current legislation and on drafting the new constitution it is required to complete
by January 1, 1987. In agreements reached last October, before the
elections, the seven political parties now represented in the assembly committed themselves, on paper, to a set of basic constitutional
principles, including: periodic national elections; freedom of the press
and free dissemination of ideas; freedom to organize; freedom of
movement; free and democratic labor unions; guarantees for personal,
private, cooperative, and state property rights; democratic election of
municipal governments immediately following enactment of the new
constitution. The FSLN insisted on a commitment to national defense, including a military draft; it agreed to a depoliticization of the
armed forces, conditioned on the willingness of non-Frente members
to serve.

However admirable the goals, it won't be possible to reach final
judgment on the integrity of the process until the constitution is in
place and its provisions tested in practice. Meantime, however, a reporter wanting to learn how seriously the assembly members take the
process — and whether the FSLN, with its nearly two-thirds majority,
is turning the legislature into a rubber stamp for the Sandinista-
dominated executive branch — can pick up evidence in plenty. I was

able to interview the leaders and other members of all four major parties. I was also able to sit in on the floor debates in the assembly. Some were tediously long, but the discussion was free and far-ranging. (It's permissible even to voice open support for the counterrevolution, and not only in the assembly, but also in the streets and in the pages of *La Prensa*, the fiercely anti-Sandinista paper.) And sometimes the debate is lively indeed; once I saw a fist fight in which both participants suffered some damage before they were separated.

In my interviews with members of the assembly, by far the most negative judgments came from Virgilio Godoy, nominal leader of the Independent Liberal party (PLI). Godoy is a brilliant pessimist, as skeptical of U.S. intentions as he is about the Frente. He described the assembly as "an institution that was practically still-born." In its first legislative act, he said, it had enfeebled itself by transferring broad powers to the presidency, including the right to suspend the assembly by declaring a state of emergency, to exercise legislative powers during the three months of the year the assembly is not in session, to control the budget, and to veto acts of the assembly.

Godoy gave other criticisms in an article in *La Prensa* (March 22) quoting his views. The rules of the Assembly, he wrote, give unfair advantage to the Sandinistas by granting the presiding officer unilateral power to close off debate when in his judgment the topic at hand has been sufficiently discussed. The rule that requires a minimum of five sponsors before a bill can be brought up for deliberation is "clearly discriminatory and antidemocratic," since it deprives the three smaller (all Marxist-Leninist) parties, with only two delegates apiece, from initiating legislation on behalf of their constituents. Godoy's most sensational (or oddest) accusation accounted for *La Prensa*'s banner headline: "35 Sandinistas Will Be Able to Approve the Constitution." It rested on legislative arithmetic. Under Assembly rules, 60 percent of the 96 members (or 58) constitute a quorum; final approval of the constitution will require a 60 percent majority of the quorum, or a minimum of 35 votes. (The arithmetic is accurate, but the parliamentary rules are hardly bizarre; it is not the rules but the election results that put the FSLN in a commanding position. Further, Godoy's argument assumes the absence of a large number of opposition delegates from the Assembly's most critical vote.)

I asked Godoy what he thought about the fate of the pre-election accords pledging all the parties that signed to creation of a democratic system. "There isn't any evidence that the FSLN intends to respect the signature it places on those accords," he said. "The first accord of the summit meetings [among the parties] was to reestablish freedom of the press, and that accord was violated the same day it was signed," when

La Prensa chose to suspend publication after government censorship of its lead story for that day (Oct. 21).

Because he was a supporter of the revolution for a considerable period, because he is *La Prensa*'s principal source on assembly actions, and because he is sometimes described in the U.S. media as "the" leading opposition figure, Godoy's opinions have to be included in an article for readers in this country. In other interviews, however, I found few members of opposition parties (including his own) who echoed his views or followed his leadership, and a number who disagreed violently.

I talked, for instance, with Clemente Guido, a medical doctor who is a vice president of the assembly and leader of the Democratic Conservative party (PCD), the assembly's second largest. Guido said Godoy's criticisms were half-truths, "and half-truths are worse than lies." Yes, he said, the president of the republic can veto acts of the assembly, but the assembly can override a veto with a 60 percent majority (in the U.S. a two-thirds majority of both Houses is required). Again, assembly actions that gave power to the presidency did not rise solely from the FSLN: Guido's own party had been advocating such provisions since well before the Frente was founded. Members of the three small parties can introduce legislation by joining together or seeking cosponsors from other parties. Other provisions attacked by Godoy, said Guido, are provisional, subject to revision in the drafting of the new constitution. (As for the charge that the "excessive" power of the assembly's presiding officer favors the FSLN, I observed later that when Guido himself presided he was far quicker to use his authority than the Sandinista president, Carlos Núñez.)

An Internal Struggle

From other sources I learned that Godoy's account of the censorship incident was less than candid: He failed to mention that the censored article was a story reporting his own decision to pull the PLI out of the elections, or that he had been able to announce that decision to the nation in a televised address on the government station, delivered on the evening of the same day *La Prensa* failed to appear.

Without defending the censorship, a fellow member of Godoy's party shed further light on the incident. He was Constantino Pereira, Godoy's vice presidential running mate on the PLI ticket in the November elections. Pereira is a coffee grower (two plantations) and a cosmopolite who speaks fluent English and French and once lived in exile in Switzerland and France. Last fall, after Godoy's announcement, Pereira made a dramatic televised appeal asking PLI members to ignore their party chief and cast their ballots. His largely successful plea rescued the PLI from political oblivion and helped restore credibility to the elections themselves.

Reflections on a New Era in the Philippines

April 7, 1986

Walden Bello

Walden Bello, a native of the Philippines and co-author of Development Debacle: The World Bank in the Philippines, *is director of the Institute for Food Policy, San Francisco.*

THE CELEBRATION of the end of a hated dictatorship continues in the Philippines. So, unfortunately, does the mythmaking in Washington.

Success has many parents, and among those claiming paternity of the new Corazon Aquino government is the United States. Washington today is awash with self-congratulations for a "triumph of American diplomacy." A frantic move to dissociate the U.S. from a loyal ally who had already been defeated by a people's uprising, however, hardly qualifies as a "triumph." Indeed, Ronald Reagan's switch from his notorious claim that the February 7 presidential elections were characterized by "fraud on both sides" to his demand that Marcos step down on February 24 will long stand as a classic example of diplomatic opportunism.

Yet Washington's claim to a share in Marcos's ouster is not entirely untrue. Though they encountered hesitation, if not outright resistance at the White House, key State Department officials had been pushing a strategy of liberalization with the end in view of eventually displacing Marcos. The snap presidential election that played such a decisive role in Marcos's fall had been the dictator's response to U.S. pressure for liberalization.

The idea of the "Third Force," a doctrine which had been shelved in the aftermath of Vietnam, was dusted off and applied in the Philippines by pragmatic American policymakers. They had supported Marcos so long as he was in full command of the situation but were now desperately seeking an alternative to the triumph of the Philippine left. The Third Force concept, writes prointerventionist columnist Charles Krauthammer, "is simple. In friendly countries ruled by dictators, America should use its influence to support a 'Third Force,' a democratic alternative to a pro-American despot on the one hand and Communist insurgencies on the other. A Third-Force strategy means not settling for the lesser of two evils, but trying to help build and support a middle, democratic way."

The government of Cory Aquino is such a Third Force. Whether it will accept or effectively play the role Washington wants it to assume is open to question. The euphoria still has to die down, but Cory Aquino's enormous personal popularity and her unquestionable integrity cannot mask for long some hard realities about her government.

One decisive reality is that, for all its rhetoric about "people power," the new government is dominated by the traditional Philippine elite and draws its support mainly from the urban middle class.

A related characteristic of the new regime: It is an unstable coalition of sharply competing factions of that section of the elite disenfranchised by Marcos with his imposition of martial law in 1972. While strongly antidictatorship in sentiment, this faction retains a strong interest in the maintenance of the country's landlord-dominated semi-feudal agrarian structure, has strong ties to the United States, and is strongly anticommunist. President Aquino is tied, by blood and marriage, to two of the most prominent landlord families in Central Luzon. Her vice president, Salvador Laurel, is the chieftain of the most powerful political dynasty in Southern Luzon.

The question in many people's minds is: Will Cory Aquino be able to transcend her class background and become a genuine representative of the 85 percent of Filipinos who come from the lower classes? Many of her past moves contained pleasant surprises; the answer to this question is a tossup. But, even if she were inclined in a socially progressive direction, it is unlikely that her landed backers would give her a free hand on matters of such vital importance to them as land reform.

Next in influence after the disenfranchised elite is that section of the Marcos coalition which defected to Aquino. Headed by Armed Forces Chief of Staff Fidel Ramos and Defense Minister Juan Ponce Enrile, this faction includes the military, which, despite some much-publicized replacements of some highly placed Marcos loyalists, remains intact. Aside from serving as a vehicle for the ambitions of Enrile, the overriding objectives of the Enrile-Ramos group are to pursue the counterinsurgency drive against the leftist New People's Army (NPA), retain the military's influence in politics, and protect it from being subject to judicial prosecution for human rights abuses à la Argentina.

The alliance between Enrile-Ramos and Aquino is even now quite fragile. How fragile is indicated by Enrile's warning that the "Armed Forces Reform Movement" — which led the successful mutiny against

Marcos — would "have a say" if Aquino were to move to replace him....

The alliance of convenience between Aquino and the Enrile-Ramos faction is unlikely to survive a serious effort by the Aquino forces to move toward democracy, dismantle the repressive machinery, and confine the army to its barracks.

Bases and Dollars

The explosive issues of the tenure of the U.S. bases, the $26 billion foreign debt, and the International Monetary Fund austerity program will provide immediate points of strain between the nationalists, on the one hand, and the traditional elite and the Enrile-Ramos group, on the other.

These tensions within the governing coalition will be aggravated by the economic crisis, the growing popularity of demands for fundamental solutions to the Philippines' basic problems, and the challenge posed by the left. The new government has raised expectations of swift, widespread, and thorough political and economic changes which it cannot possibly fulfill, given its essential character as an elite-dominated government. The post-Marcos scenario sketched out by the president's slain husband, Benigno Aquino, Jr., contains a grim warning for her:

Look, you have a situation when Marcos falls, you come in, the Communists back off, and people expect you to make miracles. How do I put back three million jobs? How do I bring down the price of gasoline, for Peter's sake.... So the people will say, "Jesus Christ, you're the guy we waited eight years for? You're even worse!"... The thing I can say is, the first guy that will come in will be blown out in six months. Then a second guy will come in and he'll be blown out in six months.

A key player is the left, whose actions will greatly determine the future of the Aquino government. Currently in motion are attempts to begin negotiations for a cease-fire with the New People's Army. It is, however, extremely unlikely that the NPA will give up its arms, despite the positive stance it has taken toward Aquino. And it is very likely that the illegal National Democratic Front and other nationalist mass organizations will take advantage of the greater "democratic space" now available to organize and press demands for land reform, withdrawal of the U.S. bases, and an end to U.S. domination of the economy.

These developments would make it increasingly difficult for the government to resist U.S. pressure to mount a stepped-up and effective counterinsurgency effort. The Reagan administration has made it quite clear, in fact, that its continued support for the Aquino government is contingent on the latter's willingness and capacity to undertake an antiguerrilla drive which would be more effective than Marcos's.

Again, Cory Aquino has consistently surprised people. She might just stand up to U.S. pressure for a military solution to the insurgency.

Caving in to U.S. pressure for a military solution to the insurgency will inevitably translate into a resurgence of the military's influence in politics, the blunting of democratic reforms, and even more intense splits within the ruling coalition. While the ultimate direction which the Aquino government will take cannot be predicted at this point, it is clear that it has only two options — to serve as a transition to a more progressive political order or to regress toward repressive rule, under U.S. pressure and in the name of "national security."

Some in Aquino's cabinet feel that the fork in the road is only six months down the line.

By Any Other Name...

November 17, 1986

Roger L. Shinn

Roger Shinn, Reinhold Niebuhr professor of social ethics emeritus from Union Theological Seminary, New York, is known for his wide variety of interests in theology, politics and society and for many books, including Forced Options, *and* Wars and Rumors of Wars.

THE HORROR AND BLASPHEMY of nuclear war are so overwhelming that we must listen to every cry of pain and outrage. The Methodist bishops in their pastoral letter have issued such a cry. I hope it will be heard.

But there is a difference between a cry and a policy, between rhetoric and reality. President Reagan expresses his moral abhorrence of the present policy of deterrence. So do the Methodist bishops. Likewise Reagan and the bishops agree in their expressed desires for a world without nuclear weapons. Those rhetorical agreements conceal — or, more accurately, fail to conceal — stark opposition on the realities of policy. Reagan's ethical objections to deterrence are joined to his advocacy of an increased budget for weapons and his Strategic Defense Initiative (Star Wars). The Methodist bishops oppose both.

That coincidence of rhetoric and clash in reality require us to examine the relation between rhetoric and reality within the pastoral letter and its accompanying "Foundation Document."

The Methodist bishops praise, but claim to go beyond, the pastoral letter of the U.S. Roman Catholic bishops, *The Challenge of Peace*. Happily the letter does not gloat over that superiority, as some Methodists are doing. (Even a few Catholics are hailing the Methodist letter as bolder than their own.) The two documents concur on many issues; the difference is on deterrence.

The Catholics, in an agonizing analysis, rejected the present deterrence policies, then gave "a strictly conditional moral acceptance" of a revised deterrence policy as a transitional stage on the way to negotiated nuclear disarmament. A committee of the Catholic bishops is now reconsidering that position, in a process that may lead to revision of it if there is no progress toward actual disarmament.

The Methodists point to the Catholic position, then stake out their own. They declare their belief that "the moral case for nuclear deterrence, even as an interim ethic, has been undermined by unrelenting arms escalation." They reject the "idolatry of deterrence," and they say: "Deterrence must no longer receive the churches' blessing, even as a temporary warrant for the maintenance of nuclear weapons."

I hope that any Christian will reject the "idolatry of deterrence," along with all other idolatries, and will affirm that the mission of the churches is not to give a "blessing" to national military policies. I doubt that the Methodists differ at all from the Catholics on those issues. But what about policy? Do we really have here a bolder rejection of deterrence than the Catholics made? If any are inclined to read the document as a total rejection of deterrence "even as an interim ethic," the text quickly moves to correct that error. The Methodists urge "an ethic of reciprocity" in the reduction and ultimate elimination of nuclear weapons — an equivalent of the Catholic position. Meanwhile they justify "the interim possession of such weapons for a strictly limited time." They do not give the name of deterrence to that "interim possession," but it is hard to think of any more accurate name. They certainly do not want to keep the weapons in order to use them. The alternative is to keep them in order to deter others from using them.

Methodist Moment of Truth

The document comes to its moment of truth when it quotes, without quite endorsing, the Sixth Assembly of the World Council of Churches (Vancouver, 1983):

We believe that the time has come when the churches must unequivocally declare that the production and deployment as well as the use of nuclear weapons are a crime against humanity and that such activities must be condemned on ethical and theological grounds.

The Methodists do not continue the reasoning of the Vancouver Assembly, which requires "the struggle to cause one's own nation to
commit itself never to own or use nuclear weapons, despite the period
of nuclear vulnerability." Instead, they say: "The rejection of nuclear
deterrence, however, does not necessarily mean immediate, unilateral disarmament." How does that differ from saying: The rejection
of nuclear deterrence does not really mean the rejection of nuclear
deterrence?

Why do they not follow out the logic of the WCC? An unstated
reason may be that such a position, quite understandable in some societies and in some communities of faith, is not a political option in
this country. There are times when political alternatives are so bad that
the church should disregard them; but if a church is to influence the
body politic, its recommendations must have some political credibility.
Radical unilateral disarmament does not.

The more important reason is plainly stated in the document: "Indeed, immediate and total nuclear disarmament by the U.S. might
well tempt other countries to develop or expand their own nuclear arsenals, thereby increasing the risk of nuclear war." In other words, the
abandonment of a deterrent — at least an interim deterrent — might
heighten the nuclear peril. I wish the bishops had added the observation that the fact of a Soviet deterrent may well have prevented the
U.S. from using nuclear weapons in some past times of temptation —
as indeed we did use them when there was no such deterrent.

It is at this point that the bishops grapple with realities that their
more rhetorical statements neglect. I wish they had done so more
consistently. Alan Geyer was the key consultant and writer of the
document. I wish the bishops had paid more attention to his opposition to "deterrence dogmatists," coupled with his awareness "of many
signs of moral sensitivity and political wisdom among some deterrence
advocates" (*The Idea of Disarmament!*, Brethren Press, 1982).

In one university faculty conversation, where the Catholic pastoral
letter was taken with some seriousness, the tendency was to dismiss
the Methodist document as more hortatory but less genuine in relating
ethical and political policy. The Catholics openly confess their moral
agony and their discontent with their own conclusions. The Methodists are up against the same problems, but are a little too pleased with
their conclusions.

One extremely sobering problem remains in both documents. They
agree in condemning the arms race, in seeking reciprocal disarmament of the great powers, in maintaining a modified deterrent (under
whatever name) during the transition. They agree that their goal
is total nuclear disarmament. Neither quite faces up to the extreme
improbability of achieving that form of disarmament.

Alva Myrdal, the Swedish Nobel peace laureate and advocate of disarmament, was probably a little more honest in saying that humanity is destined to live with nuclear weapons as far ahead as anybody can see. I don't like that opinion, but I don't see how to refute it. Arms reduction is hard but possible. Total nuclear disarmament is another matter. The fact that both Reagan and Gorbachev can so easily agree on that goal, while having so much more difficulty with nearer goals, is a sign of the unreality of their talk at just that point.

The reason is the reciprocity that the Methodists emphasize. If arms reduction comes, as I devoutly hope it will, verifiability will be important. Means of approximate verifiability are available, and approximate verifiability is good enough in a world of vast arsenals. Approximate verifiability will not be good enough when it comes to destroying the last hundred or last ten nuclear weapons in every arsenal. Nobody knows how to accomplish verification in that situation. Nobody now knows how many nuclear weapons, assembled or ready for quick assembly, there may be in the Middle East, in South Africa, in a few other scattered parts of the world. Even if the U.S. and the USSR were to achieve a miracle of trust, would they trust everybody else in the world? And would they give up their last nuclear weapons when they suspected others might have them?

Why raise such remote questions when more immediate questions are urgent? Only because so many others, whether in the White House or the Kremlin or the churches, are answering them, usually not thoughtfully. My opinion is that we cannot now solve them and had better not presuppose their solution. Meanwhile, we have a full agenda. Our genuine opportunities to reduce the risk and terror of war and to build peaceable relations need not depend on solutions to distant problems.

I have concentrated on the main difficulty, as I see it, in the Methodist pastoral letter. There is much more worth discussing. I would like to know better what the bishops mean by calling for "a new theology." They remind me of politicians advocating "new ideas" but not producing them. I see little that is new in the theological suggestions, unless it is the idea of the church "as an alternative community to an alienated and fractured world" — and that idea I do not understand. Surely it does not mean that the church is going to become the "alternative" community that produces and distributes economic goods, does the work of government, and sponsors the educational and artistic processes of this pluralistic world.

With these various reservations, I find much to commend in the document. It shows an acute awareness that peacemaking is far more than disarmament. Its attention to world economic issues is important.

Its criticisms of both the U.S. and the USSR are judicious. It is not afraid to fault both militarists and self-righteous peace activists. Its call for attention to nonviolent strategies of social change is appropriate. It is a faithful document in calling the churches to concern for the wide range of human problems that bear on peace. I find myself defending the document against its most vociferous critics and, above all, against those who say the churches should not be engaging these issues.

The Lord's Song in a Hostile Land: Time to Pay the Cost of Hope in South Africa

May 4, 1987

Charles Villa-Vicencio

Charles Villa Vicencio, professor of religion and society at the University of Cape Town, South Africa, is author of Trapped in Apartheid. *He was very much involved, through the Institute of Contextual Theology, in the 1985 South African Kairos Document challenging "state theology."*

UNTIL RECENTLY IT WAS fashionable to challenge the church to leave the security of its cloister of vestments, liturgy, and cult in order to engage the world — there to be the leaven in the lump and the salt of the earth. At a political level the church was called to thrust aside its isolation and to confront the state with prophetic diligence.

That option has passed, and the choice of the church leaving the cloister to engage the world has been preempted. Today parishioners are being detained, driven into exile, and killed. We have, in many instances reluctantly, been *compelled* to respond to the world that has encountered us. We have been drawn into the marketplace and obliged to express an opinion on economic sanctions. We have been driven onto the battlefield, compelled to make a stand in support of our young people who refuse to do military service in an army used to prop up an apartheid regime. We have been forced into a church-state confrontation as the civil authorities have curtailed our religious freedom.

Over the years conservative church leaders have insisted that the moment of resisting civil authority can come for the church only when that authority interferes in the church's right to worship God. These leaders have referred to the magnificent stand taken by Archbishop Geoffrey Clayton who, in response to the "Church Bill" of 1957, counselled his priests to disobey a law which prevented people from discharging their "religious duty of participating in public worship." "That is the point at which we can do none other than resist," church leaders have consistently told us.

That moment has in recent days been thrust on us. When Minister of Police Louis de Grange sought to prevent services (in June 1986) in commemoration of the Soweto uprising of 1976, both Desmond Tutu and Allan Boesak were compelled to inform the minister, as Archbishop Geoffrey Clayton had told Prime Minister Verwoerd in his day, that Christians would be called to worship despite his restrictions. While the minister seemed to revise his earlier position allowing for *bona fide* services to be held, the police failed to show the kind of restraint with regard to church services that was shown in 1957. This has regretfully thrust the church into overt and explicit confrontation with the state.

The banning of funerals during recent months has become a common occurrence; some communities were prevented from holding June 16 services; individual ministers were warned not to refer to the events of Soweto 1976 in their Sunday services. A congregation of two hundred people was arrested in Elsies River. In Mdantsane a church was invaded and desecrated, and in Cape Town tear gas cannisters were fired through the windows of a mosque. Try as it may, the church can no longer escape the world. State authorities have invaded the sacred space in which Christians are to be obedient to God. This is a space which includes worship services and funerals, but it is also a space which is located in the marketplace, in educational institutions, in political bodies, and in the streets of our cities, townships, and rural areas.

Large sections of the institutional church, anesthetized by an ethereal theology of escapism, manage to ignore this challenge. Yet the church *which is obedient to the gospel of Christ* is under siege. We long for the peace of days now gone, and with the Psalmist of old we weep by the waters of Babylon, and ask: "How shall we sing the Lord's song in a foreign land?" (Ps. 137). More pertinent: How shall we sing the Lord's song in our own land which has become a hostile land? How shall we hope in the midst of despair?

Suffering and Hope

Hope is so often a casualty of sustained oppression. The Bible tells the story of the degradation of the slaves in Egypt. Their oppressors' greatest victory over them was their internalized despair. Then the spirit of freedom was again engendered within them as Moses spoke of the hope of liberation. Pharaoh increased their oppression: ultimately the extent of the oppression was so bad that anything was perceived as better than what they had. They had nothing to lose, and *that* became the womb of their new-found determination, hope, and ultimately their liberation.

When people suffer most they hear the call of God. In degradation they call out to heaven. God hears their cry and a new hope is planted within them. In the biblical tradition it is this new-found hope, hope which emerges out of despair, which is seen as the prelude to God's age of peace. Says the prophet Joel: At that time "your sons and daughters shall prophesy, your old men shall dream dreams and your young men shall see visions" (Joel 2:28).

It is never easy to cross the hermeneutical gap between the Bible and the context within which it is read. Yet it is not difficult to recognize that the Pharaoh and taskmasters of this land have, like their predecessors in Egypt, overplayed their hand and driven their victims into a position where they too, having little to lose, have risen up in rebellion. The sons and daughters of Soweto, Guguletu, Kwamashu, Umlazi, Mamelodi, Winterveld, Crossroads, and elsewhere present us with a prophetic challenge that speaks of the God-given will and right of a people to be free. Our mothers and fathers in the struggle have dreamed a new dream, and even at this moment from deep underground they are directing the struggle of our people to be free. Our young people have seen new visions. Herein is our hope — that as our country is torn apart as never before, as we become trapped in the spirt of violence, as we begin to see before our eyes the slow and painful destruction of the last vestiges of economic, social, cultural, and spiritual well-being in our land, we are better poised than ever before to face the fundamental issues which constitute our crisis. This is our hope that in despair we are driven to face the real issues that destroy us. We must pray to God that we, and especially those whose place in this society has not yet driven them to despair, will not wake up to these issues only when there is nothing left to salvage.

Our hope is grounded in God's gift of life over death. Yet, because the resurrection is a response to the cross our hope can never be other than cautious and costly. Allow me to suggest three dimensions of our hope:

First, there is reason for political hope. Such words can only be hesitantly uttered, and there is certainly no cause for immediate hope. The South African regime seems as intransigent as ever. And we are reminded that no obvious evidence exists in all of history which speaks of a ruling class ever voluntarily surrendering power. Only when it is in their own obvious self-interest and when their rule is militarily and administratively on the point of total collapse does the possibility of honest negotiation emerge. Alas, the children of darkness are all too often wiser than the children of light. People of good will must not allow their hope for peace to distort their social analysis or political common sense.

Economic sanctions, other forms of international pressure, and internal protest have been hotly debated. Can they force the South African regime to its senses, allowing for honest negotiation rather than escalated violence? The question everyone seems to ask is whether such pressures will force the whites into a laager and business interests into a siege economy, which can only intensify the suffering of blacks and perhaps prolong the endurance of a defeated regime.

History tells us that those who have suffered least are able to bear the least suffering. Those who have the most to lose are less inclined to lose everything than those who already have lost virtually everything. Given these factors, there is an increase in the number of people both inside and outside of South Africa who are saying that the "pressure option" is worth trying. It offers no guarantees, but the alternative to this option for bringing the South African rulers to their senses is unrestrained war, anarchy — and perhaps even Lebanese-type carnage.

Speculation aside, we have moved into a new sphere of the struggle for liberation in South Africa. We are no longer living in a confused phase of trying to work out whether President P. W. Botha is interested in reform. He has played his hand and chosen to intensify repression in much the same way as every oppressor since Pharaoh. The chances of pressure on South Africa from outside and inside being reduced without the unqualified introduction of a political program leading to majority rule are virtually nonexistent. This means that the lines against apartheid are more clearly drawn than ever before. For those who are committed to see the unequivocal collapse of apartheid together with all revised, reformed, and modified versions of it, this is a sign of hope. This is our political hope. Small and limited as it is, we are beginning to discover what kind of beast we are dealing with in this land. It is the all-consuming, uncompromising, and deadly beast so vividly depicted in Revelation 13.

The South African government is under threat as never before. This is why we have a national state of emergency, the introduction of further draconian laws, press censorship, and police rule. This does not mean the government is about to fall, but its legitimacy is called into question by an ever-widening constituency of people. This forces the churches and individual Christians into a moment of crucial decision making. This is a sign of hope. Ours is a *Kairos*. Ours is a time when our future and that of our children is poised between damnation and salvation.

Either we shall be victims of history or agents of change. For too long have we, co-creators with God of our own history, abdicated this responsibility to those who claim to rule in our interests. These rulers never have been elected by the majority of the people in this country, so they should not be surprised when we regard them as illegitimate. They never have ruled in accordance with the broad tenets of the Bible, so they should not be surprised when we call them heretics. They never have sought to come to terms with the political realities of our time, as they keep the leaders of the people locked up in prison, so they should not be surprised when they are regarded as the enemies of the people.

No Turning Back

Simple sanity asks whether the moment has not come for all reasonable people in this country to unite in opposing the intransigence of the Botha oligarchy. Our hope is the realization that now, more than ever before, there is a group of people who are ready to do just that. Participation by exiled leaders of the African National Congress in Lusaka and elsewhere is seen by an increasing number of people as a nonnegotiable ingredient in the ultimate solution to this country's problems. This is a sign of hope. An increasing number of people are beginning to realize that white minority rule in this country is doomed. This is a sign of hope. It is only a question of time and manner, when and how this rule will be replaced. This is a sign of hope. Yet we know that hope which is more than abstract idealism is costly. We also know that before the inevitable collapse of the structures of racism, exploitation, and oppression in this country, the cost to be paid is a high one. We must pray that bloodshed will be kept to a minimum and that our commitment to nonviolent options for change may endure and produce the desired result.

Here too is our hope! Dictatorships seldom unwind slowly; they tend to collapse. "Take heed, watch, for you do not know when the time will come," said Jesus (Mark 13:33). Ours is the task to watch and to pray that we may anticipate and grasp that moment when it comes.

Secondly, there is reason to hope for reconciliation. Our theology has always taught us that neither grace nor reconciliation is cheap. Yet in our evangelical fervor we have perhaps spoken too cheaply of both. This fervor has left some people a little dismayed when these categories are tested in our conflict situation, and it is found that not everyone is prepared unconditionally to embrace an offer of reconciliation. This hardened political reality, with lines between opposing forces ever more clearly drawn, is forcing us to rediscover the meaning of the biblical teaching on reconciliation. This is a sign of hope.

The Kairos Document has generated a great deal of discussion on the Christian teaching on reconciliation. The document is clear: "No reconciliation is possible in South Africa *without justice*." The document then goes further to argue that we are not "expected to forgive the unrepentant sinner." Critics have responded by saying that the document fails to give due emphasis to the unconditional free offer of forgiveness and reconciliation which God extends to sinful humanity. In a similar vein, it is argued, Christians are obliged to offer and accept reconciliation within the human community in a similar unconditional manner.

God's offer of reconciliation is free and unconditional, but the traditional theories of atonement remind us that this reconciliation *is* not without the cost of the sacrificial death of Christ. The human appropriation of forgiveness, in turn, involves a redeemed and transformed life. A consequence of repentance is necessarily a changed relationship with both God and humankind. This is not without considerable cost to the redeemed person, the origin of which is located in the act of human *metanoia* or repentance in response to God's grace. We are beginning to discover this cost in South Africa. This is good news, the first step toward making genuine political and biblical reconciliation possible.

A colleague, Itumeleng Mosala, points out that the word "reconciliation" is used sparingly in the New Testament, and that the Christian doctrine of divine and human reconciliation is a category developed in Paul's Epistles. The Greek word used to denote the concept of "reconciliation" is *katallage* or *katallasso* and its derivatives, which is precisely the word used in the Septuagint text in Isaiah 9 to mean "restoration." The concept of "katallage," in turn, has a conceptual equivalent in Leviticus 25 where the process of *restoring* land by the landowners to the peasants becomes a central ingredient to teaching on the Jubilee Year. What this suggests is that the New Testament doctrine of "reconciliation" cannot be understood apart from the teaching on "restitution," "repossession," and "restoration" as understood in the Hebrew tradition.

The intensity of our political crisis teaches precisely this. A lot more than a few minor changes in attitude between blacks and whites will be required for genuine reconciliation to occur in this country. Limited reforms, a few modified laws which allow for cross-racial marriages, open restaurants, a multicameral parliament, and the substitution of an "identity card" for a passbook are simply not an adequate political or biblical basis for reconciliation.

A Costly Repentance

A political process designed to *restore* economic, social, political, and human relations is necessary. This we are beginning to discover. This is cause for hope. We are beginning to face the actual problem and

not hide behind a few obscure liberal slogans. The question beyond
hope is how many of those who are among the privileged people of
this country will be prepared to pay this price, and after what kind
of bloody incentives?

*Thirdly, there is reason to hope for a restoration of the Christian
church.* At least since the Constantinian settlement with the Christian church in 312 A.D., the church has traditionally been on the side
of the ruling class. Before that, evidence suggests that the church
consisted largely of socially deprived people who, inspired by the
message of the gospel, were regarded by the rulers to be politically subversive. But as a result of a series of treacherous battles
and bloody deeds, Constantine became the sole ruler of the Empire
and Christianity was practically the state religion. With this the stage
was set for the church to become wealthy and politically powerful. Through the many contours of the history of the church since
then, which include reformations and counter-reformations, the institutional church has managed to entrench itself in this favored
position. Either explicitly or by default the church has more often
than not provided the changing generations of rulers with theological
legitimacy.

This dominant tradition has not, however, been able to suppress a residual theology of resistance which has contradicted the
church's favored social location. Suppressed by the appropriation of
the Christian heritage by successive generations of rulers, this residual theological tradition has affirmed a New Testament emphasis on
the "preferential option for the poor." It is a tradition built on what
the New Testament teaches us was Jesus' obvious special concern
for the oppressed, for widows, orphans, and marginalized people in
society.

To rediscover this tradition is to reaffirm the church of the New
Testament. Could it be that as the church in this country continues
to be the focus of attack from a dictatorial government, an increasing number of believers will embrace a Christianity which locates
God on the side of the oppressed? This is a sign of hope. Experiencing sustained persecution for their faith and reading their Bibles
in this context, some Christians are beginning to rediscover what it
means to be the church in a hostile land. Some people are beginning to learn what it means to sing the Lord's song in a land where
persecution is the price to be paid not only for demanding one's God-
given rights, but for showing compassion to those who are denied
such rights.

It also, however, means that a social and theological division which
has long existed within the Christian church is becoming more explicit because not all who claim membership in the church are ready

to affirm this residual gospel of the poor and oppressed. Indeed for obvious social and economic reasons, many are prepared to defend the church of Constantine. They know of the good things to eat and drink there, even if it requires pandering to the whims of those who assume that because they control so many of the resources of this land, they can control the church of Christ as well. This intensifying division must be countered by evangelism and praxis, but ultimately we are to be obedient to the God made known in the biblical tradition rather than to those who make the church a haven for wealth and privilege.

Is there hope in our crisis? It depends to which age we cling. For those who hold to this dying age that has served a small section of the people of this land so well there is little reason to hope. For those who reach out to the new age, sustained by the sure knowledge that it is our task to share the violent birth pangs of this new day which is the God-given heritage of the oppressed, there is much for which to hope. Yet because our hope emerges out of despair, out of the cross, we must pray for grace to endure. Says Jesus: "You will be hated by all for my name's sake. But who endures to the end will be saved" (Mark 13:13).

Philosophy of the Stone

February 15, 1988

Dale Bishop

Dale Bishop, a contributing editor of C & C, *is the Middle East secretary of the National Council of Churches. He holds a doctorate in Middle East languages and cultures from Columbia University and has published articles on Lebanon, the Palestinian issue, Islam, and Iran.*

BILL COFFIN USED TO remind his Riverside Church parishioners that in matters of faith one should seek not certainty, but clarity. Although the outcome of the Palestinian uprising in the Israeli-occupied territories of the West Bank and Gaza is by no means certain, the "children of the stones" have brought a new and compelling clarity to the question of Palestine. Their revolt has swept away some assiduously nurtured Israeli and American illusions about the nature of Israel's occupation of territories captured in the 1967 War. At the same time "the kids" have sent a potent message both to the Arab states and to their own PLO leaders.

The first illusion to fall is that of the "benign occupation." It should now be quite clear that this occupation, like all occupations, is benign neither for those whose lands are occupied nor for the occupiers. Palestinian youth are willing to "bare their chests" not because of some inherent penchant for martyrdom, but because they regard themselves as having nothing to lose. An entire generation has grown up in an environment of negation: the negation of the Palestinian identity, the negation of basic human rights, the negation of hope for either a personal or a collective future. Resistance becomes a way of affirming existence; collective resistance becomes a referendum against despair.

On the other side of the barricades are other kids, kids who carry weapons singularly ill-suited for a confrontation with an unarmed populace. Thus in an age of great military sophistication, the conflict between Israeli and Palestinian is waged by children who wield the most primitive implements of warfare: the stone and the club. The Israeli military command, we are told, has sent psychologists to treat the young soldiers in Gaza who have been ordered to beat their Palestinian contemporaries into submission. Those psychologists ought first to examine the political and military leaders who have presided over the brutalization of young people on both sides of the barricades.

Clarity

Closely allied to the illusion that this has been a benign occupation is the assumption by U.S. officials that the ill effects of the occupation can be offset by an improvement in the Palestinians' "quality of life." A leading proponent of this "solution" is Secretary of State George Shultz. His assistant secretary of state, Richard Murphy, has testified before the House Middle East subcommittee that, failing a negotiated settlement between Israel and its Arab neighbors (note the absence of the Palestinians in this formulation), we should "improve the quality of Palestinian life in the territories." (You remember those ringing words of Patrick Henry, "Give me a better quality of life or give me death!") Once again, the clarity of the kids in the camps is helpful. As one said to us, "This uprising is not about poverty, nor about the conditions in the camps. You could give every Palestinian a villa. As long as we are under occupation, we will resist." Is that so difficult for the heirs of the American revolution to understand?

Nor should there be doubt any longer about who are the legitimate representatives of the Palestinian people. Clearly, no Arab state can claim that right: not Jordan, which prohibited demonstrations of sympathy by that country's own Palestinian residents; not

Syria, which has manipulated the Palestinian factions within Syria and in Lebanon in the furtherance of Hafez al-Assad's foreign policy goals; not Egypt, which is still suspect because of its separate peace with Israel. Although the young people in the streets are sending a message of frustration to their own PLO leaders, they are at the same time saying that the PLO and the Palestinian people are coterminous, that only the PLO has the right to represent them.

A theopolitical clarity is also emerging regarding the U.S. role in all this. On January 13 several American colleagues and I visited Gaza's Ahli Arab Hospital, which is operated by the Episcopal Diocese of Jerusalem. While we were talking with patients who had been admitted the day before with gunshot wounds — most of the hospital's sixty beds were occupied by casualties of the disturbances — a commotion arose in the courtyard. There we witnessed the arrival of the latest victims — a group of women in their fifties and sixties who had been beaten and gassed by Israeli soldiers. The soldiers had burst into their homes in search of husbands and sons. In frustration they had fired tear gas into the hovels that served as these women's homes and had brutally beaten the women. They had even fired a tear-gas canister into an ambulance as it transported two of the women from the scene. Earlier in the day, a lawyer who works with the Gaza Center for Rights and Law had shown us a spent tear-gas canister. It was made in the U.S.A., and bore the sort of banal instructions one might find on a game of lawn darts, "For outdoor use only."

In that hospital courtyard two angry Palestinian women accosted our small group of well-meaning Americans. One woman kept shouting *"Allahu Akbar"* ("God is great") as a kind of punctuation between her analytical comments about American policy toward the Palestinians. "Why do you vote against Security Council resolutions? Why do you give them arms? Do you think we are animals?" Her attitude was one best described as "importuning," and yet her theological punctuation marks were delivered with an air of prophetic judgment.

As I later reflected on the experience, I was reminded of a conversation with a young Muslim intellectual from the West Bank. Many young Palestinians are turning to Islam, he said, as the best hope for the liberation of Palestine. The democratic secularism of the West never seemed to apply to the Palestinians. And so the kids, now quite clear about whom and what they cannot rely on, have adopted the "philosophy of the stone," and they have done so in the belief that God, indeed, is greater than the powers arrayed against them. That is both a challenge to, and an indictment of, the West.

South Africa: The More Things Change...

September 25, 1989

Gail Hovey

Gail Hovey was managing editor of Christianity and Crisis from 1984 to 1990 and is now a contributing editor. Executive director of Grassroots International in Cambridge, Mass., she is a long-time analyst of South African politics and an activist in the U.S. antiapartheid movement.

"WE STAND ON THE THRESHOLD of a new era in South and southern Africa," F.W. de Klerk said a few weeks before the September 6 elections that made him president — in voting that excluded 73 percent of the population. One of the "new" things in South Africa is the first change in white leadership in more than a decade. De Klerk replaced P.W. Botha as head of the Nationalist party in February after Botha suffered a stroke. In August, his authority undercut, Botha angrily resigned from the government and de Klerk became acting president. Now, beating threats from both the left and the right, the Nationalists have won a very narrow victory and de Klerk is president. But that's probably not what de Klerk was referring to.

The "new era" in southern Africa would have to include the November elections in Namibia that are to end South African control and lead to independence. South Africa's efforts to manipulate the election process, however, are nothing new, but simply extend the familiar essentials of illegal occupation: intimidation and repression.

The negotiations leading to the settlement in Namibia came about because of new setbacks and circumscriptions: South Africa was defeated on the battlefield, and the cost of the war was becoming intolerable. These reverses finally forced Pretoria to accept a settlement that would allow Namibian independence to proceed under United Nations auspices. The agreement required South African troops to leave Angola and called for the phased withdrawal of all Cuban troops from Angola. But it is doubtful that de Klerk meant military defeat and economic crisis when he spoke of a new era.

Demonstrating a new *style* of leadership, de Klerk has already visited a number of European capitals. He has sought to end South African isolation on the African continent, meeting before the election with the leaders of Mozambique, Zaire, and Zambia. That presidents Chissano, Mobutu, and Kaunda each invited him to their countries is most fundamentally an indication of the war-weariness in the region. De Klerk wants these visits because he is confronted with his own version of war-weariness, despite the fact that he would try to put a different face on it.

Speaking in July to COSATU, South Africa's largest trade union federation, Frank Chikane of the South African Council of Churches (SACC) explained that the government "would stop at nothing in an effort to ease the pressure of international sanctions by creating the impression that it has reformed its ways" (*Washington Post*, July 15, 1989). Foreign investment in South Africa is at a standstill and the government can raise no substantial loans abroad. On June 30, 1990, some $11 billion in loans were scheduled to come due. Some of the loans have been converted in ways that will ease the pressure next June. But South Africa is under extraordinary pressure to convince the international financial community, and the new administration in Washington, that sanctions should be lifted because a new day has dawned. What's new about the South African government's opposition to sanctions?

SACC head Chikane suffered three attacks on his life earlier this year in a bizarre case of chemical poisoning. The building which housed the council was bombed, just a year ago. No arrests have been made in the attacks on Chikane's office or his person. But failure to apprehend and prosecute in acts of terror against blacks is nothing new.

Majority in Movement

Beginning in August a newly formed Mass Democratic movement went into action to challenge apartheid institutions and register black rejection of the segregated September elections. The first target was the segregated hospitals, and blacks demanded treatment at white institutions. The movement then went on to challenge segregated schools, buses, parks, and swimming pools in a massive defiance campaign.

But these actions by this new organization are really nothing new. They are a continuation, under a different name, of the work carried out by any number of other organizations including the now banned United Democratic Front (UDF) and the African National Congress (ANC) before it. They are a continuation, under a new name, of the majority demand for justice.

Of course, de Klerk was not speaking of these activities when he talked about a new era in South Africa. And the government response was totally predictable. Already the State of Emergency was renewed in June for the fourth year. It has made the work of the protest movement much more difficult. But if its intention was to eliminate protest, the State of Emergency has been a complete failure. The protest continues because the conditions giving rise to it continue.

Anglican Archbishop Desmond Tutu was among those tear-gassed by police as they left a church meeting in late August. Scores of people were injured and arrested. Tutu said the country is "on the brink of a major catastrophe." Before the voting began more than twenty people were killed. The government is determined to squelch the movement. It wants to insure that there will be no repeat of the 1984 protests that coincided with segregated parliamentary elections and shook the country for two years.

De Klerk wants a chance to establish himself in power and to put into effect the Nationalist party's new five-year plan. It claims to be something very new indeed: the vehicle to end apartheid and white minority rule.

And how would the Nationalists achieve this? Not by negotiations and elections leading to majority rule. Not even by a process as complex and flawed as the one under way in Namibia. In South Africa, white minority rule would be replaced by a federation of many minorities: whites, Indians, people of mixed race, and some ten different African tribes. People who reject tribal affiliation would even have their own group.

But this, again, is nothing really new. It is still a system based on group identity. Race or ethnic origin is at its core. It is still a system being imposed on the people of South Africa by the minority white government. It is apartheid with a new face.

None of this is to suggest that nothing is happening in South and southern Africa, that unprecedented negotiations are not taking place. The Soviets and Cubans were actually wined and dined by the government in Cape Town. Before P. W. Botha gave up the presidency, he invited Nelson Mandela, South Africa's most prominent political prisoner, for tea at his official residence. De Klerk will be meeting with leaders at home and abroad deliberately seeking new contacts. All of this is to suggest that we listen to what Beyers Naudé said during his May visit to the U.S. about the September elections: "My friends, don't be fooled. We have no reason to believe that there will be any fundamental political change in our country."

Externally that means pressure should be increased, sanctions tightened and expanded until they are universal, comprehensive, and mandatory. Internally it means the four basic demands of the Mass Democratic movement must be met: end the State of Emergency, release all political prisoners, unban all political organizations, including the UDF and the ANC, and allow all exiles to return. If these conditions were met, then it might be possible to assert that yes, "we stand on the threshold of a new era in South and southern Africa."

The Future of Germany

January 8, 1990

Carl E. Hester

Carl E. Hester, former director of the Carl Schurz House in Freiburg, Germany, teaches religion at Randolph Macon College in Lynchburg, Va. He has lived for more than twelve years in Germany and visits there frequently.

ERICH HONECKER, the East German leader, having been told by God that in fourteen days the world will be destroyed, goes on East German television to make the announcement. "I have some bad news and some good news," he says. "The bad news is that God exists, but the good news is that in two weeks *perestroika* and *glasnost* are going down the drain."

This joke — which circulated in East Germany during Soviet President Mikhail Gorbachev's West German visit in June 1989 — catches the *après moi le déluge* mood of the die-hard East German leadership. Two years earlier, on Pentecost 1987, East Berlin youths who had ventured up to the Wall to listen to a West Berlin rock concert on the other side began shouting "The Wall must go! Gorbachev must come!" The police intervened and made five arrests. In retrospect, it marked the beginning of the end.

While the East German government resisted reform, West Germany figured increasingly in Gorbachev's plans for East-West political and economic rapprochement. Since 1987 diplomatic relations between the Soviet Union and the Federal Republic had steadily improved. During his June visit to West Germany, the crowds were almost embarrassingly enthusiastic. While East Berlin put on the brakes, Gorbachev looked to Bonn for the capital, management skills, and technology to fuel *perestroika*.

At the end of the visit, a joint declaration spoke of the need to build a "Common House" in which "the United States and Canada have a place as well." Once again West German diplomacy had found its balance: tied to the West, but open to the Soviet idea of a Common European House. Along this dual track, West German policy has encouraged change, without appearing to initiate it, sought to overcome divisions, but abjured the broker's role, remained ever the team player, never the star, ever loyal, never unilateral. This idea always held out the promise that unnatural boundaries would come down, though few if any could have foreseen the momentous events which lay just ahead for Eastern Europe and Germany.

Yet the historic changes in Central Europe that hold such promise and are in part fruits of West Germany's dual-track diplomacy may create conditions which call that diplomacy into question. At a pace which defies diplomatic prudence and conventional wisdom, Central Europe has proceeded to reinvent itself politically. The opening of the Berlin Wall on November 9, 1989 forms the dramatic centerpiece of these developments. As media happening and political event, it symbolizes historic change and the crumbling of a much larger edifice. Europe is shifting its center of gravity and reconstituting a central position which can only be occupied by Germany. Central Europe's reinvention poses once more the question of Germany's future.

On November 21, 1989 Hans-Dietrich Genscher, West Germany's foreign minister, presented President George Bush a chunk of the Berlin Wall. It was a gesture rich in diplomatic symbolism: the fruits of *Ostpolitik*, Willy Brandt's opening to the East, offered to the leader of the Western Alliance. Such exercises in public diplomacy are calculated to underscore the Federal Republic's continuing commitment to the West and its values and to allay fears of a radical revision of West German priorities and policies.

While gestures of this sort may express current intentions, they cannot eliminate concerns over the changes in Europe's postwar security order. The transformation of the frontline states in opposing alliances into one Central European country with the power to dominate the region has profound implications for the entire continent. Erhard Eppler, a leading Social Democrat political strategist and Protestant layperson, made this point in a remarkably prescient address June 17: "There is a difference between what bubbles up, let us say, in the Baltic or Yugoslavia and what could happen in Germany. If Slovaks, Serbians, or Croatians want to live in one state, it's their business. The partitions which they can erect, at most, between themselves do not affect the statics [architectural balance] of the European House. The ugly partition of iron and cement that stretches through Germany has more to do with the statics of this European House than we would like. The one who wants to tear it down must calculate the statics of the entire House and possibly rebuild the entire House. What happens to Germany interests all Europeans."

Out of Tutelage

What we have been witnessing in East Berlin, Leipzig, and other cities is nothing less than the first peaceful revolution on German soil and the emergence of a people from political tutelage. Most of the traumatic changes in modern Germany have been brought about by war. Both the German Democratic Republic and the Federal Republic are states born out of military defeat, with political systems imposed by occupying forces. Now, without the leadership of a Lech Walesa or a Vaclav Havel, East Germans are deciding their own political future.

Jens Langer characterizes these events as a Protestant revolution. Certainly the roots of the current national awakening go back to the church-sponsored unofficial peace movement of the early 1980s. On both sides of the border the peace movement raised the consciousness of Germans about their own peculiar dangers and responsibilities. Over the years the Protestant church has provided the main institutional bridge between the people of the two German states. Churches in East Germany were, until recently, the only organizations to enjoy independence from both the state and the party, including the right to free assembly. The Lutheran church there, with some seven million members, is, at present, the single most important force for change and stability in the society. In early December Gottfried Forck, Lutheran bishop of Berlin-Brandenburg, chaired the roundtable talks among rival political groups. The Protestant churches seek to promote orderly change and above all to preserve the nonviolent nature of the protests.

The churches may also play a key role in determining whether the GDR can reform itself in a manner which will win the loyalty of its citizens. If the economy can be stabilized and calls for reunification slacken — there are already reports of *Trabi* [the small East German car] trashing in West Germany — the church, together with other reform groups, may be able to convince the people in the street that the ideal of democratic socialism, and the GDR, are both worth preserving.

One possible scenario that would reassure Germany's neighbors might be an East German socialist democracy, confederated with the Federal Republic, but with its own independent identity. Such a confederation would not attempt to preserve an untenable status quo in the heart of Europe, or to thrust Germany back into the past. Long ago George Kennan proposed to widen the horizon of German national aspirations and loyalty by embedding them in a federated Europe. Aspirations and loyalties can, of course, also be directed to something smaller than the nation. Germany has a long history of decentralized rule, regional traditions, dialects, and cultures. An East German socialist democracy within a confederated Germany might represent not only socialism with a human face, but democracy on a human scale.

Whatever the form, German unity will be something new, something we have not seen before. Unity is desirable, and probably inevitable. To argue against it is to argue against the right of self-determination and to deny the very values that are supposed to hold the Western democracies together.

It is also bad politics. To renounce the pledge to support this goal would certainly produce a backlash in West Germany not limited to extremes of the left or the right.

Middle Position

Germany is emerging once more as the major economic and political power in the center of Europe. West Germany has already begun to reassess its position and play a political role commensurate with its economic strength. In the words of Federal President Richard von Weizsaecker, "We are not a great power, but we are also not a plaything for others."

In its middle position — and with a combined population of over 75 million — Germany may inherit once more the difficult problems which plagued the Second Reich after German unification in 1871. Too small to stabilize the center, but too large to fit into the existing architecture of Europe, the Second Reich (1871–1918) became under Bismarck the broker of Central Europe. The shifting alliances this created, especially after Bismarck's genius was removed, contributed significantly to instability in Europe. When Konrad Adenauer developed his policy of *Westintegration*, he consciously rejected Bismarck's swing diplomacy, insisting that Germany must not create the impression that it can maintain a neutral position: "Long ago I made a great decision: We belong to the West and not to the East."

The dramatic events of the last months have put German unification back on the agenda of world affairs. How will this process of unification be related to two other historic tasks: the construction of a Western European Union in 1992, and the healing of the divisions of an Iron Curtain turned Rust Belt? While the French give priority to the Europe of 1992, West Germany, true to its dual-track orientation, has adopted a Central European perspective which connects West European Union with the larger, more complicated process of pan-European integration. Social Democrat (SPD) politicians, in particular, have urged that any West European Union remain open for a meaningful bringing together of all parts of the continent. At the same time, only a tightly integrated Western Europe of 1992, with its complex web of economic, political, and cultural institutions, can attract and anchor a resurgent Germany.

It remains to be seen if West Germany can continue the balanced diplomacy which has allowed it simultaneously to maintain Western commitments and exploit Eastern opportunities while pursuing German unification. Not since the 1950s has West Germany faced such fundamental and fateful choices. And though the East German revolution shows signs of outpacing the European evolution which might contain it, the new decade begins full of hope and promise.

Just War, Jihad, and Abuse of Tradition

March 4, 1991

Alan Geyer

Alan Geyer, professor of political ethics and ecumenics at Wesley Theological Seminary in Washington, D.C., is author of Christianity and the Superpowers: Religion, Politics and History in U.S.-U.S.S.R. Relations. *He is a contributing editor of* C & C.

THE PREACHER AT the Religious Broadcasters Convention on January 28 was not Billy Graham, Jerry Falwell, or Pat Robertson, but George Bush. After citing Matthew's reminder that "the meek shall inherit the earth," the president proceeded, not so meekly, to offer a rousing homily on the righteousness of the Gulf War.

The pivotal sentence contained two clauses that proved contradictory: "The war in the Gulf is not a Christian war, a Jewish war, or a Moslem war — it is a just war." The first clause followed a well-deserved reproach to Saddam Hussein for trying to portray the conflict as a "religious war." But the second clause was prelude to the invocation of Christian just war principles and specific citations of Saints Ambrose, Augustine, and Thomas Aquinas. The theological exhortation that followed was a homiletical exercise begging to be challenged by those who oppose the offensive military action that began on January 16.

The piosities continued with the assurance that "America has always been a religious nation — perhaps never more than now. Just look at the last several weeks. Churches, synagogues, mosques reporting record attendance at services.... Why? To pray for peace." Not content, however, with these impressive evidences of a prayerful people, Bush three days later announced at a prayer breakfast (with Billy Graham again at his side) that February 3 would be an official day of prayer for peace. Graham himself fervently added: "There comes a time when we must fight for peace."

The day after Bush's Religious Broadcasters sermon, the *Wall Street Journal* — in suspect synchronization — offered half its editorial page to a two-thousand-word blast from Richard John Neuhaus, now a bugle boy for Bush, who commended the president for his recitation of just war principles. Neuhaus devoted more than half his article to a sarcastic assault on the National Conference of Catholic Bishops, the National Council of Churches, and "the declining churches that used to be mainline" for failing to agree with George Bush on the morality of the war. In fact, however, Neuhaus avoided any substantive application of just war criteria to the Gulf War itself, obviously preferring to seize one more occasion to beat up on religious leaders who don't share his brand of neoconservatism.

Politicians often resent the intrusion of churches and religious rhetoric in public policy debates — at least when that intrusion challenges their policies. In this case, the Chief Politician of the land has implicitly challenged the churches to a public debate over the application of Christian principles to the war he has launched. Here goes.

Few would argue with Bush's claim that Iraq's "naked aggression" against Kuwait raises the first principle of a *just cause*. What is raw cant, however, is the boast that "our cause could not be more noble" or "we seek nothing for ourselves."

Complicity

The heavy record of U.S. complicity in the causes of this conflict includes the following: a decade of irresponsible energy policies that (as Senator Bob Dole candidly admitted) have made oil a primary motive for war; years of inconstancy and procrastination on the Camp David Accords' promise of Palestinian self-government, giving Saddam his own most incendiary appeal to a just cause; billions of dollars of U.S. arms dumped all over the Middle East, compounding the region's rivalries and tensions; a strong tilt toward Iraq in its long war with Iran, with conspicuous neglect of Saddam's brutalities and oppressions, and with assurances by U.S. Ambassador April Glaspie eight days before the invasion of Kuwait that the U.S. would not take sides in the Iraq-Kuwait dispute; and years of default on the UN imperative for an authentic multinational peacekeeping force.

The principle of *just intent* (or "right reasons," as Bush invoked it) has been degraded as U.S. actions have escalated from defense of Saudi Arabia and economic sanctions to a massive offensive deployment; to the initiation of history's most devastating air assault, which has severely disrupted civilian life; to the imprudent demand for unconditional surrender. Postwar reconstruction and stability in the Middle East loom as horrendously costly and difficult responsibilities — for somebody.

The principle of *last resort* rigorously requires pursuing all possible nonmilitary alternatives before undertaking military action. The president gave the Religious Broadcasters a highly quantified report on the administration's efforts between August 2 and January 15 to avoid war: "more than 200 meetings with foreign dignitaries, ten diplomatic missions,...over 103,000 miles traveled." But behind those big numbers and Bush's earlier boast that he had gone "the last mile for peace" is the really big fact that he refused to practice any constructive diplomacy: no arbitration of claims; no discussion of a wider Middle East conference; not even any "face-saving" device for a proud Arab dictator that just might have freed Kuwait and prevented the present carnage (we shall never know). And, curiously, Bush avoided mentioning his own economic sanctions policy, the continuation of which had been persuasively urged by two former chairmen of the Joint Chiefs of Staff, six former secretaries of defense, and forty-seven senators.

Last resort? Suspicion grows that George Bush and Jim Baker are grievously lacking in diplomatic imagination and/or they made up their minds last August to go to war if Saddam refused to yield to their threats.

Canons of "Success"

The traditional requirement of *legitimate authority* was met, according to Bush, by "unprecedented United Nations solidarity" through twelve Security Council resolutions. The UN warrant and the extravagant "new world order" rhetoric, however, are diminished by the operational unilateralism of U.S. policy in the Gulf and by years of abuse of the United Nations as a delinquent, a dropout, and a downright obstructionist in most fields of international cooperation. Reagan-Bush rejection of World Court jurisdiction, the Law of the Sea Treaty, and minimal UN norms of economic equity have severely impaired prospects for an authoritative new world order.

In the Carnegie Endowment study *Estrangement: America and the World*, Richard Ullman observes that "the most significant estrangement" of the U.S. in the past decade has been "from the entire idea of cooperation through a formal structure of international organizations," especially the United Nations — an estrangement that has "verged on contempt" for the rest of the world. In short, beyond the hard-lobbied UN seal for U.S. military policies in the Gulf, the administration has shown little disposition to strengthen the political and moral authority of the UN on the great constructive tasks of world order, human development, and global survival.

Whether the criterion of *reasonable prospect of success* can be met depends on the canons of "success." An overwhelming U.S. military victory may create more problems in the Middle East than it can solve, such as an unlimited U.S. military presence, more intractable Israeli-Palestinian hostilities, intensified Arab anti-Americanism, masses of refugees, Syrian and Iranian ascendancy, immense economic burdens, and unending terrorism. Bush, however, seems not to have focused very much on such matters. Witness his confident benediction to the Religious Broadcasters: "And we know that, God willing, this is a war we will win." The just war tradition continues to provide a helpful set of serious moral issues concerning war and peace. The misuse and abuse of that tradition, however, are among the most terrible facts of political, and religious, history.

Part 5

Sexual Politics/AIDS

Few domestic issues proved so divisive in the society as well as the churches during the last twenty-five years as the movements for women's and gay liberation. This was the core of what was called "cultural politics."

Within the churches that cultural debate has focused on the ordination of women, and gay men and lesbians, and on women's legal right to abortion.

That debate has much to do with sexual ethics: the meaning of sexuality and gender, the relationship between procreation and sexuality, and the role and status of women in U.S. society. Within the churches it has led to conflict over the relevance of the traditional sexual ethic to the actual lives of many Christians.

Clarifying the conflict has not been easy. The debate is often acrimonious, if not vicious. But it has also tended to focus on civil rights and right to privacy to the exclusion of frank discussion of fundamental moral judgments.

Christianity and Crisis's contribution to the debate began in earnest with the publication of James McGraw's "The Scandal of Peculiarity" (1973), a special issue on the "irregular but valid" ordination of eleven women to the Episcopal priesthood (1974), Howard Moody's description of the efforts of the Clergy Consultation Service on Abortion (1971), and the publication of James Nelson's groundbreaking theological reflection on homosexuality reprinted here.

AIDS, it may be hard to remember, has not always been with us. In fact Acquired Immune Deficiency Syndrome did not burst into public awareness until the middle of the 1980s. It struck as a horrifying kind of plague: diagnosis was a death sentence. And, although globally the virus causing the disease was prevalent among heterosexuals, in the U.S. it seemed at

167

first to be a "gay disease." It soon became obvious that AIDS was also widespread among intravenous drug users, but that did little to change the social stigma and led far too often to claims that AIDS was God's retribution for sinful behavior.

Those infected were thus dealt multiple blows. Suffering from an incurable disease, they were frequently treated as lepers. And the anxious attention paid them as symbols of our collective insecurity was matched by a very slow federal policy response to combat the AIDS epidemic.

In this situation, the church has had a crucial ministry — both to those dying from AIDS and to the broader constituency of frightened, confused Americans. To complicate matters, the churches have had to confront a major obstacle to their ministry: their complicity in stigmatizing gays and drug users, and their social distance from the groups they would help.

Homosexuality and the Church

April 4, 1977

James B. Nelson

James Nelson is professor of Christian ethics at United Theological Seminary of the Twin Cities. He has written extensively on sexual ethics and on sexuality and spirituality, including The Intimate Connection: Male Sexuality, Masculine Spirituality, and Embodiment.

THE GAY CAUCUSES now active in virtually every major American denomination no longer will let us forget that the church must face the issue of homosexuality more openly, honestly, and sensitively than it has yet done. Beyond this legitimate and appropriate pressure, however, there are other compelling reasons for the church to reexamine its theology and practice:

1. Homosexual Christians are sisters and brothers of all other Christians, earnestly seeking the church's full acceptance without prejudgment on the basis of a sexual orientation regarding which they had no basic choice.

2. While antihomosexual bias has existed in Western culture generally, the church must take responsibility for its share in shaping, supporting, and transmitting negative attitudes toward homosexuality.

3. The Christian mandate for social justice will not let us forget that discrimination continues today against millions of gay persons in employment, housing, public accommodations, education, and in the enjoyment of fundamental civil liberties.

4. The church is called to do its ongoing theological and ethical work as responsibly as possible. Fresh insights from feminist theologians, gay Christians, and those secular scholars who frequently manifest God's "common grace" in the world remind us of the numerous ways in which our particular sexual conditions color our perceptions of God's nature and presence among us. If the Protestant Principle turns us against absolutizing historically relative theological judgments, so also our openness to continuing revelation should convince us, with some of our ancestors-in-faith, that "the Lord has yet more light and truth to break forth."

5. The heterosexually oriented majority in the church has much to gain from a deeper grappling with this issue: an enriched capacity to love other human beings more fully and with less fear.

The Bible and Homosexuality

A brief survey of pertinent scriptural passages must begin with a word about our interpretive principles. My first hermeneutical assumption — and the most fundamental one — is that Jesus Christ is the bearer of God's invitation to human wholeness and is the focal point of God's humanizing action; hence, Jesus Christ is the central norm through which and by which all else must be judged. Second, I believe that the interpreter must take seriously both the historical context of the biblical writer and the present cultural situation. Third, we should study the Bible, aware of the cultural relativity through which we perceive and experience Christian existence. And, fourth, our scriptural interpretation should exhibit openness to God's truth that may be revealed through other disciplines of human inquiry.

With these assumptions in mind let us turn to the Bible, noting first that nowhere does it say anything about homosexuality as a *sexual orientation*. Its references are to certain kinds of homosexual *acts*. Understanding homosexuality as a psychic orientation is relatively recent. It is crucial that we remember this, for in all probability the biblical writers in each instance were speaking of homosexual acts undertaken by those persons whom the authors presumed to be heterosexually constituted.

While the Onan story (Gen. 38:1–11) does not deal directly with homosexual activity, it gives us important clues to some of the reasons for its ancient condemnation. Onan's refusal to impregnate his widowed sister-in-law, a refusal expressed in his deliberate withdrawal before ejaculation, was interpreted by the biblical writer as so serious a violation of divine decree that Onan was killed by Yahweh.

Three interpretive observations are important to our subject. First, the story clearly represents the strong procreative emphasis characteristic of the Hebrew interpretation of sexuality. Our awareness that the very survival of a relatively small tribe struggling against external challenges depended significantly upon abundant procreation helps us to understand this emphasis. Yet, our own situation on an overcrowded planet is markedly different, and faithful response to God's humanizing activity in Christ should compel us to reassess this procreative norm.

Second, the story is based in part upon a biological misunderstanding present throughout the Bible. The prescientific mind, and more particularly the prescientific male mind, believed that the man's semen contained the whole of nascent life. With no knowledge of eggs and ovulation, it was assumed that the woman provided only the incubating space, "ground for the seed." Hence, the deliberate and nonproductive spilling of semen was equivalent to the deliberate destruction of human life. When such occurred in male masturbation, in male homosexual acts, or in *coitus interruptus,* the deserved judgment was as severe as that for abortion or for murder. The third observation follows from this. Male masturbatory and homosexual acts have been condemned far more vigorously in the Judeo-Christian tradition than have similar female acts. The sexism endemic to a patriarchal society ironically bore with its logic a heavier burden upon "deviants" of the "superior" gender.

It is, however, another Genesis account (19:1–29) that we associate more directly with homosexual activity — the Sodom story. Contemporary biblical studies persuasively indicate that the major theme of the story and concern of the writer were not homosexual activity as such but rather the breach of ancient Hebrew hospitality norms and persistent violations of rudimentary social justice. That inhospitality and injustice are "the sin of Sodom" is evident when one examines parallel scriptural accounts as well as explicit references to Sodom elsewhere in the Old Testament. Further, the story is not given an explicitly and dominantly sexual interpretation until several centuries after it was written — in the intertestamental Book of Jubilees.

Given this general agreement, scholars do differ as to whether homosexual activity actually played any role in the story at all. However, within the context of the story's major theme, what if we assume that the writer did intend to condemn certain homosexual acts as particularly illustrative of human guilt in the face of God's righteousness? Even then, in fairness to the text, it is difficult to construe the Sodom account as a judgment against all homosexual activity, for its condemnation then would be directed against homosexual rape. Indeed, as John McNeill has observed, the use of the Sodom story in the Christian West may be another of those ironies of history. In the name of a biblical account whose major theme is inhospitality and injustice, countless homosexually oriented persons have been subjected to precisely that.

What are we to make of those Old Testament passages that in addition to rape condemn other homosexual acts? (See, for example, the Holiness Code in Lev. 18:22 and 20:13; also Deut. 23:17 and 1 Kings 14:24, 15:12 and 22:46.) Cultic defilement is the context of these passages. Canaanite fertility worship, involving sacral prostitution and orgies, constituted a direct threat to Yahweh's exclusive claim. Yahweh was the God who worked through the freedom of human history and not, primarily, through the cycles of biological life. Thus, sexuality was to be seen not as a mysterious sacred power, but rather as part of human life to be used responsibly in gratitude to its creator. In this context these texts are most adequately interpreted, and this central message is utterly appropriate to the norm of the new humanity that we meet in Jesus Christ.

Also, remember that a common Middle East practice during this period was to submit captured male foes to anal rape. Such was an expression of domination and scorn. As long as homosexual activity was generally understood to express such hatred and contempt — particularly in societies where the dignity of the male was held to be of great importance — any such activity was to be rejected summarily.

In the New Testament we have no record of Jesus saying anything about homosexuality, either as a sexual orientation or as a practice. The major New Testament references are found in two Pauline letters and in 1 Timothy. The context of Paul's widely quoted statement in Romans 1:26–27 is clearly his concern about idolatry. Three things should be noted. First, concerned about the influence of paganism upon the Roman Christians, Paul sees homosexual expression as a result of idolatry, but he does not claim that such practices are the *cause* of God's wrath. Second, in this passage we have a description of homosexual *lust* ("consumed with passion for one another") but not an account of interpersonal homosexual love.

Third, Paul's wording makes it plain that he understands homosexual activity as that indulged in by heterosexuals, hence that which is contrary to their own sexual orientation. Thus, it is difficult to construe Paul's statements as applicable to acts of committed love engaged in by persons for whom same-sex orientation is part of the givenness of their "nature." Indeed, Paul uses "nature" as a flexible concept expressing varying concerns in different contexts. An ethical position that condemns homosexuality as a violation of natural law must turn to a nonbiblical philosophical position — but not to Pauline material — for its content.

Remembering Human Historicity

Paul's other reference to homosexual acts (1 Cor. 6:9–10) is similar to that of the writer of 1 Timothy (1:8–11). Both passages list practices that exclude people from the kingdom — acts that dishonor God and harm the neighbor, including thievery, drunkenness, kidnapping, lying, and the like. Thus, if it is apparent that here homosexual acts are not singled out for special condemnation, it could also be argued that there was general disapproval. What, then are we to make of Paul's moral judgment in this case?

Perhaps we should accept Paul for what he was — a peerless interpreter of the heart of the gospel and one who was also a fallible and historically conditioned person. If the norm of the new humanity in Jesus Christ obliges us to question the Apostle's opinions about the proper status of women and the institution of human slavery, so also that norm obliges us to scrutinize each of his moral judgments regarding its Christian faithfulness for our time — including his perception of homosexuality.

Surely, the central biblical message regarding sexuality is clear enough. Idolatry, the dishonoring of God, inevitably results in the dishonoring of persons. Faithful sexual expression always honors the personhood of the companion. Sexuality is not intended by God as a mysterious and alien force of nature, but as a power to be integrated into one's personhood and used responsibly in the service of love.

A typology of four possible theological stances toward homosexuality can begin with the most negative assessment. A *rejecting-punitive* position unconditionally rejects homosexuality as Christianly legitimate and bears a punitive attitude toward homosexual persons. While no major contemporary theologians defend this position and while official church bodies have moved away from it, this stance unfortunately is amply represented in Christian history.

If we have been ignorant of the persecutions of homosexuals, it is not without reason. Unlike the recognized histories of other minority groups, there has been no "gay history." Heterosexual historians usually have considered the subject unmentionable, and gay historians have been constrained by the fear of ceasing to be invisible. A conspiracy of silence has resulted. Yet, the facts are there. Stoning, sexual mutilation, and the death penalty were fairly common treatment for discovered homosexuals through centuries of the West's history. While the church frequently gave its blessings to civil persecutions, in its internal ecclesiastical practice its disapproval was even more frequently shown through the refusal of sacraments and ostracism from the common life.

The rejecting-punitive stance today may be milder in its usual manifestations, though it continues to bear highly punitive attitudes along with its theological arguments. If the latter are based upon a selective biblical literalism, the former are rooted in familiar stereotypes. All lesbians are hard, and all male gays effeminate; homosexuals are compulsive and sex-hungry; male gays are inherently prone to child molestation; homosexuals are by nature promiscuous. Each of the preceding stereotypes has been thoroughly discounted by reliable research; yet they persist in the minds of many, buttressed by untenable biblical interpretations. But the key criticism of this stance is simply the incongruity of a punitive orientation with the gospel of Jesus Christ.

The *rejecting-nonpunitive* stance must be taken more seriously, for no less eminent a theologian than Karl Barth represents his view. Since humanity is "fellow-humanity," says Barth, men and women come into full humanity only in relation to persons of the opposite sex. To seek one's humanity in a person of the same sex is to seek "a substitute for the despised partner," and as such it constitutes "physical, psychological and social sickness, the phenomenon of perversion, decadence and decay." This is idolatry, for one who seeks the same-sex union is simply seeking oneself: self-satisfaction and self-sufficiency. While Barth says homosexuality thus is unnatural and violates the command of the Creator, he hastens to add that the central theme of the gospel is God's overwhelming grace in Jesus Christ. Hence, homosexuality must be condemned, but the homosexual *person* must not.

William Muehl argues for the rejecting-nonpunitive position from a more consequentialist stance. Maintaining that "the fundamental function of sex is procreation" and that homosexuality is an illness comparable to alcoholism, Muehl then turns his major attention to social consequences. Sheer acceptance of homosexuality would have "implications for our view of marriage, the limitations appropriate to sexual activity, the raising of children and the structure of the family." Since we are relatively ignorant concerning such potentially grave social results, Muehl argues, we should respect the historic position of the church, which rejects homosexuality.

The rejecting-nonpunitive stance appears to rest upon two major stated arguments and two major unstated assumptions — each open to serious question. The first stated argument is that of natural law and idolatry. At this point Barth seems to forget our human historicity, apparently assuming that human nature is an unchangeable, once-and-for-all substance given by the Creator. Actually, our human nature is shaped in some significant part by the interaction of people in specific periods of time with specific cultural symbols and specific historic environments. Committed to this alternative interpretation, Gregory Baum fittingly writes, "In other words, human nature as it is at present is not normative for theologians.... What is normative for normal life is the human nature to which we are divinely summoned, which is defined in terms of mutuality. This, at least, is the promise of biblical religion." After examining the evidence of mutual fulfillment in committed gay couples, Father Baum concludes: "homosexual love, then, is not contrary to human nature, defined in terms of mutuality toward which mankind is summoned."

Is Sex Orientation Chosen?

Barth's idolatry judgments appear to rest upon several additional — and equally questionable — assumptions. One is that procreative sex is divinely commanded and normative. Yet, in light of the gospel and of our current human situation, we might better say that while responsible love and sexual expression cannot be sundered, procreation and sex cannot be irrevocably joined. Another assumption is that there can be no "fellow humanity" apart from the opposite sex. But is it not more biblical to maintain that there is no genuine humanity apart from *community?*

Still another assumption is that homosexuality means a "despising" of the other sex — an assertion without logical or factual foundation. Indeed, many homosexuals exhibit the ability to establish deeply meaningful and loving relationships with members of the opposite sex precisely because sexual "conquest," in whatever form, is excluded from the situation. And the logic of Barth's argument at this point would seem to be that *heterosexuals* by their nature should despise members of *their* own sex. Finally, Barth maintains that homosexuality is idolatrous because it is basically self-worship. It is as if the classic syllogism were to be changed to read as follows: "I love men; Socrates is a man; therefore, I love myself." Non sequitur. In actuality, compared with heterosexual couples committed gay couples show no intrinsic or qualitative differences in their capacities for self-giving love.

The second major argument of the rejecting-nonpunitive position is that undesirable social consequences probably would result from homosexual acceptance. This argument appears to rest upon a major unspoken assumption: that homosexuals in fact do have meaningful choices about their same-sex orientation. If one makes this assumption, then one might (as Muehl appears to do) draw a further conclusion: that societal acceptance would bring in its wake a significant increase in the numbers of those choosing homosexuality.

Such assumptions must be radically questioned. Actually, statistics show no demonstrable increase in homosexual behavior in the quarter-century since Kinsey's study, in spite of somewhat less punitive social attitudes in recent years. Further, it is probable that greater acceptance of homosexuality would have desirable consequences for families and child-rearing: Emotional intimacy among same-sex heterosexual family members would be less inhibited by unrecognized homosexual fears, and syndromes of alienation and destructive rejection of the homosexual child in the family would be lessened.

The great majority of homosexuals do not appear to have a meaningful choice concerning their orientation any more than do the great majority of heterosexuals. There exists today no general agreement about the cause of homosexuality. Major theories cluster around two different approaches, the psychogenic and the genetic, but both remain in dispute. It is significant, however, that in 1973 the Trustees of the American Psychiatric Association removed homosexuality from that association's list of mental disorders, saying, "Homosexuality per se implies no impairment in judgment, stability, reliability, or general social or vocational capabilities."

Moral Responsibility and Self-Acceptance

The minority of gay persons who have sought therapeutic treatment to reverse their sex orientation have experienced an extremely low success rate. Behavioral modification programs using aversive therapy have conditioned some homosexuals against attraction to their own sex, but most frequently they have been unable to replace that with attraction to the opposite sex, a dehumanizing result. Indeed, Dr. Gerald C. Davison, who developed and popularized the "orgasmic reorientation" technique, recently disavowed his own treatment, calling upon behavior therapists to "stop engaging in voluntary therapy programs aimed at altering the choice of adult partners."

The other underlying assumption appears to be this: that theological positions and ecclesiastical practices which reject homosexuality can, in fact, be nonpunitive toward those persons so oriented. This, too, must be radically questioned, and we shall do so in the context of the next major position.

The third major theological option is that of the qualified acceptance of homosexuality. Helmut Thielicke provides its best articulation. His argument follows several steps. First, similar to Barth's contention, Thielicke maintains, "The fundamental order of creation and the created determination of the two sexes make it appear justifiable to speak of homosexuality as a 'perversion'...[which] is in every case not in accord with the order of creation." But Thielicke is more open than Barth to the results of contemporary psychological and medical research. Thus, he takes a second step: "But now experience shows that constitutional homosexuality at any rate is largely unsusceptible to medical or psychotherapeutic treatment, at least so far as achieving the desired goal of a fundamental conversion to normal-ity is concerned." Further, homosexuality as a predisposition ought not to be depreciated any more than the varied distortions of the created order in which all fallen people share.

But what of sexual expression? If the homosexual can change his or her sexual orientation, such a person should seek to change. Admittedly, however, most cannot. Then such persons should seek to sublimate their homosexual desires and not act upon them. But some constitutional homosexuals "because of their vitality" are not able to practice abstinence. If that is the case, they should structure their sexual relationships "in an ethically responsible way" (in adult, faithfully committed relationships). Homosexuals should make the best of their painful situations, without idealizing them or pretending that they are normal.

More than Barth and Muehl, Thielicke is empirically informed and pastorally sensitive on this issue. But his position is still grounded in an unacceptably narrow and rigid version of natural law. As such, in spite of its greater humanness his argument becomes self-contradictory. In effect the gay person is told, "We heterosexual Christians sympathize with your plight, and we believe that any sexual expression in which you engage must be done in an ethically responsible way — but do not forget that you are a sexual pervert!"

An ethics of the gospel ought never forget that moral responsibility is intrinsically related to self-acceptance, and that self-acceptance is intrinsically related to acceptance by significant others and, ultimately, by God. Gay persons in our society frequently have been told by their families that they do not belong to them, by the church that they are desperate sinners because of their sexual orientation, by the medical profession that they are sick, and by the law that they are criminals. In the face of such rejection, the amazing thing is that so many are emotionally stable and sexually responsible. If emotional problems still have a higher incidence among gay persons (as they do within any oppressed social group), we should cut through the vicious circle of self-fulfilling prophecy and recognize where the root of the problem lies — in societal oppression. Thielicke fails to do this. More humane though his position is, by continuing to label same-sex orientation as a perversion of God's natural law, he encourages continuing punitive attitudes toward homosexuals and in consequence undercuts his own hope for more responsible sexual relationships.

Realizing Our Intended Humanity

The fourth major theological possibility is full acceptance. While it usually makes the assumption that homosexual orientation is much more a given than a free choice, even more fundamentally this position rests upon the conviction that same-sex relationships are fully capable of expressing God's humanizing intentions.

Though still in a minority, the advocates of full Christian acceptance are increasing in number. In 1963 the English Friends state in their widely read *Towards a Quaker View of Sex:* "One should no more deplore 'homosexuality' than left-handedness.... Homosexual affection can be as selfless as heterosexual affection, and therefore we cannot see that it is in some way morally worse."

Among individual theologians Norman Pittenger has articulated this position most fully. God, he affirms, is the "Cosmic Lover," ceaselessly and unfailingly in action as love, and manifested supremely in Jesus Christ. God's abiding purpose for humankind is that in response to divine action we should realize our intended humanity as human lovers — in the richest, broadest, and most responsible sense of the term. Our embodied sexuality is the physiological and psychological base for our capacity to love.

For all of its continuity with animal sexuality, human sexuality is different: As persons our sexuality means the possibility of expressing and sharing a total personal relationship in love. And such expression contributes immeasurably toward the destiny to which we are all intended. Hence, abnormality or deviance should not be defined statistically, but rather in reference to the norm of humanity in Jesus Christ. Gay persons desire and need deep and lasting relationships, just as do heterosexual persons, and appropriate genital expression should be denied to neither.

Thus, the ethical question according to Pittenger is this: What sexual behavior will serve and enhance, rather than inhibit, damage, or destroy, our fuller realization of divinely intended humanity? The appropriate answer is a sexual ethics of love. This means commitment and trust, tenderness, respect for the other, and the desire for ongoing and responsible communion with the other. On its negative side such an ethics of love mandates against selfish sexual expression, cruelty, impersonal sex, obsession with sex, and against actions done without willingness to take responsibility for their consequences. Such an ethics always asks about the meaning of any particular sexual act in the total context of the persons involved, in the context of their society, and in the context of that direction which God desires for human life. It is an ethics equally appropriate for both homosexual and heterosexual Christians. There is no double standard.

It is obvious by this point that my own convictions favor the full Christian acceptance of homosexuality and its responsible genital expression. I have felt quite personally the force of each of the other stances described in this article, for at various earlier periods in my life I have identified, in turn, with each one — beginning as a teenager with the full complement of antihomosexual stereotypes. In recent years, both through theological-ethical reflection and through personal friendships with some remarkable gay persons, I have become increasingly convinced that the positions of both Barth and Thielicke inadequately express the implications of the gospel on this issue.

Homosexuality: A Heterosexual Problem?

Reinhold Niebuhr has powerfully argued that Christians must learn to live with the tension of "having and not having the truth." "Tolerance" in its truest sense, he maintained, is experienced when, on the one hand, a person can have vital convictions that lead to committed action and, on the other hand, that same person can live within the reality of forgiveness. The latter means experiencing divine forgiveness for the distortion of one's own understanding and having the willingness to accept those whose convictions sincerely differ. Hopefully, it is in such spirit that this personal note is written, and in such spirit the heterosexual reader is invited to wonder with me at this point about three possibilities.

One possibility is that "the homosexual problem" may be more truly a heterosexual problem. We are learning that "the black problem" is basically the problem of white racism, and that "the woman problem" is basically the problem of male sexism. So, also, we might well wonder whether or not "the homosexual problem" could be rooted in a homophobia frequently experienced by heterosexuals.

My own experience suggests this. While in the preceding paragraphs, for the sake of economy, I have simply used the terms "heterosexual" and "homosexual" (or "gay"), the best available evidence indicates that we are all bisexual to some degree. True, most of us, for reasons not yet fully understood, develop a dominant orientation toward one or the other side of the continuum. But Kinsey's early research repeatedly has been confirmed: On the scale of sexual orientation relatively few persons fall near the "zero" end (exclusively heterosexual) and relatively few approach the "six" mark (exclusively homosexual).

Though, for the majority of us, our adult genital expression may have been exclusively heterosexual, it is quite probable that we do experience homosexual feelings even if such are frequently relegated to the unconscious level. And males in our society generally have the greater difficulty with this, inasmuch as we have been continuously subjected to exaggerated images of masculinity. Thus, I believe it is worth pondering whether some of our common reactions against homosexuality might be linked to secret fears of homosexual feelings in ourselves — Freud's "reaction formation," defending against an impulse felt in oneself by attacking it in others.

Gay people may also represent threats to us in other related ways. The gay man seems to belie the importance of "super-masculinity," and his very presence calls into question so much that "straight" males have sacrificed in order to be manly. Homosexuals appear to disvalue commonly held public values related to marriage, family, and children. Because we so frequently judge others by our own standards, those who obviously deviate from them appear to be seriously deviant. And, strangely enough, homosexuals may awaken in heterosexuals a dimly recognized fear of death. Sometimes our hopes of vicarious immortality through our children and grandchildren are stronger than our resurrection faith. Then the presence of the gay person who (usually) does not have children may reawaken the fear of death, even though its conscious experience may be a nameless anxiety. I wonder.

Second, I wonder how much of the heterosexual reaction against homosexuality is related to male sexism. I suspect that some of our responses are. Surely, the more severe biblical condemnation of male homosexuality was not unrelated to the status of the male in a patriarchal society. For a man to act sexually like a woman was serious degradation (literally loss of grade). And in our own society, where male sexism remains a serious problem, it is still the male who more commonly experiences homophobia. Indeed, the striking parallelism between so many arguments against homosexual acceptance and arguments against full acceptance of women-men equality ought to make us reflect upon this.

Third, I wonder about the possibilities of augmented liberation for us all were a greater acceptance of homosexuality to come. Many of us have experienced some diminution of our own homophobia bringing new possibilities of tenderness, lessened competitiveness, and greater emotional intimacy with those of our own sex. Many of us males have become more conscious of the connection between the uses of violence and our needs for assurance of our virility, and we wonder whether greater understanding and acceptance of our own homosexual impulses might not well contribute to a more peaceful society. The list of liberating possibilities could be expanded, but perhaps the point is clear. In any event, I wonder about the relation between Jesus' apparent silence concerning homosexuality and Jesus as the image of authentic human liberation.

Precisely because we must live with "having and not having the truth," it is important that we share our serious wonderings. Perceptions of sincere Christians will differ on this issue, but we can all attempt to invite each other into our quests for fuller understanding of that humanity into which God invites us all.

Some Implications for the Church

The church's firm support of civil rights for gay persons ought not depend upon agreement concerning the theological and ethical appropriateness of the homosexual orientation or of specific same-sex acts. Civil rights support ought to be considered an expression of Christian concern for basic social justice.

The present legal situation is still very uneven. Some states and municipalities have legislated civil protection for gay persons, while others (the majority) have not. Most states still have punitive legislation on their books, though in actual practice enforcement is varied and often unpredictable. In any event, laws labeling "sodomy" or "unnatural sexual intercourse" as punishable offenses have a number of inherent problems. They violate the rights of privacy. They are ineffective and virtually unenforceable except through objectionable methods such as entrapment and enticement. However, enforced or not, sodomy laws stigmatize as criminal the person whose only crime is preference for the same sex, and inevitably such laws have considerable effect upon the gay individual's sense of self-worth. Further, an important principle of church-state separation is involved. What some Christians on fairly narrow doctrinal grounds consider a sin ought not to be made a crime unless that moral judgment can be defended on broader grounds of public interest and unless the behavior in question constitutes a demonstrable threat to human well-being and public welfare.

Beyond the civil rights, if and when churches were to affirm homosexuality and its responsible expression as fully appropriate to those persons so constituted, the implications for church life would be many, and their implementation might well be complex.

What about the full acceptance of gay Christians in the ongoing life of congregations? Because such acceptance still is largely absent, the movement toward congregations organized principally for gay persons will undoubtedly continue. This movement is completely understandable, but regrettable, for the majority's lack of acceptance then continues to fragment the body of Christ.

To be sure, congregational affirmation of gay persons would involve significant attitudinal changes on the part of many heterosexual Christians. With full acceptance, for example, all of those gestures and behaviors appropriate to heterosexuals in church gatherings must be affirmed for homosexuals as well. This should mean, then, no double standards concerning the hand-holding couple, the kiss of greeting, or the appropriate partner at the church dance.

The ordination question continues to be difficult. Not only division over theological and ethical issues but also differing patterns of ministerial placement and job security cause deep concern for many otherwise sympathetic church leaders. While no doubt there are presently ordained homosexual ministers in every major denomination, the vast majority of them continue secrecy about their sexual orientation. Only one major denomination has ordained a stated homosexual: The Rev. William R. Johnson was ordained by the United Church of Christ in 1972 and then only after prolonged study and debate in his association.

The recommendation made by the United Church's Executive Council in 1973, if difficult to implement, is the appropriate stance: "It [the Executive Council] recommends to associations that in the instance of considering a stated homosexual's candidacy for ordination the issue should not be his/her homosexuality as such, but rather the candidate's total view of human sexuality and his/her understanding of the morality of its use." This, indeed, is the logic of full acceptance. It is not the gay person's sexual orientation that would cause difficulty in ministerial leadership, but rather the misunderstandings and prejudices held by those whom he or she would lead. (Should a dominantly white denomination ordain black persons to the ministry? The parallel with racism seems clear.)

Most difficult of all gay-related questions for the present denominational church is that of homosexual marriage. The ordinance of marriage has a very long theological and ecclesiastical history, and that history is a heterosexual one. Profound symbols are organic. They must grow and develop, and sudden changes in their understanding cannot successfully be legislated. Marriage, involving a wife and a husband and the possibility of children, is clearly a heterosexual symbol.

But new rites can be created to meet legitimate needs unmet by existing symbols. There are, indeed, gay Christian couples living in long-term, permanently intended covenantal relationships who earnestly desire the affirmation of their religious communion. A "blessing of union" rite (by whatever name) could function in ways not identical but parallel to marriage rites. Such an ordinance could give the church's recognition, sanction, and support to a union whose intention is lasting and faithful. Indeed, if the church encourages responsible sexual expression among gay persons and then denies them its ritual and communal support, it engages in hypocrisy. If and when the church moves toward such liturgical recognition, it should also work for legal recognition of homosexual unions, involving such matters as tax laws and inheritance rights.

The ecclesiastical implications of full acceptance are undoubtedly complex. Very understandably, however, many gay Christians are tired of waiting for such complexities to be resolved. They have waited — and hurt — long enough. Their impatience, I believe, is a call for repentance and for urgent work by the rest of us. At its root the basic issue is not about "them," but about us all: What is the nature of that humanity toward which God is pressing us, and what does it mean to be a woman or a man in Jesus Christ.

Coming Out: Journey without Maps

June 11, 1979

Carter Heyward

Carter Heyward, one of the first eleven women ordained Episcopal priests in 1974, teaches theology at Episcopal Divinity School in Cambridge, Mass. A contributing editor of C & C, *she is author of* Speaking of Christ: A Lesbian Feminist Voice *and* Touching Our Strength: The Erotic as Power and the Love of God.

IN ANOTHER ARTICLE of mine that is being published this week, I speak of my resistance to all categorizing of human beings, including the use of sexual categories such as homosexual, heterosexual, and bisexual. The reason I cite for resisting is that "being human — being sexual — is not a matter of 'qualitative analysis' in which relationships of highest value become genital equations: woman plus woman equals gay; woman plus man equals straight." In my view, the labels we use do not express, but rather distort, the most important things we can know and say about our own sexuality and human sexuality in general.

If I believe this — and I do — why then break through my own resistance and "come out"?

The answer does not come easily. The difficulty here does not rise out of diffidence, for this article will not be primarily biographical but rather an analytic attempt to make sense out of biographical journeying. Quite apart from personal meanings, however, the subject being addressed does not yield readily to our efforts for comprehension. We live, all of us, in uncomfortable ambiguity. We live with contradictions and partial truths. In ambiguity we seek the meaning of ourselves and of the world, and the words to communicate the meanings we find. In its enormous vital complexity, sexuality may draw us as close as we will ever get to the heart of ambiguity. It is to escape from our anxiety-producing uncertainty, I think, that we so readily accept labels and resist our own questing and questioning.

People tend to think of sexual "identity" (or "preference," or "orientation") as something innate. I do not believe this is true. It seems to me that our sexual feelings and behavior are shaped by a variety of interweaving factors. Biology — our bodily glands and their powerful secretions, along with anatomy itself — is one, but only one, of these factors. We are shaped also by our ethnic, religious, and class heritages, by our schooling, by the events in our early experience, and certainly by our parents — by the specifically sexual models they provide, by their values, and by the ways they relate not only to each other, but also to us, and to others.

We are *born* sexual; our sexuality is indeed a given. But it is from a myriad of sources, and by a process closer to osmosis than to either inheritance or deliberation, that we *learn* how to feel and act sexually. That is why, I believe, we ought not identify the categories of "sexual identity" with sexuality itself, as though the categories were fundamental and fixed; as though they too were gifts to be accepted and valued without question. To celebrate our sexuality is to make a theological and anthropological affirmation of the pulsating dynamic of created life, the force within us that moves us beyond ourselves toward others. But this powerful affirmation of both creation and Creator is diminished in its truth when sexuality is equated with such categories as "gay" and "straight." For these categories can be boxes; they can be imposed from without, not truly chosen, not reflective of who we are or might have been or might become.

A Dominant Worldview

Yet these categories — boxes — are real. We live in them. We are in some significant part creatures of the social structures in which we participate; the boxes we call our sexual identities can be not only influenced, but even determined, by them. These structures, then, demand recognition and responsible attention. With regard to sexuality, what must be realized is that historically the predominant effect of cultural conditioning has been to squeeze all humanity into a single large box labeled "heterosexual." This social structure, this box, is so huge and so all-pervasive that we cannot easily see it; because we are enveloped by it, we cannot often find the distance we need to see and examine it. We accept this boxing of our sexuality as natural, the way things are and therefore ought to be.

Thus the heterosexual box becomes god of our social structures (including the church), our relationships, and our self-images. Functionally the heterosexual box becomes critical to and definitive for patriarchy, nuclear family, private enterprise, male-headship, and derivative boxes such as "masculine" and "feminine."

The social order is constructed, thus, upon a box largely invisible to its inhabitants. The moment a boy child learns that little boys don't cry, the instant a girl child learns that little girls don't fight, the child takes a step further into the heterosexual box. If, for reasons that may have little if anything to do with sex or gender, the child is drawn to protest against boxes, specifically against the heterosexual box designed to transform vulnerable little boys into big strong men and feisty little girls into soft, sweet ladies, the very social effort to implant a heterosexual identity may begin a contrary process. The point is that the result in either case is that the sexuality within is confined, shaped, limited, perhaps diminished by the container built around it.

The reason this is important is that sexuality drives toward relationship. It is a movement shared by all creatures and the creator, an impulse that we are capable of celebrating in every aspect of our lives. A significant aspect of sexuality is that it brings us to physical and emotional ecstasy in partnership. The ecstatic power of the sex act can lead us to identify it wrongly with the whole of sexuality, when in truth sexuality is, I believe, the one most vital source of our other passions; of our capacities to love and to do what is just in the world. I would go so far as to suggest that the capacity to celebrate sexuality is linked inextricably with the capacity to court peace, instead of war; justice, instead of oppression; life, instead of hunger, torture, fear, crime, and death.

Sexuality, which finds its most intimate expression between lovers, moves us into an active realization, and great relief, that we are not alone; that we are, in fact, bound up in the lives of others; and that this is good. That is why, I think, many (but too few) Christians speak of love and justice together; justice is the moral act of love.

This has personal meaning for me. Recalling my past, I can see now that coming out has been a long and puzzling journey out of the heterosexual box, in which I was no more comfortable at age five than I am now at thirty-three. The experience is hardly rare, as we are coming to know from the testimonies of women and men who, when they were girls and boys, were continuously reminded that anatomy is destiny and that sex-role expectations are not to be evaded. My own parents made no conscious attempt to teach me rigid sex roles. Yet, both they and I lived in the heterosexual box that was far larger, and more deeply formative, than either they or their children could realize. Accordingly, I experienced the larger social order as squeezing something out of me, pressing something in on me and eventually depressing into me feelings of shame about wanting to do things and be things that "weren't for girls."

Why did I want to be Superman and not Lois Lane? Matt Dillon and not Miss Kitty? Because Superman and Matt Dillon were more interesting to me. They led exciting lives. They made things happen. They were confident, assertive, energetic. Somewhere inside I knew (and knew *rightly*) that unless I felt *myself* to be an interesting, confident, and assertive person, completely capable of exerting as much "will" and leadership as the next person, I could never really love, or allow myself to be loved, by anyone. Not mutually. Not really. I *knew* also that any effort I might make on behalf of justice would be triggered by my own lack of self-esteem and by the painful inclination to identify with the underdog, rather than by the human and *sexual* impulse to work for justice on the basis of a strong confidence in both myself and the power of God to love.

In our history, in our society, in our churches, the heterosexual box is that into which girls are pressed into ladies who *should* marry and who must be held within the social order as subordinate to husbands, fathers, or father-surrogates — regardless of the unique and individual capacities, needs, and desires of either women or men. There is too little room in this enormous socially constructed box for real mutual love between the sexes and no allowance at all for mutual love between women or between men. There is too little room in the heterosexual box for either spouse in a marriage to develop fully her or his capacities for loving humanity and God out of a sense of self as *both* strong and gentle, confident and vulnerable, assertive and receptive, equally able to lead and to follow. As a social structure, the heterosexual box intends to permit no androgyny or gynandry; nor does it encourage us to cast off the burden of sex roles — because the heterosexual box is built entirely out of sex roles.

New Priorities

Feminism challenges the legitimacy of sex roles. Along with other social movements, feminism is rooted in the critique that a society so constructed that certain people and groups *profit* from inequalities — between men and women, rich and poor, black and white, etc. — is a society in which money is more highly valued than love, justice, and human life itself. Feminism moves toward the reversal of these values: Human life must be first; all else, second. As sex roles fall, as more and more women and men refuse to play along for profit and social gain at the expense of our true selves, the heterosexual box begins to weaken. This is exactly what is happening today in our society. The box is collapsing: Women and men are coming out.

For many women, and I am one, coming out means that we are beginning to value ourselves and our sisters as highly as we have been taught to value men. Coming out means loving women, not hating men. Coming out means beginning to feel the same attraction, warmth, tenderness, desire to touch and be touched by women as we have learned to feel in relation to men.

For about fifteen years I have been coming out sexually, experiencing my attraction to women as well as men to be a valuable dimension of myself — as friend, lover, Christian. I have been aware that there is a box, another box, a less constrictive box, for people with this experience: "bisexual." As boxes go, bisexuality isn't bad. It may be (if unknowable truths were known) the most nearly adequate box for *all* persons. The problem with bisexuality in my life (and I can speak only for myself) is that it has been grounded too much in my utopic fantasy of the way things "ought" to be and too little in the more modest recognition of myself as a participant in *this* society at *this* time in *this* world, in which I have both a concrete desire for personal intimacy with someone else and a responsibility to participate in, even witness to, the destruction of unjust social structures — specifically, the heterosexual box.

If our world and civilization have a future, it may be that in some future decade or century sex roles will be transcended; persons will be defined as persons and modes of relationship will be chosen, not imposed. It has been my experience that to live now as bisexual is to live somewhat abstractly in anticipation of a future that has not arrived. That is why, for several years, I have been coming out of bisexuality, coming out of utopic vision in order to focus my sight on the urgency and immediacy of the concrete present.

At present, I am a student writing a doctoral thesis on a theology of mutual relation, believing as I do that the future of both humanity and God depends upon human beings' willingness to relate as equals. I am a teacher in a seminary in which both women and gay people have to struggle fiercely to keep themselves from being squeezed into the heterosexual box in which women must submit, and gay people must repent. I am a priest in a church which, like most churches, threatens to collapse under the weight of a perverse notion of a sexuality that is to be neither celebrated nor related to other issues of love and justice. I am a woman in a church and a society that patronize women with reminders of how far we have come and of how much we have been given. And I am a lesbian — a woman who has come out of the heterosexual box and into another box, which, as boxes go, is far superior for my life as a responsible person, a Christian woman, in this world at this time.

Coming out, I come into the realization of myself as best able to relate most intimately — to touch and be touched most deeply, to give and receive most naturally, to empower and be empowered most remarkably — best able to express everything I most value — God in human life, God in justice, God in passion, God as love — in sexual relationship to a lover who is female.

It is with another woman in this world at this time that I am able to experience a *radical mutuality* between self and other, a mutuality that we have known since we were girl children, a mutuality that has shaped our consciousness of female-female relationships as the first and final place in which women can be most truly at home, in the most natural of social relations. It is, moreover, with other lesbian feminist Christians that we can *witness* to the power of God's presence in mutuality — relationship in which there is no higher and no lower, no destructive insecurities fastened in the grip of sex-role expectations, but rather a dynamic relational dance in which each nurtures and is nurtured by the other in her time of need.

A romantic portrayal? No, it is not easy. There are tensions, fears, the possibility of cruelty and abuse — just as in any relationship. It is not that lesbian relationships are always, or even most often, characterized by mutuality. It is just that, in the present social order, lesbian relationships offer an opportunity for a mutuality of remarkable depth. Lesbian relationships can make prophetic witness within and to society: a witness not on behalf of homosexuality per se, but rather on behalf of mutuality and friendship in all relations.

Gains and Losses

Coming out, there are things lost: the bearing of my own children and the learning how to live better with male lovers. But the gain outweighs the loss: Coming out, I begin to envision and embrace the children of the world as my own; and the men of the world as my brothers, whom I can better learn to know and love as friends. Coming out involves a recognition of the co-creative power I have always experienced in relation to women. Coming out is a confession that I need and want intimacy with someone whose values and ways of being in the world can support and be supported by my own. Coming out means realizing and cherishing my parents' way of loving and of being in the world; of valuing who they have been and who they are, and of knowing myself both as bound to them and as separate from them in my journeying. Coming out means remembering my other relatives and early friends, in the hope that they can trust, and celebrate, the parts we have played in the shaping of one another's values.

Coming out is a protest against social structures that are built on alienation between men and women, women and women, men and men. Coming out is the most radical, deeply personal, and consciously political affirmation I can make on behalf of the possibilities of love and justice in the social order. Coming out is moving into relation with peers. Not simply a way of being in bed, but rather a way of being in the world. To the extent that it invites "voyeurism," coming out is an invitation to look and see and consider the value of mutuality in human life. Coming out is simultaneously a political movement and the mighty rush of God's Spirit carrying us on.

Coming out, I stake my sexual identity on the claim which I hold to be the gospel at its heart: that we are here to love God and our neighbors as ourselves. Each of us must find her, or his, own way to the realization of this claim. I have given you a glimpse into my way. Where the journey began, where it will end, I don't know. I know only that I am glad to be coming out.

Thinking about Abortion

July 14, 1986

Vivian Lindermayer

Vivian Lindermeyer is managing editor of Christianity and Crisis. *During her twenty years on the staff she has paid particular attention to feminist and ethnic issues. Twice her work — for editorials and for reviews — was singled out for Awards of Merit by the Associated Church Press.*

THE RECENT SUPREME COURT DECISION upholding Roe *v*. Wade marks a temporary resting point in the social and political battle over women's legal right to abortion. During the last five years, as this conflict has escalated, prochoice feminists have become increasingly articulate in presenting their case for a feminist ethics of reproductive freedom, including the legal right to abortion. In its broadest outlines, their approach has drawn on the principles of bodily integrity and socially determined need.

Bodily integrity and the control over one's body that it implies are central to the liberal tradition's view of the individual. Pregnancy, prochoice feminists emphasize, is an event within a woman's body. If we genuinely view women as persons with needs, rights, and responsibilities, we must recognize that despite possible conflict between the survival of the fetus and the claims of the mother, women must retain the final choice about their reproductive lives, including the right to choose abortion.

The appeal to socially determined need stems from the recognition that sex, pregnancy, child-bearing, and child-rearing are structured by society. Women don't just become pregnant; they do so in a society that enhances or limits — but in all cases structures — their options. Accessibility of birth control, the class and race to which a woman belongs, the level of health care, nutrition, and employment: These are only a few of the social factors that set the stage for choice. Since women are primarily responsible for rearing children, and since they do so under specific and complicated social circumstances, they should control the process of deciding about abortion.

The interplay between these two strands of the argument is intricate. Some feminists have said that in a society that assumed genuine communal responsibility for women's and children's well-being, women's right to decide might be subject to some type of social intervention. In good part, however, prochoice feminists have not accepted this approach, believing that it ignores the central importance of bodily integrity — pregnancy happens in a woman's body.

C & C holds an editorial position favoring women's right to choose. We do not intend to keep rearguing our position. What we do intend is to create a forum for prochoice feminists to reflect not on why but on *how* women should decide about abortion. Granted the persuasiveness of the feminist case for legal abortion, what do feminists have to say about the moral values and reasoning, the moral or religious imagination, and the notion of moral responsibility that women should bring to their individual choices about abortion?

Many prochoice feminists have noted that reflection on a feminist morality of abortion decision-making has been frustrated by the need to wage the political battle over who should decide. Prochoice feminists have been careful to distinguish between the political-legal and the moral aspects of the abortion issue, but such fine points have often been lost in the din of political battle.

The result is a kind of vacuum. Despite the groundwork already laid in women's experiences and conversations, in counseling centers, and in feminist writing and research on how women make abortion decisions, we have seen little sustained public discussion of feminist criteria for abortion decision-making. In our judgment, confusion has filled this vacuum.

In the past few years, prolife feminists have argued that support for legal abortion is inconsistent with other feminist social goals and with the feminist vision of humankind. The prolife position has found forceful articulation in a recent article by Sidney Callahan ("A Case for Pro-Life Feminism," *Commonweal*, April 24, 1986). Callahan's comments on women's moral obligations to fetal life underline the need for more discussion of prochoice criteria. "The woman's moral obligation," says Callahan, "arises both from her status as a human being embedded in the interdependent human community and her unique life-giving female reproductive power. To follow the prochoice feminist ideology of insistent individualist autonomy and control is to betray a fundamental basis of the moral life."

But, prochoice feminists appeal to individual autonomy in arguing for women's *right to choose*. That does not make individual autonomy or liberal individualism their ideology. The argument for legality does not tell us anything definitive about the values and concerns prochoice feminists think should guide women as they choose. It does not, for one thing, tell us whether women should exercise their autonomy in an individualist fashion. In fact, in the absence of more sustained reflection on criteria, Callahan is on slippery ground in concluding much at all about what a feminist morality of abortion might be. Unless we grant with Callahan that fetal claims have stronger force than women's claims because of the fetus's extreme need — and prochoice feminists don't grant this conclusion — we are still left with the substantive questions: *How* do we translate our concern to "choose life" into our concrete decisions? *How* do we affirm obligations to ourselves and to the "interdependent human community" in reflecting on our choices? In the absence of this kind of moral analysis, appeals to moral imperatives remain merely abstract.

Confusion is also apparent in the prochoice community. In a column entitled "Is Abortion Really a Moral Dilemma?" (*New York Times*, February 7, 1985), Barbara Ehrenreich credits the right-to-life movement with "getting even prochoice people to think of abortion as a 'moral dilemma.' . . . In liberal circles it has become unstylish to discuss abortion without using words like 'complex,' 'painful,' and the rest of the mealy-mouthed vocabulary of evasion."

It is hard to know exactly who Ehrenreich has in mind. Beyond doubt, appeals to moral complexity are used again and again in the abortion debate as a cover for saying that abortion should be illegal. But the term "moral dilemma" is not always used this way. Many prochoice people use it to mean that choosing abortion requires moral deliberation. Ehrenreich's choice of language and tone can easily be taken to suggest that the decision to have an abortion is of little moral significance.

Ehrenreich may fear that talk about the complexities of abortion plays into the hands of the right-to-life movement. It might. But not talking about complexity also poses a danger. It can stifle constructive discussion. It lends credence by default to the argument that prochoice feminists consider abortion to be a private choice, because they view it as being outside the realm of social morality, morally insignificant. It can lend credence to cultural stereotypes of women as unserious, not capable perhaps of being moral agents.

In the midst of all this, it is crucial to affirm again and again that it is necessary and possible to make morally justified choices about abortion and that prochoice feminists insist on women's right to choose not because they don't appreciate the moral significance of abortion, but because they appreciate just how morally significant abortion is.

Feminist Realism

July 14, 1986

Beverly Wildung Harrison

Beverly Wildung Harrison is Carolyn Williams Beaird Professor of Christian Ethics at Union Theological Seminary in New York City. Her study of the ethics of procreative choice, Our Right to Choose *(1983), stands as one of the definitive texts on the morality of abortion. She is a contributing editor of* C & C.

FEMINISM GENERATES a profound commitment to social justice. This commitment originates in an awareness of the fundamentally relational, interdependent, and finite character of life. At the same time, feminist reflection on the particularity and diversity of women's lives and on the integrity of their historical struggles cautions us against thinking too rigidly about what social justice and morality mean. Because religious feminism sets the context for my thinking about abortion decisions, I want to elaborate on some of its particular insights.

A feminist religious vision urges us to understand social justice within the radically pluralist nature of creation. As feminist theory affirms and celebrates, reality is not pregiven and static, but an ongoing, changing process. The world and the cosmos are inexhaustibly rich in potential for moral fulfillment in spite of the active and powerful presence of evil. Moral life that is authentically feminist must honor this insight.

Ethical reflection does not consist in the static repetition of inherited patterns of obligation. Such patterns help us locate the claims the past bequeaths to us. But thinking ethically requires us to take these claims and continuously test and reformulate them. It requires us to reorder values and to forge hope and virtue out of conflicting values. A feminist religious ethic enables us to grasp that all our decisions — including a decision about a specific pregnancy — are made "in a world in which there is a call to do good, a call to be generous, a call to self-fulfillment," a world, also, in which "it is certain that creation both recovers from wrong decisions and continues to be alive to the processes of creation" (Jean Lambert).

A caveat: We should not talk about abortion dilemmas in a way that removes them from the living *continuity* of women's lives. The approach we need is an ethic of procreative choice, not merely an ethic of abortion. In one sense, abortion is a negative therapeutic or corrective act, not an act of positive moral agency at all. From the standpoint of a woman's experience, we have to ask a more basic moral question: What am I to do about the procreative power that is mine by virtue of being born female? In thinking about this question, in acting on this question, one consideration remains paramount: the *active moral agency* to create a world where conditions actually exist that enable women to exercise real choices about the role of procreation in their lives. A genuinely reflective, value-respecting morality cannot fully develop where conditions of choice are absent.

Our moral arguments either for choice or about particular abortion decisions must never be severed from our historical analysis of the absence of choice. (This interrelationship is not understood by some writers, notably Sidney Callahan and Madonna Kolbenschlag, who criticize prochoice feminists for excessive individualism and voluntarism.)

Feminists recognize that human fertility and reproduction have always been shaped by human activity, decision, and control. We must be suspicious of any purported feminist theory which does not recognize that basic social institutions, including the church, are implicated in institutional systems of control aimed at dictating the use of women's reproductive power.

The recent availability of legal, elective abortion provides, at best, an increased degree of self-directive power. It enables women to maneuver more meaningfully amid incredible pressures and limited options. For many, the availability of abortion does little more than increase the margin for survival. It certainly does not assure full and optimal conditions for spontaneous choice or even for full deliberation about choice.

We make a dreadful error, in thinking about abortion decision-making, if we do not acknowledge that the conditions needed *to choose to bear and rear children* are worsening. The accelerating pauperization of women and their dependent children is a massive and global phenomenon. While the conditions for procreative choice among the minority of the really affluent improve dramatically, the possibilities for providing food, shelter, health care, and adequate education for children deteriorate for most. Increasingly, children are dependent — *exclusively* dependent — upon the maternal life line. It is those who neglect this historical setting who are individualistic in their ethics.

The Moral Situation

Here, then is the full complexity of the moral situation in which we must set a discussion of criteria regarding abortion: We need the guidance moral reflection can give, but we must insist that women be *fully realistic* about what it means to have children. The historical situation suggests that the decision to bear and raise children is likely to be made either out of an immense amount of psychological denial — for females are still rewarded with spiritual approbation for unconscious conformity to a naturalistic myth of women's fulfillment — or out of a well-considered commitment that requires an element of moral courage.

How much moral courage do feminists have a right to expect from ourselves and our sisters? No more than the prudential wisdom our theological-moral tradition has commended to men. No doubt without full conscious intent, traditionalist Christian moral theology has managed to make the pregnant women the most conspicuous expectation to the general rule that theological fidelity enables us to live conscientiously even when we must act in situations where none of the options is optimal morally. (All females are excepted, but *especially* the pregnant woman.)

We can envision some of the elements of optimal decision-making, but we must do so while remaining aware that individual cases are not simply occasions to express consistent value commitments or principles of action. They are rather particularly vexing settings for value-balancing decisions where an individual women most frequently has little power to shape the moral quality of life. Individual women do *not* bear all of the moral accountability for the complex social-moral equation that confronts them when a pregnancy is unplanned. (Why, then, are the most censorious denouncers of the morality of women who do choose abortion often those who accept no part of the moral burden for altering the many constraints on women's lives?)

Nurturance Is Active

Certainly one of the values most normative for the feminist moral vision — and the one "feminists for life" distort and make the *exclusive* norm — is our obligation for "caring" and "nurturance" of others. I see no reason to retreat from this value in feminist approaches to abortion decisions. It is a distinctive feature of women's culture and women's historical experience to nourish a fundamental respect for the irreducible moral value of nurturance. This, however, is an active, not a passive value; it can be expressed in myriads of ways, through all of the social roles in which we participate.

What we must be clear about is that active caring and nurturance are *not* the same as some "natural " female (or worse, "feminine") need for motherhood which, if denied, renders us morally inept. Here again, an insufficiently historical feminist theory tempts us to confuse the irreducible value of active caring with some purported "special vocation" of motherhood. It tempts us to place women who don't choose this vocation outside the moral pale of true femininity, to make them enemies of feminism.

But the social institution of motherhood is as historical as any other, even though bourgeois ideology portrays maternal desire as the peculiar, a-historical "essence" of womanhood. When feminists join this ideology of motherhood with nurturance, caring, and all active efforts to maintain a familial quality in our common life, we fall into the trap of being bourgeois propagandists. Unfortunately, Christian feminists are particularly tempted to this pitfall.

We all know at heart that good mothering requires clear and consistent differentiation between a child and a parent. Its goal is always mutual empowerment and the transformation of infant dependence into mutuality. That is not the same thing as entrapment in "maternal thinking." A compulsive maternalism has its own forms of pathology and provides a poor basis for social decision-making of any sort: It tends to romanticize dependency, and, as philosopher Sarah Ruddick has shown, it makes it difficult to maintain distance from personal feeling when that is appropriate to moral discrimination.

Compulsive "maternalism" (like paternalism, of course) also erodes a woman's (or a man's) capacity for growth and self-direction; it invites us to seek our fulfillment indirectly, through manipulation of another's need. The often unconscious use of another's dependency to provide ego-enhancement for oneself is surely the besetting sin of parenting. We can say that child-rearing requires extraordinary artfulness in the moral expression of caring precisely because the child's dependency makes him or her vulnerable to aberrant caring. In other words, especially under modern conditions, motherhood is a morally demanding relation; it therefore ought not to be entered into lightly. That is certainly no reason for insisting that women who find themselves pregnant are moral degenerates if they discern they are not at this point well-equipped for the assignment.

Romanticizing motherhood threatens also to tilt the understanding of caring and nurturance in feminist ethics away from an insistence that shared or mutual relationship is the morally highest mode of caring. It is perfectly legitimate to insist that in having children women should not be motivated by a strict and legalist sense of obligation. I suspect all "motives to maternity" that do not participate in a gracious recognition that children are not mere helpless, dependent, or innocent beings but rather, in all their adamant separateness, abundant sources of joy, appreciation, and wonder. Should any women choose childbearing who does not see this?

A Shifting Moral Equation

I also tend to think that many women's inability to differentiate between a moral evaluation about terminating early fetal life and a moral evaluation of one's attitude toward children stems from an inability to distinguish claims regarding dependency. Appeals to "fetal innocence" and "helplessness," for example, resonate deeply for those raised in the Christian tradition. Unfortunately, traditional Christian symbolism yields a special valence to such claims because in it only what is *not* sexual is seen as truly innocent. Clearly, in orthodox Christian tradition, a pregnant women is perceived as tainted; *only* fetuses can be "truly innocent." No matter how much we value early fetal life, we cannot say that only fetal helplessness counts as a relevant moral claim. That would give absolute privilege to the fetal/maternal relationship. To opt for child-bearing always means we take a path toward realizing some critical moral value. But it also invariably involves excluding some other moral values. Pressures not to consider the conflicting claims of the many values involved only aggravates the socially underdeveloped ability of women to recognize that everything in life requires continuous value-balancing and moral choice.

I recognize the need for a shifting moral equation within the ongoing process of gestation. Until neurological development has occurred, the claims of a woman's well-being and of her existing obligations have a clear, overriding validity. Adequate understanding of gestation leads me *not* to impute intrinsic value to a fetus — certainly through the first four months of pregnancy.

Nor does my conviction that a woman should extend active human value to her fetus in later decision-making lead me to think in terms of some overriding "right to life" prior to birth. It does mean that weightier considerations are needed to justify late abortion. And it means that I would want second-trimester abortions to become a rare exception.

A feminist moral agenda includes active efforts to encourage women to detect pregnancy early, and — if the pregnancy is unplanned — to make decisions about it with speed and clarity. In fact, more and more women are learning to do this. The mean term of abortions has dropped in the U.S. in all areas where abortion services are adequate. The experience in Sweden also makes it clear that further reductions can happen, but only in a society that respects women's right to choose. Failure to extend this respect through social policy aimed to encourage early decisions only increases many individual women's ambivalence and evasion.

Certainly morally dubious reasons for having an early abortion exist, as do morally vacuous reasons for carrying a pregnancy to term. Obviously, the rightness or wrongness of these decisions inheres in the violation of responsibility to one's own integrity and to relationships with male partners, family, and others. But even when a women considering an unwanted pregnancy does not share my views about fetal life, and considers the fetus to be already a human life, I would still urge that she not treat the moral prohibition against taking human life to be an unexceptional rule.

It is morally wiser for a woman deliberating about abortion early in pregnancy to recognize that she has an *active* obligation to think of the embryo or fetus *not* as an existing human life, but as a powerfully potential soon-to-be human life that will require deep moral commitment and claim her obligations dramatically. The most conscientious decisions at this point in pregnancy can be made only if a woman or girl can free her imagination to ponder what it may mean to have a child. There is much to be gained morally from helping pregnant women to learn to think this way.

I reject any position that portrays as "frivolous" or as "matters of mere convenience" reasons for terminating pregnancy that relate to the basic material and spiritual conditions of a woman's own life as well as her obligations to others. A woman must consider how a specific pregnancy affects her plans for her life. How can our deliberations over unplanned pregnancy have any genuine moral quality if our plans for our life count for nothing, if reasons based on our goals are considered trivial?

How Much Moral Courage?

Nor does my principled recognition for the increasing moral ambiguity of late abortion lead me to conclude that good reasons for early abortion have no weight at a later point. The act itself becomes increasingly dubious morally as fetal life actively individuates and approaches stages analogous to the biological complexity of existing human life, but pregnancies can become unwanted at some point in the process. The life circumstances of a pregnant woman can change dramatically, and for the worse. Marriages come apart suddenly, jobs are lost, basic support systems collapse. There will always be some late abortions, and in my view many will be fully justifiable morally.

Furthermore, the largest number of late abortions are due to lack of access to affordable abortion services or to the current incapacity of the young to detect pregnancy. It is increasingly distressing to see so few people — including liberal prochoice proponents — making connections between the rate of resort to late abortions and the largely successful "prolife" crusade to limit abortion services (and in some cases, contraception) and cut off public funding for abortion. These connections make me even more willing to acknowledge that my reservations about late abortion must be held with great tentativeness. I want no part of anathematizing poor women or the confused pregnant young.

One category of late abortions that is on the increase has to be considered a *sui generis* type of dilemma: The dramatic escalation of prenatal medical technology, in particular, the availability of genetic screening, has created a distinctive dilemma for many women and their partners. All but invariably, the dilemma arise for a women who wants to be pregnant and have a child: She is confronted with information — some of it certain, much of it imprecise projection — about the health of her fetus.

Everyone who has faced this situation has attested to the extraordinary trauma involved. The pregnancy has proceeded with growing anticipation, shaped by general experience. But now the woman experiences yet a further testing of the values and moral commitments that led her and her partner to want a child: All will not be as they hoped.

For me, some cases pose no ambiguity morally. I rejoice that women who are carriers of some severe degenerative genetic diseases learn their fetus is afflicted in time to be spared the ordeal of watching a child die. Conversely, I am appalled that some few women and their mates are willing to use the new technology to select gender. For reasons, I cannot develop here, I believe abortion-for-gender choice is an unqualified moral wrong.

But what of the greater number of cases where what is involved is some projection, often inexact, about mental retardation or physical disability? Discussion of these issues among women — deeply painful discussion — is only now beginning. It requires feminists to press value-clarifications even further. I, for one, must confess that so far the issues raised have produced more agony than clarity.

On the one hand, it is obvious that the sin of "ableism" is at work in the widespread assumption that mental retardation and physical disability provide privileged reasons for having abortions. Clearly morally serious feminists must *not* share in such assumptions. They are fueled by sexism and by the "body-perfectism" hype that ravages the lives of the differently abled, and also twists and warps the lives of many girls and women.

Yet when I ask myself what I would do in this situation, the limits of my values come screaming forth: "Not too much mental retardation! I couldn't cope...." Posing the question this way, however, has put me in touch not only with the bias and limits of my own values, but also with the extent to which such a decision forces me to confront both fear and the genuine question of limits. With even greater urgency, I find myself asking again: "How much moral courage do feminists have a right to expect from our sisters?"

If realism in moral reflection is required at any stage in pregnancy, then surely we have some obligation to insist that it is even more appropriate here. Truth to tell, after struggling to envisage a personal response to such a dilemma, my chief reaction was relief: As a women beyond child-bearing years, I will never actually face the situation.

Increasingly, though, women are facing it. And I trust that women will forge the moral wisdom to deal with this dilemma also. My trust is no cop-out, but a confidence consistent with my feminist commitment.

Global AIDS: The Epidemic(s)

June 12, 1989

Jan Zita Grover

Jan Zita Grover is a critic living in Sacramento, Calif. She has written widely about the cultural politics of AIDS for publications in the U.S., Canada, and the U.K.

AIDS and the Third World, by the PANOS Institute/Norwegian Red Cross (Philadelphia: New Society, 1989).

AIDS: Profile of an Epidemic (Washington, D.C.: Pan American Health Organization, 1989), 350pp.

A Strange Virus of Unknown Origin, by Jacques Leibowitch (New York: Ballantine Books, 1989).

The Global Impact of AIDS, Proceedings of the First International Conference (New York: Alan R. Liss, Inc., 1988), 460pp.

THE FIRST and most important step in understanding AIDS as a global epidemic is to understand that *the* AIDS epidemic does not exist. Rather, AIDS follows different paths of transmission from country to country, depending on location, economic structure, degree of industrialization, and population patterns. The World Health Organization (WHO) has identified four distinct transmission patterns for AIDS (in *AIDS: Profile of an Epidemic*), and we need to keep our eyes on all four.

- In some parts of Africa and the Caribbean, transmission began before the 1970s, with high levels of HIV [Human Immunodeficiency Virus] infection, the virus being transmitted predominantly through heterosexual contact, perinatal contact (mother-to-child before birth), and blood transfusions.

- In the United States and Western Europe, transmission typically began toward the end of the 1970s, with high levels of infection among homosexual and bisexual males and intravenous drug abusers. Transmission through blood transfusions has been limited. Persistent but low levels of heterosexual transmission have occurred, as has perinatal transmission in high-risk areas.

- In Latin America outside the Caribbean, transmission began in the early 1980s, with moderate levels of infection among groups engaging in high-risk practices, chiefly homosexual and especially bisexual males. Blood transfusions have played an important role in transmission, one that has not been completely eliminated, but the proportions of cases occurring as a result of intravenous drug abuse and perinatal contact have been low.

- In Asia and Oceania, transmission began in the mid-1980s among groups engaging in high-risk practices. However, as yet no evidence of transmission through blood products exists, and levels of perinatal transmission are low.

Significantly, although Pattern 1 was widely recognized in Europe, Africa, and the Caribbean by the early 1980s, U.S. epidemiologists, clinicians, and journalists, as well as the U.S. government, ignored it in favor of what Jacques Leibowitch, the French immunologist (in *A Strange Virus of Unknown Origin*), calls the "lavender peril."

So convinced were many of our researchers that AIDS *had* to be related to homosexuality, says Leibowitch, that they "raised the semantic ante by inventing the label GRID (for Gay-Related Immuno-Deficiency)." On the other hand, clinicians in France and Belgium (two countries tied by their colonial history to Central Africa) were seeing a pattern distinct from the one acknowledged in the United States — heterosexual Africans afflicted with AIDS.

Faced with the Europeans' evidence, most American researchers initially refused to incorporate it. Instead, they argued that seemingly heterosexual Africans and Caribbeans were in fact covertly homosexual. Thus, Haitians with AIDS were seen as liars too embarrassed by their homosexual acts to admit them. Presumably, so were most Central Africans.

This hypothesis gave way only after the isolation of a retrovirus, LAV, in the laboratories of the Pasteur Institute in Paris in 1983–84. In America, however, most of the damage was already done: The precipitate rush of scientists, journalists, and conservative politicians to embrace the equation of AIDS with *homosexual lifestyle* has persisted to this day.

Persisting in Prejudice

This persistence is what makes the books under review here so important. They offer readers a far more balanced and detailed picture of the global AIDS/HIV epidemic. Equally important, they provide a corrective picture of the U.S. approach to AIDS, and our place within the worldwide epidemic(s).

Until we move beyond our first crude characterizations of AIDS, we cannot hope to recognize — much less respond to — the complex

AIDS epidemics facing us, both domestically and overseas. Even an understanding of the changing U.S. epidemic offers few useful policies or guidelines for dealing with the epidemic in some of our nearby neighbors, e.g., Mexico and the Caribbean. Nor does the U.S. picture help us comprehend the reaction of individual countries to their AIDS epidemics. In order to understand that, we need to grasp the importance of *difference*.

AIDS: Profile of an Epidemic and *The Global Impact of AIDS* document the profound cultural, economic, social, and political differences among nations that make international practices and policies on AIDS often difficult and sometimes impossible to enforce. For example, in Cuba all pregnant women undergo mandatory HIV testing. If positive, they must have an abortion. The Cuban government tested 103,583 persons in a little over two months (*AIDS: Profile*). It also quarantines all persons found positive (*AIDS and the Third World*). These are measures that are unlikely to be enacted in the United States — despite the fears of many AIDS activists — for the simple reason that we do not live in a closely managed economy and society.

Interestingly, Cuban efforts to isolate persons with HIV infection place many American conservatives in the uncomfortable position of having to acknowledge the resemblance of their own call for quarantine to what can be read as the "fascist" or "communist" program of the Cubans. But Cuba's quarantine measures are too complex to be written off as "fascism"; they also reflect the country's vastly different (and thanks in part to the long-term American economic blockade, significantly poorer) economy.

"Our country is a poor country," said the deputy minister of public health, Hector Terry, in 1987. "If many Cubans become infected and sick, I do not know how we would take care of them. It would cost too much. We really have to prevent such a situation" (*AIDS and the Third World*).

Nonetheless, Cuba's approach looks more like a *cultural* choice when we compare it to the policy adopted by an even poorer nation: Nicaragua opposed all mandatory and compulsory testing of its population. It also honors the resolution of the World Health Organization upholding unimpeded international travel for persons with HIV infection. (Cuba, in contrast, requires that all foreigners, except tourists, and Cubans returning from AIDS "endemic areas" take an HIV test.) As these examples make clear, governments with superficially similar economies and social organizations can arrive at very different policies on the issue of AIDS.

For governments with even fewer resources than Cuba's and Nicaragua's, the prospect of containing the epidemic and protecting both the infected and the uninfected appears even more remote. Here again we confront the importance of *difference* in conceptualizing the global dimensions of AIDS. Citizens of high-technology cultures, accustomed to believing that diseases can be cured and that "most people" live into their seventies or eighties, are likely to view AIDS as "the epidemic of the century." But in countries where childhood mortality is already high and resources are scarce, AIDS is just one more disease, as a speaker from Sierra Leone noted last year at the (London) Global Impact of AIDS Conference (her paper is not included in *The Global Impact of AIDS*). Poor African countries like hers witness the deaths of tens of thousands of children each year from malnutrition, malaria, and childhood diseases. Compared to these losses, AIDS is "way down the list" of health problems.

Unlike malnutrition and malaria, most HIV infection in countries that follow Patterns 1 and 4 can be prevented by providing information and support to sexually active persons. Such programs can utilize already-existing healthcare networks as well as those less commonly used by public health educators: families, traditional healers, unions, prostitutes, pop music, and churches. (Several papers in *AIDS: Profile of an Epidemic* and *The Global Impact of AIDS* describe these programs, and *AIDS in the Third World* devotes a short chapter to the subject.)

The problem of transmission through blood transfusions and blood products is technologically more demanding, though potentially easier to solve than altering voluntary human behavior. In Pattern 1 and 3 countries, a significant number of people develop AIDS as a result of receiving HIV-contaminated blood. Their risk is higher than in the West for several reasons: the unavailability and (often) high cost of medical care, which causes people to wait until their medical needs are acute; malnutrition, which often necessitates transfusions; lack of prenatal care; and a high incidence of near-fatal vehicle accidents. Because of these factors, people in developing countries are more likely to receive transfusions than people living in Western countries. And in many of these same parts of Africa, the Caribbean, and Latin America, blood for transfusion is far more likely to be infected with HIV than it is in the West. Widespread HIV screening is uncommon outside the largest cities in Pattern 1 and 3 countries, yet it is primarily outside the largest cities that untreated malnutrition, acute diseases, pregnancies, and vehicle accidents are most likely to result in transfusions. Only massive international cooperation can resolve this and similar prevention problems.

Treating the Have-nots

When we move beyond prevention to treatment issues, the world is even more dramatically divided between the haves and the have-nots. To America's shame, we harbor more than our share of Third World treatment practices, thanks to our structural impoverishment of entire classes of people: the urban poor, runaway adolescents, those made homeless by drugs and diseases. The haves of the U.S. (those with private health insurance, particularly insurance that pays for drugs) and other Western countries have access to whatever treatments for HIV infection, AIDS cancers, and opportunistic infections our governments and national health services make available. The have-nots of the U.S. (people lacking private health insurance or having insurance that does not cover expensive drugs like AZT, as well as many people at the mercy of their state's Medicaid program) and Third World countries have few treatments available to them. They are either too expensive, too difficult to obtain, or too untested to be safe. In effect, entire populations of young adults are being written off because of individual nations' lack of resources or the diversion of resources to other uses (in the case of the U.S., to our military and to interest on the national debt). Particularly in nations with crushing debts and low production for domestic consumption, losses in productivity due to HIV/AIDS threaten to disrupt or substantially weaken entire economies. Several contributions to *AIDS: Profile of an Epidemic* and *The Global Impact* address this problem in detail.

In 1988, the (London) Global Impact of AIDS Conference gathered together the ministers of health of 148 countries to discuss AIDS prevention. The meeting resulted in a number of general and specific resolutions, several of which are addressed in the books under review. Significantly, the U.S. government opposes several of the World Health Organization's positions. WHO opposes mandatory testing in prisons (the U.S. federal prison system does it) and affirms the need for antidiscrimination statutes for HIV-infected people and people with AIDS (Presidents Reagan and Bush have ignored the Presidential Commission on the HIV Epidemic's recommendations for such statutes). The WHO resolutions

urge the media to fulfill their important social responsibility to provide factual *and balanced* information to the general public on AIDS and on ways of preventing its spread [my emphasis].

U.S. electronic media, thanks to the Reagan administration's appointment of now-retiring Federal Communications Commission chairperson Dennis Patrick, no longer have to maintain even *the pretense* of balance in broadcasting. (Patrick, in fact, cited abolition of the Fairness Doctrine as his greatest accomplishment in office.)

WHO supports unimpeded international travel for those infected with HIV and those with AIDS. The U.S. Immigration and Naturalization Service has already prevented the immigration or naturalization of significant numbers of resident aliens on the grounds of an infection they were most likely to have contracted here. Now it is extending its reach to include international travelers.

Such federally pursued practices bode ill for international cooperation and make it unlikely that San Francisco can remain the site of the 1990 Sixth International Conference on AIDS. International health officials are already calling for all AIDS conferences in the U.S. to be canceled in favor of sites in countries with less draconian and isolationist policies.

The books under review are important, not only to policy planners and health and social-service administrators but to all informed citizens. Their perspectives, however, are largely those of government officials. The news from below is often decidedly different. Hence, their most immediate use will be in comparing our own government's response to the epidemic with the record of other nations.

The U.S. record has been decidedly mixed. After a slow start, U.S. federal research programs to identify and isolate HIV are well funded, if often poorly administered. The American blood-banking industry — which despite its "voluntary" image *is* a profit-making industry — was slow in safeguarding the U.S. blood supply. The federal government has treated the industry in a *laissez faire* manner, and only the threat of extensive litigation forced blood banks into rigorous HIV screening. The federal government has spent very little on public education about AIDS and has consistently supported local and state efforts to stifle blunt discussions of transmission risks when those discussions involve the use of public monies. Moreover, the first public monies for a nationwide, coordinated preventive campaign were not appropriated until 1986. Nor was funding initiated or supported by the White House, which sought instead to cut the appropriations made by Congress.

In most respects, in fact, our record is far worse than those of comparably developed countries (Canada, Sweden, the U.K., Denmark, the Netherlands). Given our immensely greater resources, this is utterly contemptible. For the committed American reader, then, one of the chief benefits of reading about other nations' responses to this epidemic should be righteous anger — at our government's reluctance to extend the benefits of assured health insurance, accurate and timely prevention information, and the protection of individual rights to all its citizens, and at its failure to comply with internationally agreed-upon policies and practices affecting travel and migration. But anger can only begin with knowledge. Thankfully, that is on offer here.

The Last Committee on Sexuality (Ever)

February 18, 1991

John Fortunato

John Fortunato has been a psychotherapist for fourteen years and directs studies at an Episcopal diocesan agency training health care chaplains. He is the author of Embracing the Exile: Healing Journeys of Gay Christians *and* AIDS: The Spiritual Dilemma.

AFTER A GOOD DEAL of prayerful reflection and counsel from friends and colleagues, I have, as a gay Episcopalian, decided to withdraw from my diocese's Committee on Sexuality. In fact, I have finished with all such committees.

My tolerance for debating whether I am sinful or sick by virtue of being homosexual has, after sixteen years before the mast, reached nil. My intolerance is the result of an intentional, uphill journey toward self-acceptance, a purging of the internalized self-hate that all gay and lesbian people ingest at the hands of a hostile society.

It is rather like an allergy. A single sting of homophobia, and I swell. I suppose I hold the unrealistic belief that gay and lesbian children of God deserve to live in a wasp-free environment.

In any event, even though this last-in-an-unending series of sexuality committees (which inexorably become homosexuality committees) was clear that it was not to come up with a definitive statement on sexuality, it did ask us to "respectfully hear one another." In addition, to encourage "open-minded dialogue" in the diocese, it asked that we invite any who wanted to speak with us to come and have their say.

More, the bishop appointed to the committee someone who was supposed to help us maintain "balance."

I scanned several of his articles on sexuality. He was, among other things, an articulate and rigorous homophobe. While he did not make the first meeting of the committee, I could not imagine respectfully listening to him. Nor could I imagine listening "open-mindedly" to the couched or flagrant antigay sentiment that gallops through the diocese. The more I thought about these scenarios, the more I realized I did not want to do this to myself.

I have two objections to being asked to put myself in this position. The first is that no self-respecting gay man or lesbian should have to listen to his or her ontology debated ever again, and the church should be the last institution to sponsor such a forum.

Imagine, if you will, asking black clergy to sit on a "Committee on Race" and listen open-mindedly to a discussion of whether or not black people are by nature intellectually inferior to white people (discussions that have not been unknown in South Africa). No one with a conscience would ask a black person to sit through that, and no self-respecting black person would agree to do it. Or again, imagine asking Desmond Tutu to sit with Pieter Botha and engage in a "balanced" dialogue about the pros and cons of apartheid.

The appropriate response to injustice is outrage and protest — not polite dialogue. But I am even past the point of protest, and that brings me to my second objection.

The Kingdom Coming

I simply cannot be bothered with these endeavors. If the church needs to continue its "tempest in a tabernacle" about sexuality for another 150 years, so be it. But I have no energy for it.

Curiously, at a time when people are becoming increasingly tolerant of varied expressions of sexuality, only the church still clings tenaciously to a sex-negative worldview stemming from its dogged commitment to docetism. Let it live with its heresy — and obsess over it if it must.

Myself, I take seriously my baptismal call to be faithful in kingdom making. Sadly, the church is one of the last places I can find companionship on this mission lately. It is too busy consuming its gifts and graces — resources both human and financial — feeding ego mills and dysfunctional parishes and agencies, fostering "edifice complexes" and learning to "hate all the people our relatives hate." I am bored with it. The kingdom is at hand.

So I shall continue to embroider at the institutional edges, ministering with dying crack babies and their ruined parents while rejoicing in my sexuality and the rest of God's phenomenal creation; suffering with my sisters and brothers as they die of AIDS and training others to minister to those who are ill; joining people who come to me for psychotherapy in the abysses of their souls as we try to heal unbearable brokenness.

And in the meantime, the church has my full permission to continue debating whether I am sinful or sick, worthy of being ordained or even to sit in the pew.

And when at some point the Frozen Few glance around and note that the pews are alarmingly empty, those deemed worthy to minister to them might convince them to break just one precious stained glass window and look out and see the kingdom coming. They may be surprised to recognize the ushers. They will be soup kitchen hands and street workers, nurses and housekeepers, therapists and social workers. With them will be many other good folks (both gay and straight) who have mostly left the church and stopped judging people because they are too busy being Christ for them.

Part 6

The Life of the Churches

In the U.S., in the world, the last twenty-five years have been extraordinary times for the churches. Vatican II produced a much different Roman Catholic church; liberation theology in particular led to a dramatic increase in grassroots biblically based activity.

Black churches in the 1960s provided the essential energy for the civil rights movement and continue to play a key role in the African-American community. Evangelical and Pentecostal churches exploded numerically, especially in the U.S. and Latin America, and also became more politically involved.

Women everywhere began to play more central roles. For example, from eleven "validly but irregularly ordained" Episcopal women in 1974, by 1991 the Episcopal church had ordained almost two thousand women.

The mainline church tradition from which this journal emerged has struggled with declining numbers and declining influence. One illustration: Robert Spike, who headed the National Council of Churches Commission on Religion and Race, deeply involved in the civil rights movement, helped draft President Lyndon Johnson's famous "we shall overcome" speech just before passage of a key civil rights bill in 1965. During his presidency Ronald Reagan scarcely saw mainline religious leaders, let alone listen to what they had to say. (The NCC itself had almost two hundred program staff in 1965; now it has fewer than fifty.) Neo-conservatives and right-wing groups attacked the liberal churches through the media in often scurrilous tones.

In fact, as Larry Rasmussen says earlier in this book, Christianity has shifted in recent decades from the religion of the rich to the faith of the poor, and "the vitality of Christian faith has passed from the European and North American world to peoples in Africa, Latin America, and Asia,

*to the women's movement most everywhere, and to the communities in
our own midst who are most in touch with these."*

*As the articles in this section suggest these new realities — and the
pluralism they imply — need first to be recognized, and then accepted
as opportunities — however discomforting or confusing — to move to a
richer, fuller understanding of the Christian expression in the lives of
God's people around the world.*

The King's Chapel and the King's Court

August 4, 1969

Reinhold Niebuhr

Reinhold Niebuhr, C & C's founder, had perhaps the greatest impact on a secular audience
of any U.S. theologian and ethicist in this century. This article, which he wrote not long
before his death in 1971, ran on the front page of newspapers across the country.

THE FOUNDING FATHERS ordained in the first article of the Bill of
Rights that "Congress shall pass no laws respecting the establishment
of religion or the suppression thereof." This constitutional disestab-
lishment of all churches embodied the wisdom of Roger Williams
and Thomas Jefferson — the one from his experience with the Mass-
achusetts theocracy and the other from his experience with the less
dangerous Anglican establishment in Virginia — which knew that
a combination of religious sanctity and political power represents a
heady mixture for status quo conservatism.

What Jefferson defined, rather extravagantly, as "the absolute wall
of separation between church and state" has been a creative but also
dangerous characteristic of our national culture. It solved two problems: (1) it prevented the conservative bent of established religion
from defending any status quo uncritically, and (2) it made our high
degree of religious pluralism compatible with our national unity. By
implication it encouraged the prophetic radical aspect of religious life,
which insisted on criticizing any defective and unjust social order. It
brought to bear a higher judgment, as did the prophet Amos, who
spoke of the "judges" and "rulers of Israel" who "trample upon the
needy, and bring the poor of the land to an end..." (Amos 8:4).

As with most prophets, Amos was particularly critical of the comfortable classes. He warned: "Woe to those who lie on beds of ivory,
and stretch themselves on their couches, and eat lambs from the flock,
... who sing idle songs to the sound of the harp..." (Amos 6:4–5). It

is significant that Amaziah, a court priest of Amos's time, also saw the contrast between critical and conforming types of religion. However, he preferred the conventional conforming faith for the king's court; and, as the king's chaplain, he feared and abhorred Amos's critical radicalism.

Then Amaziah, the priest of Bethel, sent to Jeroboam, King of Israel, saying: "Amos hath conspired against thee in the midst of the house of Israel: the land is not able to bear all his words. For thus Amos saith: 'Jeroboam shall die by the sword, and Israel shall surely be led away captive out of their own land.'" Also Amaziah said unto Amos: "O thou seer, go, flee thee away into the land of Judah, and there eat bread, and prophesy there. But prophesy not again any more at Bethel: for it is the king's chapel, and it is the king's court" (Amos 7:10–13).

We do not know the architectural proportions of Bethel. But we do know that it is, metaphorically, the description of the East Room of the White House, which President Nixon has turned into a kind of sanctuary. By a curious combination of innocence and guile, he has circumvented the Bill of Rights' first article. Thus, he has established a conforming religion by semiofficially inviting representatives of all the disestablished religions, of whose moral criticism we were naturally so proud. Some bizarre aspects have developed from this new form of conformity in these weekly services. Most of this tamed religion seems even more extravagantly appreciative of official policy than any historic establishment feared by our Founding Fathers. A Jewish rabbi, forgetting Amos, declared:

I hope it is not presumptuous for me, in the presence of the president of the United States, to pray that future historians, looking back on our generation, may say that in a period of great trial and tribulations, the finger of God pointed to Richard Milhous Nixon, giving him the vision and wisdom to save the world and civilization, and opening the way for our country to realize the good that the century offered mankind.

It is wonderful what a simple White House invitation will do to dull the critical faculties, thereby confirming the fears of the Founding Fathers. The warnings of Amos are forgotten, and the chief current foreign policy problem of our day is bypassed. The apprehension of millions is evaded so that our ABM policy may escalate, rather than conciliate, the nuclear balance of terror.

When we consider the difference between the Old World's establishment of religion and our quiet unofficial establishment in the East Room, our great evangelist Billy Graham comes to mind. A domesticated and tailored leftover from the wild and woolly frontier evangelistic campaigns, Mr. Graham is a key figure in relating the established character of this ecumenical religion to the sectarian radicalism of our evangelical religion. The president and Mr. Graham have been intimate friends for two decades and have many convictions in common, not least of all the importance of religion.

Mr. Nixon told the press that he had established these services in order to further the cause of "religion," with particular regard to the youth of the nation. He did not specify that there would have to be a particular quality in that religion if it were to help them. For they are disenchanted with a culture that neglects human problems while priding itself on its two achievements of technical efficiency and affluence. The younger generation is too realistic and idealistic to be taken in by barbarism, even on the technological level.

Naturally, Mr. Graham was the first preacher in this modern version of the king's chapel and the king's court. He quoted with approval the president's inaugural sentiment that "all our problems are spiritual and must, therefore, have a spiritual solution." But here rises the essential question about our newly tamed establishment. Is religion per se really a source of solution for any deeply spiritual problem? Indeed, our cold war with the Russians, with whom we wrestle on the edge of the abyss of a nuclear catastrophe, must be solved spiritually, but by what specific political methods? Will our antiballistic defense system escalate or conciliate the cold war and the nuclear dilemma?

The Nixon-Graham doctrine of the relation of religion to public morality and policy, as revealed in the White House services, has two defects: (1) It regards all religion as virtuous in guaranteeing public justice. It seems indifferent to the radical distinction between conventional religion — which throws the aura of sanctity on contemporary public policy, whether morally inferior or outrageously unjust — and radical religious protest — which subjects all historical reality (including economic, social and radical injustice) to the "word of the Lord," i.e., absolute standards of justice. It was this type of complacent conformity that the Founding Fathers feared and sought to eliminate in the First Amendment.

(2) The Nixon-Graham doctrine assumes that a religious change of heart, such as occurs in an individual conversion, would cure men of all sin. Billy Graham has a favorite text: "If any man be in Christ, he is a new creature." Graham applies this Pauline hope about conversion to the race problem and assures us that "If you live in Christ, you become color blind." The defect in this confidence in individual conversion is that it obscures the dual and social character of human selves and the individual and social character of their virtues and vices.

If we consult Amos as our classical type of radical nonconformist religion, we find that he, like his contemporary Isaiah, was critical of all religion that was not creative in seeking a just social policy. Their words provide a sharp contrast with the East Room's current quasi-conformity. Thus Amos declared:

I hate, I despise your feasts, and I take no delight in your solemn assemblies. . . . Take away from me the noise of your songs; to the melody of your harps I will not listen. But let justice roll down like waters, and righteousness like an everflowing stream (Amos 5:21, 23–4).

Amos' last phrase was a favorite text of the late Martin Luther King. He used it in his "I Have a Dream" speech to thousands at the March on Washington. It is unfortunate that he was murdered before he could be invited to that famous ecumenical congregation in the White House. But on second thought, the question arises: would he have been invited? Perhaps the FBI, which spied on him, had the same opinion of him as Amaziah had of Amos. Established religion, with or without legal sanction, is always chary of criticism, especially if it is relevant to public policy. Thus J. Edgar Hoover and Amaziah are seen as quaintly different versions of the same vocation — high priests in the cult of complacency and self-sufficiency.

Perhaps those who accept invitations to preach in the White House should reflect on this, for they stand in danger of joining the same company.

Old Wine, New Bottles:
The Institute on Religion and Democracy

March 21, 1983

Leon Howell

Leon Howell is editor of Christianity and Crisis.

THE CAMERA ZOOMED IN on St. Mark's United Methodist Church in the east Texas town of Marshall. This, said Ben Wattenberg, the narrator of the public television documentary, is as close as one might come to a typical American town. Like the people here, "the polls show that the majority of Americans are moderate and traditionalists."

On this Sunday morning in Marshall the camera soon moved inside and showed the congregation (all white) at worship. Later, outside the church, Wattenberg interviewed the Rev. Ed Robb, who had preached that day in the church. The program was titled "Protestants Protest."

Wattenberg asked: "Well, exactly what are the national church officials doing at those upper levels that you and your parishioners would specifically disagree with?"

Robb answered, in part: "They support many questionable organizations. And many of them — they feel that the Marxist option is a valid option, in the Third World particularly. They would be very opposed to the traditional American foreign policy. . . . They would support the Marxist guerrillas in El Salvador, for instance."

The program was part of a series that ran in late 1981 called "Ben Wattenberg at Large." Like the controversial "60 Minutes" program, "The Gospel According to Whom?" aired in January of this year, it featured interviews with officials of the National and World Councils of Churches and sought to establish the existence of a major gap between their values and those of down-home church folk.

Both shows drew charges of unfairness from some viewers, but Wattenberg's had dimensions that only the best-informed in its audience could have known. Ed Robb, the sole "protesting Protestant" given a voice on the show, was introduced as a "Methodist evangelist," and viewers would have been hard put to conclude that he was anything but a local pastor agitated about the policies of his national church and the ecumenical movement.

In reality Robb has no congregation of his own, and the people of St. Mark's are not his "parishioners." He is a traveling preacher, head of the Ed Robb Evangelistic Association, and as a leader of the Good News movement has made something of a career of criticizing the national leadership of the United Methodist Church.

Even more relevant, Robb is a founder and chairman of the board of directors of the Institute on Religion and Democracy (IRD), an organization that says it exists "to revitalize our religious institutions by reaffirming the link between Christianity and democratic values." Claiming to have no political purposes of its own, the IRD to date has found affronts to democratic values exclusively in asserted ties between U.S. church bodies and allegedly "leftist" or "Marxist-Leninist" groupings.

There were other aspects of "Protestants Protest" that would have helped viewers to judge its aims, had they been disclosed:

— From its founding in 1980 until late in 1981, the IRD shared offices in Washington with the Coalition for a Democratic Majority (CDM), which is co-chaired by Wattenberg and Senator Daniel Patrick Moynihan (D-N.Y.). In the months before "Protestants Protest" was aired, Ed Robb had been a frequent visitor to the CDM-IRD suite.

— Penn Kemble, who served as producer for *Ben Wattenberg at Large*, is an IRD director, maintains his office in its headquarters, co-signs letters with Robb, and has more to do with IRD's day-today operations than anyone else. Until November 1982, when IRD received tax-free status, it was legally a project of Kemble's small "hip-pocket" (his words) Foundation for Democratic Education; gifts meant for IRD were accepted on its behalf by the foundation. Kemble's politics are close to Wattenberg's and Moynihan's: From 1972 to 1976 he was director of the Coalition for a Democratic Majority, created in 1972 by such rightward-drifting neoconservatives and conservatives as Senator Henry Jackson, Michael Novak, Jeane Kirkpatrick, and others intent on recapturing the Democratic party from the McGovern liberals.

A Question of Identity

The point is, of course, that on a program that had a great deal to say about political alliances on the left, nothing was said about the close ties between host and producer of the show, both intensely political beings, and its star, who came on as an indignant small-town cleric intent only on saving the gospel from leftist politicization. Despite doubts about journalistic integrity that such reticence might raise, and despite or because of its own invisibility on the program, IRD was and remains pleased by its content; it has made copies to rent for showing by local groups. And this, along with other things, raises the question: Is the IRD what it says it is?

The stated purposes are clear enough. IRD's self-defining basic statement, "Christianity and Democracy," puts it like this:

We are keenly aware that not all Christians share our understanding of democracy and America's role in the world. Especially is this true of some leadership circles in the churches, and most especially of many who are professionally involved in shaping the social witness of the churches. It is our purpose to illuminate the relationship between Christian faith and democratic governance. It is also our purpose to propose policies and programs in the churches which ignore or deny that relationship.... We will speak privately when possible, publicly when necessary. We do not seek controversy, but we will not shrink from controversy. Basic questions about the meaning of freedom, of peace and of justice must be examined anew. In these ways we would contribute to renewing the social witness of the churches.

Ed Robb spoke more bluntly in an interview with me: "It seems to me [that] a clear policy [exists] in the NCC and the WCC to side with the radical left, and in the Third World, in particular, to side with the revolutionary Marxist-Leninist left."

The IRD office is in the basement of the Solar Building on Connecticut Avenue three blocks from the White House. Tucked away inside a larger warren of disparate offices, it is a beehive of activity. The phones ring often. Each month IRD issues a newsletter, *Religion and Democracy*, with a lead article highlighting some concern about the churches' activity: hunger programs, the nuclear freeze, Nicaragua, Poland. The screens of word processors are filled with materials and mailing lists that contain about 2,500 names. Visitors come often. IRD held a regional conference in Winston-Salem last year and plans three for this year in Seattle, Dallas, and Washington. Three secretaries, sometimes four, appear busy.

Kerry Ptacek does the research. Dianne Knippers handles journalism and membership (she came from the editorial staff of the *Good News* magazines in Wilmore, Kentucky; Jim Robb, the son of Ed, left Washington to go to *Good News*). Maria Thomas is the administrator, and Penn Kemble oversees the daily activity. Ed Robb comes in from Texas frequently, and others — like David Jessup, who works two blocks away at the AFL-CIO offices, and Michael Novak, whose office is a few blocks further away at the American Enterprise Institute — drop in frequently.

Membership had been growing slowly but jumped to about one thousand in recent months. The annual membership fee is $25. Ed Robb says, "We are just now going into mass mailings with the *Reader's Digest* article and that kind of thing. We should expand rather rapidly. Until now our profile had not been very high."

I heard the story of IRD's founding in a two-hour interview with the three most active members of its board of directors: Ed Robb, Penn Kemble, and David Jessup. IRD emerged, they recounted, from the 1980 General Conference of the United Methodist Church (UMC), where Robb, long-time champion of a strongly anticommunist campaign within the church, first met Jessup, who had recently joined the Marvin Memorial UMC in suburban Washington.

Robb recalls that "David was there with his preliminary study of the pro-Marxist funding pattern on the part of UMC agencies. The 'Jessup report,' as it came to be known, made quite an impact on the General Conference. I had never heard of David Jessup before, but I was impressed with his work. We found we had many common concerns. IRD really began to take shape at that time."

Robb soon visited Jessup in Washington, and people like Michael Novak helped the two meet others with a common perspective. They linked up with Kemble, recruited Lutheran theologian Richard Neuhaus, added Catholics like Fr. James Schall of Georgetown University and George Weigel of the World Without War Council in Seattle, mixed in several other *Good News* members such as Paul Morrell and Ira Gallaway, and formed IRD.

What Are You For?

The first of IRD's twin purposes, as set forth in "Christianity and Democracy" — "to illuminate the relationship between Christian faith and democratic governance" — gave it a sanctum from which to pursue the second: "to oppose policies and programs in the churches which ignore or deny that relationship." The energy that has gone into IRD's program to date has not cast much, if any, light on how — in practical terms — Christian respect for freedom is to be realized in the political order. That would require accepting the risk of offering affirmative proposals dealing with complex relationships between churches and governments in murkily ambiguous situations all over the world. Instead the emphasis has fallen on attacking the real and alleged errors of others, a relatively soft self-assignment....

Dialogue. At various points in our interview, Kemble, Robb, and Jessup all expressed disappointment over their perceptions that denominational and ecumenical leaders have been reacting angrily and defensively to IRD criticism rather than entering into "constructive dialogue."

"They just cannot conceive that those who come from the mainstream can be critical," Robb said. "Though people may disagree with our philosophy, I hope they will recognize our basic integrity."

"They have treated us as if we were outside the bounds of civil discourse," said Kemble. "That has naturally made us feel that the only way to make our case is to get it out through the media."

But in the eyes of some, IRD's use of the media has not been all that constructive. On a radio show in Washington February 17, right-wing columnist Pat Buchanan asked Richard Neuhaus how one could expect to enter into dialogue with people after accusing them of being "in bed with guerrillas and Communists." Neuhaus's main invitation to dialogue on "The Gospel According to Whom?" was a broad-brush assertion that church leaders are "telling lies."

But IRD has indeed excelled in getting noticed by the media. Apart from the *Reader's Digest* and "60 Minutes" triumphs, it garnered generous space in the *Washington Post.* Charles Austin, religion writer for the *New York Times,* has done at least four stories on the IRD, each time leading off with the same or similar IRD charges and following up with defensive-sounding responses from NCC and WCC officials. The headline over the first article (November 15, 1981) read: "New Church Group Assails Support of Left." On February 15 of this year — fifteen months later — the headline was "New Clergy Group Assails Church Aid to Leftists." In between, on November 3, 1982, another Austin story was titled: "National Church Council Faces New Type of Critic." For advocacy groups, getting noticed even once by the *Times* is enough to gain visibility, since other news media often follow its lead. For IRD, getting essentially the same news about its doings reported four times in The Newspaper of Record was to be certified as important.

Two days after the "60 Minutes" program, IRD called a press conference at which Robb and Neuhaus appeared. The program was "fair and I appreciate what it has done," said Robb. The IRD switchboard had lit up with calls from all over America. "Significant churches said, 'We are going to put money in escrow until we have an accounting of the charges made in the *Reader's Digest* article and the "60 Minutes" program, and the other issues IRD is lifting up.'"

With some qualifications about the *Digest*'s limited space and the style of "60 Minutes," Neuhaus, Novak, Kemble, and Jessup have all affirmed both presentations of the issues as basically accurate and fair.

Dissent within the Ranks

...Prof. Richard Lovelace of Gordon-Conwell Theological Seminary is a member of IRD's advisory board and was co-signer of the letter of invitation to the workshop. He told me that, far from approving the "60 Minutes" show, he had written a letter to CBS demanding that it present another side of the story.

Was he disturbed about IRD's close involvement with the two media presentations? "The problem, as nearly as I can tell, is that IRD — a lot of it — is unconscious that it has been used in two hatchet jobs."

What about the uncritical approval expressed by IRD spokespersons for the "hatchet jobs"?

That was a very stupid thing to do, although my good friend Ed Robb did it. Because every evangelical with whom I have been in touch says that the credibility of the WCC has gone up with them, the credibility of "60 Minutes" has gone down, and the credibility of IRD is down the drain. IRD has a great public relations problem now, because the churches have been hit with a large meteorite of which IRD is a small but important globule....

What Is Victory?

What does the IRD want? ...Most of the IRD's charges against the NCC and the WCC have been recycled many times, and have been answered as often — if not succinctly, then specifically enough to give most church people what they regard as an adequate chance to form their own judgment. Nobody at IRD has yet disproved, or even tried to disprove, the WCC's contention that it is impossible to contribute to its most controversial program, the "Special Fund" of the Programme to Combat Racism, without knowing what the money will be used for. For years, Robb has tried in vain to use the elaborately democratic processes of his United Methodist Church to get the church to adopt his anticommunist priorities. What do he and his IRD colleagues hope to accomplish?

At the exultant news conference following the "60 Minutes" show, Robb repeated a favorite slogan: "We don't want out, we want in." By that, he told me later, he means that he wants the IRD's viewpoint to get a real hearing in the two councils and the mainline churches. "We want pluralism in the church."

And if Robb's view of pluralism does not prevail? He said he was confident that "we are going to see some meaningful response." "The vast majority of persons within the mainline churches appreciate the position of the IRD. We speak for them more than the NCC speaks for its constituency. We will be open to new strategies if this present one does not work out."

One possible strategy, mentioned by Neuhaus at the same news conference, was the proposal by David Preus of the American Lutheran Church for a more inclusive ecumenical institution that would include Roman Catholics, evangelicals, Southern Baptists, and Lutheran entities not now represented in the NCC. "The NCC," he added, "while it is called 'mainline' numerically is not the mainline even of American Protestantism."

Asked whether he had a deadline, Robb replied, "No, not at this point."

Though Robb, Preus, and Neuhaus are hardly the only American Christians who talk of a broader ecumenical organization, it is fair to suggest, on the basis of IRD's makeup, funding, and tactics to date, that defense of theological orthodoxy and promotion of ecclesiastical togetherness are not its first concerns:

• Most of the money that sustains IRD comes from sources that have not previously shown interest in supporting the cause of ecumenism, or anything else relating to religion; they do give money, in large bundles, to strongly conservative *political* causes.

(IRD received 89 percent of its total income for the first twenty-six months of its life from six conservative foundations. The bulk came from three that often work in concert to fund neoconservative political thought: Sarah Scaife Foundation [$300,000], Smith Richardson Foundation [$140,000], and John M. Olin foundation [$20,000].)

• Michael Novak and Richard Neuhaus have credentials for debating the implications of Christian social witness. Ed Robb gives dynamism to the institute and in turn gains prestige from it — partly through association with Novak, Neuhaus, and other intellectuals on its letterhead, and in large measure from the national publicity conferred on him by Ben Wattenberg, the *Times*, and "60 Minutes."

Of the other two who, with Robb, constitute the central core of the operation, Penn Kemble does not attend church and David Jessup has only a brief record of church activity. Kemble and Jessup are long-time political organizers, having moved together from Students for a Democratic Society through the Young People's Socialist League to the Social Democrats/USA, a fervently anticommunist grouping that is small in numbers but rich in talent and in connections to cold-warrior elements of the Democratic party and the AFL-CIO. Two other members of the IRD board are also Social Democrats, Mary Temple and Paul Seabury.

The stance of the SD/USA is, of course, well within the American political mainstream. The question is how Jessup and Kemble, given their background and primary interests, can put themselves forward as qualified to provide expert guidance, à la *Consumer Reports*, on the churches' vast array of involvements in social action. And the mystery is why the media have not pressed that question, but have taken them and the IRD at face value.

• IRD's tactics have been examined in detail elsewhere, but a new example is provided by its latest publication, "A Time for Answers," an effort to demonstrate the churches' tilt toward the left — or, in IRD's favored language, toward Marxism-Leninism — on foreign policy issues. In its preface the booklet says the IRD does not want to "discredit these institutions" (the NCC, the WCC, and the mainline churches), and adds that "we take no pleasure in bringing these problems to light." Much of the evidence for the existence of the problems has to do with the Cuba Resource Center, an organization begun in 1970 to reduce U.S.-Cuba hostility, in part by putting U.S. churches into direct contact with churches in Cuba. But the center has received no church support since 1979 and exists now only in skeleton form. Asked about this, Kemble said the IRD was going ahead with "A Time for Answers" because "we are not so much concerned with the flow of money at a particular time as we are the philosophy of it. The views espoused then are still very much with us."

And so they are. For example, one "view" repeatedly cited in the booklet as proof of Marxist-Leninist sympathies is the judgment that the U.S. ought to abandon its trade and travel embargo against Cuba. That's an opinion shared by a good many Americans in the center and on the right of the political spectrum — including (a) entrepreneurs and investors who would like to get a crack at business opportunities now being developed by Canadian and other interests, and (b) mainstream liberals who think the embargo diminishes any hope of reducing the strength of Cuban ties with the Soviet Union.

So what is the Institute on Religion and Democracy? After wending his way, step by step, through its opening declaration of purposes, Peter Steinfels concluded (*C & C*, March 29, 1982):

A careful examination of "Christianity and Democracy" uncovers nothing to contradict the original suspicions raised by the founding of IRD: that it was a conservative-neoconservative alliance intended to advance a distinct political agenda while claiming only a broad Christian concern.

The record the IRD has written by its activities in subsequent months confirms that finding, in spades. Something could be added now to characterize the methods the IRD prefers for promoting its ends. But that's a separate task. For the purposes of this report, it's enough to mention that, given its ample funding, the talents of its key people, and its winning ways with the media, the IRD seems likely to be with us for a long time.

Which lends interest to the huge sign outside the building where the institute is housed: "America's Best Contacts." Actually, it reads in full: "America's Best Contacts and Eyeglasses." But you get the point.

Religion and American Politics: Beyond the Veil

April 29, 1985

Gayraud Wilmore

Gayraud Wilmore, a contributing editor, recently retired as professor of church history at the Interdenominational Theological Center in Atlanta.

IN THE WRITINGS of W. E. B. Du Bois there is a recurring theme: the Veil of color that hangs between black existence and American reality. In some places Du Bois says that the world we blacks look out on is "beyond the Veil." In other contexts he says that our own world is "within the Veil." I never understood the full meaning of this metaphor until I reflected back on an experience that for many years I tried to blot out of my memory.

It happened when I was in the army during World War II, traveling by train through the South from Shreveport, La., to Washington, D.C. As we sped through the night, I sauntered back to the dining car to get something to eat. It was full of white people who gawked, forks poised between mouth and plate. I must have looked sharp in my freshly pressed uniform and T/5 stripes. A stony-faced black waiter ushered me to a table for one. He then reached up and pulled a curtain completely around me and my table so that I suddenly found myself seated in a little world all my own, behind the Veil of a Jim Crow curtain.

Beyond that curtain I could hear the chatter of the voices of my fellow passengers and the clatter of their glasses and silverware. But I remember something else. Through the slightly opaque scrim that separated us I could make out the natural gestures and postures of the white people without the distraction of accidental and consequential detail. In other words, I saw what really mattered — the essential aspect of the reality beyond that curtain. And when I looked the other way, out of the window at my side, with the curtain as a barrier to the glare of the dining car lights, I could see the dark world outside through which our train was moving — instead of my own reflection.

We've heard a lot lately about religion and politics in America. What I am suggesting is that blacks bring to this discussion what is, perhaps, a unique perspective. It may be described as the privileged disprivilege of an outsider, a kind of perception that both deforms and informs our vision as we stand in the shadows, out of the harsh and glaring reality of the American experience — within the Veil.

What do we see? Much of the same world that everyone else sees, but from a different perspective. Most of us vote either Democratic or Republican, like most Americans. But I think we see realities about American politics that others may miss. One example must suffice.

For most of our lives we have heard white Christians say that "religion and politics don't mix." And yet from where we sit they seem to mix very well. American religion and American politics seem to make quite comfortable bedfellows even though they like to pretend that they're not really in the same bed. We have found that when that game is being played somebody is going to get screwed and we are usually that somebody. Why? Because both religion and politics in this country are programmed to maintain the ascendancy of white over black, the middle classes over the underclass, males of all colors over females of all colors.

The institutional church has seemed exceedingly unreliable when it comes to trying to understand the relationship between religion and politics in the U.S. During the nineteenth century several major denominations protested that because churches had no business mixing religion with affairs of state they could not decently undertake political agitation against slavery. But many churches changed their minds when they saw a profitable economic and political union going down the drain. Similarly, the same churchpeople who did not want to mix religion and politics over the question of slavery joined forces to organize the Anti-Saloon League under strong church sponsorship and succeeded in getting the Eighteenth Amendment ratified in 1920 — no mean political trick for apolitical churches. In the South at the turn of the century, many Holiness Christians were politicized within the Ku Klux Klan. Charles Fox Parham praised the Klan for its "fine work in upholding the American way of life." Other conservative Christians who eschewed partisan politics when the labor unions and the civil rights movement tried to get their churches to cooperate had no problem mixing religion and politics in the postwar Christian Anti-

Communist Crusade and, more recently, the mobilization of the Moral Majority behind the election of Ronald Reagan.

Getting Hands Dirty

I don't want to oversimplify complex issues, but from where we stand it appears that many white churches are inconsistent about when they may or may not soil their hands in the dirty linen of politics. When a fair economic wind is blowing and politicians are preserving white supremacy, controlling the levers of social power and guaranteeing material security for the middle and upper classes, religion and politics are presumed incompatible and the walls go up between church and state. But when Anglo hegemony is threatened by external forces like communism, or by marginated minorities within the society, like blacks, atheists, and women, then it becomes a holy cause to send church lobbies to Washington and march church members to the polls to vote "for the sake of our Lord and Savior, Jesus Christ." One cannot help being suspicious about the theological seriousness of such self-serving inconsistency.

Now to be sure, the black churches have their own problems. It may be that because they lack squeamishness about political activity (with some notable exceptions, like the former Colored Methodist Episcopal church) some of them have been shamefully used by big city machines. But at least they have never pretended that politics could get along without religion. They have rather assumed that it was their moral responsibility to marshal the votes that would force the powers that be to loose the bonds of the victims of poverty, discrimination, and human injustice of every kind.

Nor have black churches expressed the kind of panic recently observed when white liberal Christians, like Walter Mondale, met ebullient conservative Christians, like Jerry Falwell, going to the polls to take an opposing position on presumably religious grounds. Black folks, after years "behind the Veil," take such things in stride. When the 1984 presidential election returns were in and we realized that we had again backed the losing side, the general attitude on the street was: "So what else is new? The struggle continues." For many black churches the bottom line has been not so much winning or losing, but being faithful to what they are convinced is the "right thing to do."

As a matter of fact, most black churches probably have more in common with the white Christian right than some of us like to admit. But on fairness and justice issues they are usually on the side of those who expect government to take greater responsibility for those who hurt the most in our society. If the white Evangelicals will now open themselves to the spirit of Jesus in using their new political power to minister to the poor and oppressed, blacks will be the first to welcome them. But if not, Brother Falwell and his cohorts had better be prepared for a fight.

Perhaps the major difference between the white Christian right and the mainline black churches with respect to religious attitudes that influence political choices is what may be called the ambivalence of black Christians about what white conservatives like to call "the traditional values of American life," or "the values of our Christian culture," or "bringing America back to God." Such slogans ring false to people for whom religion, for all its exuberance, is something poor, sinful human beings find comfort in at the foggy bottom of life — where judges deal and preachers steal, presidents tell lies and legislators play shady games behind oak-paneled doors. Somehow black folks have always believed that honest religion has to have a strong stomach for the nitty-gritty world we live in and help people survive by keeping their feet on the ground even when their souls may be rising to Pentecostal heights. For such down-to-earth religiosity the new Christian right slogans sound a bit too precious to be real, and just a mite too hypocritical. Beware of people who want to be more religious than God. Frederick Douglass wrote in 1845: "Were I to be again reduced to the chains of slavery, next to that enslavement, I should regard being the slave of a religious master the greatest calamity that could befall me. For of all slaveholders with whom I have ever met, religious slaveholders are the worst."

Black and Jew and America

In an article in *Soundings* (Winter 1970), Professor William H. Becker of Bucknell compares Jews and blacks in terms of their intense ambivalence that "derives from certain basic affinities within the life and thought of each community." We need to recall these affinities during this period of our estrangement. Becker argues that blacks and Jews share an ambivalence about the basic goodness of secular, democratic, and scientific America; about assimilating with this supposedly enlightened nation; about its Christianity and about the vocation of black or Jewish suffering for its ultimate redemption.

I think Becker is dead on target. When black theologians merge the thought of Martin Luther King, Jr., with that of Malcolm X, that is precisely what we get — a hardnosed realism about America as a den of thieves slightly moderated by a compassionate hope that by the power of God it might someday become better than it is. That is what I like to call "pragmatic spirituality." Malcolm and Martin were developing it together (although quite independently) — complementing one another like yin and yang; weaving a tapestry of tough love, a down-home but surprisingly sophisticated religion that is neither fundamentalist, evangelical, nor liberal, Protestant, Catholic, or Jewish. In a way that we have not yet begun to understand, it is Afro-American, deeply spiritual and unabashedly political.

What kind of politics is the consequence of this kind of religiosity? I want to suggest that it is something like what we saw in Jesse Jackson last year. Jackson's campaign was visionary without self-delusion, rhetorical without meaninglessness, conflictual but hanging loose, telling it like it is, risking defeat rather than selling a friend down the river for a principle, yet being willing to go down rather than to cave in on what seems "only the right thing to do" — and bouncing back to try it one more time. Underneath all the glamor and all the contradictions was the apparently inexhaustible patience of the black folk and their faith that God will make a way somehow for the poor and the downtrodden, that "God may not come when we want him to, but he's always on time," that all you have to do is trust God and, as Fannie Lou Hamer used to say, "keep on keeping on."

I think that the black politicians who were committed to Mondale during the primaries understood that this peculiar relationship between black religion and politics was what they were up against in the Jackson campaign. They held their peace as much as they could. We are not mad with them. They too were committed to bread-and-butter issues like jobs, housing, health care, better schools, majority rule in South Africa, and cutbacks in defense spending, but the way they read it one must finally work through white-dominated systems, and movement-oriented politics cannot produce in the 1980s. But that's not all that must be said.

Many of us who were disappointed with their weak support if not outright rejection of Jackson understood where they were coming from, and we have not yet abandoned them — not yet. But the handwriting is on the wall. Black churchpeople mistrust conventional party politics and cigar-smoking, back-slapping politicians. They also know that their preachers are not angels, but they have more confidence in them and in the church when it comes to accountability to the black community. Unless black office-holders make themselves equally accountable they will be thrown out of their jobs.

It is fair to ask, just what are the implications of all this black talk for American politics as a whole? That question is worth exploring at greater depth, but I believe that Jesse Jackson, fueled by the dynamic of the black and progressive white religious communities, has inserted a new element into American politics that will not soon be dissipated. At first glance it may seem too brash and 1960-ish to have an impact on post-civil-rights America. But under the banner of the Rainbow Coalition it can shake up a few local baronies and have an influence out of all proportion to its numerical strength.

For my part, I would welcome consideration of Jackson leading an

honest-to-goodness third party. Americans need another option today
that is more inclusive of those who are not satisfied merely to work
the system, but who want to change it. Three and a half million votes
for an amazingly few dollars spent is not to be scorned. And there are
many more people out there who are tired of the present stalemate.

There is still another contribution that Jackson's brand of religion
and politics has to make to American politics in general. It is an openness to and respect for people of color everywhere. I remember that
when I was in college the great Paul Robeson came to our campus
and said, "One day an African from the bush will come here and secure your liberation." Well, it may not turn out to be an African, and
she or he may not need to come here. It may be done from Central
America, from Asia, or from some obscure island in the Pacific. But I
firmly believe that in the economy of God, the Third World — suffering and bleeding while we glory in our power and prosperity — will
have its day. Desmond Tutu said recently, "When that day comes, we
will remember who were our friends."

Black Christians, Muslims, and Jews, with allies from a few other
ethnic groups, are more oriented to that possibility than are most
white Christians. We are more willing to work for it on the domestic front and to shape U.S. foreign policy around it. Rainbow politics
is, in a sense, the politics of a Third World people encapsulated in the
first world. We do not have to be reminded that we are a minority. We
know what it is like to live within the Veil, and we are prepared to
make the most of it. But we are not alone. We are not unaware of the
potential power of other submerged peoples in various parts of the
world and are sensitive to their present suffering. Because we believe
in the God of the oppressed we are willing to link our destiny with
theirs in the ongoing struggle for liberation and a new humanity.

The NCC in a New Time:
Finding a Place in the Culture

January 9, 1989

William McKinney

William McKinney is dean and professor of Religion and Society at Hartford Seminary in
Connecticut and co-author of the much-discussed American Mainline Religion.

THE INTERSECTION OF Claremont Avenue and Reinhold Niebuhr
Place (120th Street) on Manhattan's Morningside Heights has been in

the news lately. On the northeast corner, Union Theological Seminary is selling a dormitory to help cope with operating deficits. Across the street, on the northwest corner, the Riverside Church is looking for a senior minister and for ways to maintain its programs in the face of a severe money crunch. On the southwest corner, at 475 Riverside Drive the National Council of Churches is asking fundamental questions about its identity, mission, and structure.

The intersection of Claremont and Reinhold Niebuhr Place comes as close to being "sacred space" as liberal Christians have in North America, and what happens there is of more than passing interest to those of us who have looked to its institutions for leadership and guidance over the years.

One hears lots of explanations of "what went wrong" in the Union-Riverside-475 neighborhood: the arrogance of church bureaucrats, faculty orneriness, bad management, personality and ideological conflicts, too much affirmative action, too little support from essential constituencies. I suspect there's something in some of these interpretations (and very little in others!), but that all of them miss the mark.

The real significance of what's happening at the intersection of Claremont Avenue and Reinhold Niebuhr Place is in what it symbolizes about the place of a certain brand of Protestantism in the late twentieth century. I hope I'm wrong, but I suspect what's happening to Union, Riverside, and the National Council of Churches is going to be repeated in lots of theological seminaries, local churches, and denominational headquarters in the 1990s.

In his report to the October "Tarrytown Conference" called to explore options for the National Council of Churches, General Secretary Arie Brouwer observes that "one way to read the history — mostly failed history — of attempts to restructure the council is to read it as an attempt of the member churches to define their place together in the culture. Little wonder then that we have encountered so much difficulty or that now in this time of shifting places in the culture, the accumulated pressures have put us in crisis."

I think the council's controversial general secretary is correct on this point, and that any attempt to re-envision the council's identity, mission, and structure must begin with a tough-minded examination of the council's (and the council's constituent bodies') place in the culture. I'd go even further than Arie Brouwer goes. The future of the National Council of Churches, Riverside Church, Union Seminary, and their "old-line" Protestant partner institutions depends on their coming to grips with what Wade Clark Roof and I, in *American Mainline Religion*, have called their "postestablished" status.

Old-line, New Time

Inevitably, when I address a clergy or lay audience about the changing cultural place of old-line Protestantism someone argues that Protestantism was never really as "established" as Roof and I seem to imply. I've come to rely on a fairly simple device to make my point. "Tell me," I say, "what's the name of the local Catholic hospital?" In my town the answer is Saint Francis. "How about the Jewish hospital?" "Mount Sinai, of course." "And the Protestant hospital?" "Oh, yes, Hartford Hospital." "How about the social service agencies?" "... Catholic Family Services, Jewish Family Services, Child and Family Services": The Protestant identification is assumed.

Most of the institutions of old-line Protestantism came into being in a time when these groups' established status could be taken for granted. One suspects that when the *National Council of the Churches of Christ in the United States of America* came into being in the 1950s, few eyebrows were raised at what today seems an oddly presumptuous name. In the 1950s the name made sense, just as it made sense for the council to locate itself in New York City, the seat of the nation's established institutions. John D. Rockefeller was an obvious source of funds to help construct the council's new headquarters, and what more obvious choice in October 1958 to lay the cornerstone at 475 Riverside Drive for the "national home of the churches" than former Morningside Heights neighbor and president of the United States Dwight D. Eisenhower?

That's changed, of course, but we haven't caught up with the importance of the change and what it means for our institutions. Before announcing his candidacy, President-elect Bush didn't journey to 475 Riverside Drive or visit the presiding bishop of his own Episcopal church: He paid a courtesy call on a pastor in Lynchburg, Virginia. It's been awhile since a national news magazine has done a cover story on the leader of an old-line Protestant church, but we're not surprised to see Jesse Jackson or Pat Robertson on the cover of *Time*.

I'm not terribly worried about the institutions at the intersection of Claremont and Reinhold Niebuhr Place. They're going to survive. If Union Seminary can survive the reallocation of its faculty apartments, it will remain as good a place to study theology as we have in North America. Riverside Church will find a new senior minister, get over the pain that comes with down-sizing, and remain the church of choice for lots of us when we have a Sunday in New York. And the National Council of Churches will survive as well. Its name, shape, leadership, and program may change but it will continue in some form.

So what's the big deal? The big deal for me is whether the National Council of Churches and its partner institutions use the current moment to help the larger religious movement of which they are both part and symbol to obtain a reading on its future options.

And what are these options? One option, which I suspect will probably prevail for another round or two, will be to continue to tinker with structures and budgets in the hope that somehow things can be made right. We'll sell a dorm, consolidate a couple of offices, close a wing to save on heating costs, and long for leadership that will catalyze our hopes and aspirations — a Protestant Lee Iacocca who can turn things around and restore the old-line churches to their earlier position of dominance.

The other option, the one for which I fear we're not quite ready, is to ask what God is calling postestablishment churches to be about in a culture that no longer takes us as seriously as we take ourselves. If the leaders of the National Council of Churches can help us get some handles on that question and what it means for the way we shape our ministries, they'll have done something far more important than save an ecumenical agency.

The question at the intersection of Claremont and Reinhold Niebuhr Place needs to shift from how we restore these institutions to their prior glory, to what kind of institutions we need to define and carry out our mission in a new time.

Talking Ecumenism, Walking Assimilation

April 9, 1990

Samuel Solivan

Samuel Solivan is an ordained Assembly of God minister (Spanish District) and an associate professor of Christian Theology at Andover Newton Theological School in Newton, Mass.

Reforming Fundamentalism: Fuller Seminary and the New Evangelicalism, **by George Marsden (Grand Rapids: Wm. B. Eerdmans Publishing Co., 1987), 299pp.**

HOW DOES an institution founded on fundamentalism take the whole church seriously? How does it acknowledge — even incorporate — diversity, while remaining faithful to orthodoxy? These and related questions frame the background to George Marsden's history of Fuller Theological Seminary, the preeminent evangelical seminary, located in Pasadena, California.

Reforming Fundamentalism is not a conventional institutional history. Rather, Marsden uses Fuller as a kind of focal point for looking at the role played by the "new evangelicals" in shaping contemporary fundamentalism. The book covers the period from the founding of the seminary in 1947 to about 1968 — with the last two chapters devoted to a brief examination of important shifts since then.

Reforming Fundamentalism tells the story of the "new evangelicals," a small group of white middle-class conservative Calvinists, and their attempt to forge a distinct place for their worldview within world Protestantism. It highlights their personal commitment, ambition, sacrifice, even triumph, as well as their pursuit of modernity and inclusivism, albeit an exclusive inclusivism.

Fuller was founded as a multidenominational seminary with no formal denominational affiliation. Indeed, as a careful reading of Marsden makes clear, Fuller initially went to great lengths *not* to be identified as "ecumenical" — a term tied to modernist notions of the church.

From its inception, the school had been haunted by the legacy of fundamentalist separatism. The call to "come out from among them" could still be clearly heard, and to ignore it was to endanger the support of a large number of benefactors. This became evident in the seminary's decision to dismiss Bela Vassady, one of the founding members of the World Council of Churches, who had arrived on the faculty to teach biblical theology and ecumenics. In 1949 Vassady wrote a short essay, "Through Ecumenical Glasses," in which he praised ecumenism, arguing that U.S. Christians needed to develop a "one-church consciousness." Apparently he was unaware that evangelical and fundamentalist dispensationalist eschatology identified the oneness of the church with the reign of the anti-Christ.

Charles Fuller, founder of the seminary and president of its board of trustees, himself held to dispensationalism. The pressures the Vassady article brought to bear on him were so serious that he violated his policy of noninterference in faculty affairs. Through a series of maneuvers, including a binding directive that faculty avoid approval of the WCC, Vassady was dismissed.

Fundamentalist dispensationalist separatism, then, mitigated against an inclusive ecumenism; "multidenominationalism" was the closest to ecumenism fundamentalists and new evangelicals came in expressing their understanding of the "Church Apostolic and Catholic." (Later in the 1980s, the term "ecumenical" was reintroduced at Fuller.)

"Neoevangelicalism"

Nonetheless, Fuller did seek an inclusive evangelicalism, what it called "neoevangelicalism." It participated in some of the most important evangelical ecumenical activities of the past two decades, including the National Association of Evangelicals, the World Evangelical Fellowship, and the World Congress on Evangelism.

What informed Fuller's notion of ecumenicity was not federal union à la the WCC but mutual support in the task of world evangelism. Practicality required that those who thought alike, who believed in evangelism as the "saving of souls," would work together. But it did not require that they unite. The programmatic implications of this approach were manifest in the importance placed on the contributions and insights of people who represent differing evangelical viewpoints: people of color, and, supposedly, people with heterodox theologies such as Pentecostals and charismatics. Case in point: Hispanics and other under-represented minorities at Fuller.

The 1970s were a time of change for Fuller. William Pannell became the first black member of the board of directors and later the first black full-time member of the regular faculty. Black and, later, Hispanic and Asian studies programs were also instituted. By 1982 over two hundred members of under-represented minorities were enrolled at Fuller, and the seminary had a few Hispanics on the faculty and administration. This "white gentlemen's" seminary had opened its doors partially to persons of color, even to some who, on Calvinistic standards, were semi-pelagians. This opening, in turn, posed a different set of challenges to Fuller's understanding of multidenominationalism.

Fuller restated the nature and content of its "ecumenical experiment" in the "Mission beyond Mission" statement drafted in September 1983. The statement identified five imperatives: Go and make disciples; call the church of Christ to renewal; work for the moral health of society; seek peace and justice in the world; and uphold the truth of God's revelation. "Mission beyond Mission" concluded by asking for support and critical appraisal.

As a North American Hispanic Pentecostal Christian, I would like to engage with my brothers and sisters at Fuller in this critical reflection. I am concerned about the impact of Fuller's mission on the Hispanic community in particular and the church at large because I believe it has serious implications for the entire seminary enterprise in the United States.

Reforming Fundamentalism consistently raises the same question: Which evangelicals is Marsden writing about? The neoevangelicals of Fuller surely do not represent the community I and many other evangelicals of color belong to. Marsden has written the history of a small group of white, conservative Calvinist men, and it is through their theological grid that Fuller understands itself and the world. Fuller's "ecumenical experiment" is, then, a bold attempt to address its cultural and theological bondage, and the seminary should be applauded for its progress. At the same time, the Hispanics, blacks, and other "minorities" at Fuller are, at best, engaged on the periphery of Fuller's vision and preferences. We have been invited to the back room, not to the kitchen where we can join in preparing the soup.

Fuller's explicit imperative to make disciples is undermined by its implicitly defining disciples as those who are willing to conform to its worldview. Its assumptions continue to interfere with the inclusiveness it says it seeks. They may also interfere with its imperative to work for the moral and social well being of society — a task that requires the efforts of hosts of Christians working from a variety of perspectives.

"Signs and Wonders"

Perhaps the most concrete example of the tensions and contradictions at Fuller is to be found in the problems raised by the "signs and wonders" course the seminary offered and in how the seminary addressed them.

In 1982 the School of World Missions at Fuller offered a course entitled "The Miraculous and the Growth of the Church." It was designed to address, in both theory and practice, the place and function of miracles in the ministry of the church. In 1986 the course was suspended as a result of heated debate over two questions: Do the Scriptures warrant the belief that miracles are a recurring feature of the church's ministry today? Is a course on miracles appropriate in an academic setting?

Fuller's resounding "no" to both questions reflects its cultural and class perspective. In explaining its decision, Fuller listed the following sources as informing its understanding of evangelical commitment: the Protestant Reformation, the great work of God on the "continent" (*which* continent? Europe?), and the piety of John Wesley and of other evangelistic movements in Great Britain and the United States.

How do evangelicals outside this Anglo-American circle factor into the current definition of evangelicalism? How do race, ethnicity, gender, language, and class inform the content and the practice of ministry? Fuller's formal report on the controversy alludes to views that are "uncongenial to the evangelical tradition" and "not in accord with traditional evangelical theologies of ministry." It implies that non-Anglo-American perspectives "could subtly subvert our theological basis and rather than enrich our evangelical tradition, deflect us from it." If that is the case, exactly what should we make of the seminary's explicit statements of openness to multicultural and multiethnic contributions in its midst?

In the final analysis, the people who make up a given hermeneutical community determine the legitimacy of the questions raised and the answers given. Fuller's hermeneutical community has not really changed much since the 1940s. Yet the seminary seeks to draw students from an evangelical community that has *greatly changed*. The fastest growing evangelical group in the U.S., and for that matter the world, are Pentecostals, and a large percentage of them are poor people of color and from other cultures. They *believe* that signs and wonders are or should be a normal part of ministry, especially in the heathen kingdom of North America.

In explaining its reasons for suspending the signs and wonders class, Fuller said that as a multidenominational seminary it did not want to favor the viewpoint of any single tradition, in this case pentecostal-charismatics. Yet in most other areas of the curriculum, the school favors a narrow Reformed approach, in spite of the multidenominational, non-Reformed view of a large segment of its student body. This approach is suspect at best, inconsistent with claims of respecting and being informed by the various expressions of the evangelical church's diversity.

How does Fuller responsibly train Hispanic, black, and Asian students for ministry when the evangelical traditions that have formed them and to which they will return are sometimes at variance with the traditional brand of evangelicalism? How can an evangelical theology informed by a middle-class, Anglo-American perspective equip these saints for ministry in the urban centers of our nation?

Generic evangelicalism will not suffice, neither on biblical nor on theological grounds. The gospel takes most seriously our particularity of class, color, gender, and language. As on the day of Pentecost the Holy Spirit empowered the disciples to address diversity by speaking in tongues, so may Fuller be empowered to equip the saints in light of their particular needs and realities.

As the signs and wonders controversy makes clear, if Fuller is to fulfill its role as a seminary for the third millennium it must seek to embody in its inner circle a globalizing principle at both the national and the international level. The authenticity of its commitment to reach the *whole world* will be measured in direct proportion to its commitment to incorporate at all levels of its institutional life persons and perspectives who are representative of the multiethnic and multilingual evangelical community *already present in its midst*.

God and Neighbor

A first step in this transformation is to take seriously its own backyard as the place of engagement in missionary methodology and strategy, taking seriously North American Hispanics, Afro-Americans, Amer-Indians, Amer-Asians. This requires a conversion to one's neighbor that transcends allegiances to received theological tradition and cultural biases. The mission of the church can no longer continue to be a ministry of assimilation into the North American status quo. Rather, the churches' vocation is to call all people into a liberating relationship with God and their neighbor as modeled by Jesus the Christ. It is an invitation to those on the boundaries to inform and shape the center. It is the Galilee principle expressed by Mexican-American theologian Virgilio Elizondo: "What human beings reject, God chooses as his [sic] very own."

Fuller Seminary represents a great possibility for the church in the third millennium. Its grounding in the Scriptures, its christological center, its social awareness, its use of the social sciences as tools for mission — together with the unfolding of the Holy Spirit's power in signs and wonders — can well be the wholistic expression and incarnation of the faith that we so desperately need. But this kind of mission requires us to stop seeing each other as objects of evangelism, or converts to our ideologies. Instead, we must start seeing each other as persons we are called to love and respect.

At the same time, Fuller's experiment should raise questions for *all* seminaries that identify themselves as multidenominational or ecumenical. Can they in good conscience seek and receive students from nontraditional traditions, such as Pentecostals, yet deny the importance of their theological perspectives and contributions to the whole? Or are we faced once again with the contradiction between our talk and our walk, between orthodoxy and orthopraxis?

When History Is All We Have

September 24, 1990

Will Campbell

Will Campbell, a C & C columnist, has described himself as a Baptist preacher of the South, which is different from being a Southern Baptist preacher. Known as the sage of Mt. Juliet Tennessee, he is author of Brother to a Dragonfly *and* Forty Acres and a Goat, *among other books.*

THEY SAY THAT Baptists have always fought among themselves. And that there is no fight like a family fight. The latter is probably true. But the original Baptists, whether the Anabaptists of sixteenth-century Europe or the English Separatists of the seventeenth, were too busy struggling for physical survival to engage in internecine squabbles. However, on July 17 Baptists in Nashville, Tennessee, were fighting each other. With the force of arms.

I suppose I had no reason to be there. Probably had not even a right to be there, having deserted the steeples a long time ago. "I just came to smell the flowers," I answered when a reporter asked me what I was doing there. Really, I had just gone to watch. I soon discovered that I was not prepared for what I was watching: Hired guards — armed with .38-caliber revolvers or 9mm automatic pistols — standing between two hostile groups, each claiming to be authentic Baptists. What's going on here?

C & C readers are familiar with the events leading up to the show-down. For twelve years the event has been brewing, since Paul Pressler, a Houston judge who, as a magistrate, would not have been allowed to join the original Baptist movement, and Paige Patterson, a Dallas preacher, underling of W. A. Criswell, senior pastor of that city's First Baptist Church, met at Café du Monde in New Orleans and devised a scheme to wrest control of the Southern Baptist Convention from those they considered too liberal to be trusted with the business of God.

Their plan was simple. Members of all boards of trustees and committees are appointed by the president on a rotating basis. By electing a president sympathetic with their views for ten successive years, total control would be theirs.

It worked. Year after year thousands of messengers (the Southern Baptist term for delegates) poured into convention centers in Dallas, Miami, St. Louis, Atlanta, San Antonio, Las Vegas for the annual gathering. They came in cars, church buses, recreation vehicles, airplanes, and on trains to cast their ballots. Each year the Pressler-Patterson faction won. The mission was accomplished.

Divided into what came to be known by the press as moderate and fundamentalist camps, neither group pleased with what it was called, the struggle escalated. This year 38,000 gathered in the New Orleans Superdome and elected Morris Chapman of Wichita Falls, Texas. It was the twelfth victory for the fundamentalists. The occasion was marked by a raucous celebration at Café du Monde where plaques were presented to the founders of the "takeover" movement. The moderates cried "foul!" The fundamentalists went about it.

To the victors belong the spoils. Two years ago, perhaps to test their strength, they took on the administration and faculty of Southeastern Seminary, a school many considered to be the most progressive of their six theological schools. Southeastern, in Wake Forest, North Carolina, is now an academic skeleton of what it had been; the president replaced by one to the liking of the fundamentalists, the faculty in disarray.

Caesar's Centurions

All of that was prelude to what happened in Nashville on July 17. Immediately following the New Orleans convention, members of the Southern Baptist Executive Committee — a body of seventy-seven members appointed by past and present presidents to carry on the business of the church between annual meetings — demanded the resignations of the director and news editor of Baptist Press, an agency charged with writing and distributing news stories concerning Southern Baptists. For some years they had drawn fire for filing news stories many considered not in the best interests of Pressler and the fundamentalist side. When the two men, Al Shackleford and Dan Martin, both nationally respected journalists, refused to resign, a special session of the Executive Committee was called for July 17.

The meeting was scheduled to begin in the auditorium of the Baptist Building at 901 Commerce, Nashville, Tennessee, at ten o'clock in the morning. Two hours earlier more than two hundred people had gathered in support of the two men. And in support of the historic Baptist notion of freedom of information. Speculation inside the auditorium was that the first order of business would be a vote for executive session. Instead, at about a quarter past the hour word spread that the Executive Committee was in secret session in a room upstairs. Earlier, barricades of tables and chairs had blocked the stairs to the second floor. Discovering that they had been removed, the group hurried upstairs. Instead of a barricade armed guards blocked entry.

It was strange for me at first. Why were we surprised? Why did any of us even care? Had we not seen the so-called moderate group, when they were in control, do little better? Had we not watched as they said little, and did less, during the civil rights era? Vietnam? Who among them lifted an editorial voice? And who among them offered leadership to give equality to the women in their ranks, who constituted more than 50 percent of their numbers? Had we forgotten that sometimes our own writings had been kept from the shelves of their bookstores? Was it not they who built the abomination in which we were now standing from the tithes of the poor?

What are we to make of this multimillion-dollar building with its flaunting display of opulence and tight security dedicated to the lowly Galilean? Where are they at this moment, the holdover moderates who have not yet been purged from their plush offices here but probably will be soon, who hang onto the security of Mammon and vow to speak out as soon as retirement age is reached? Why do they cringe behind their own closed doors instead of storming the guards and money changers screaming, "In the name of Almighty God, stop it!" Why don't we? What freedom of information, what historic principles are we defending with our silent presence? Is this not what many of us thought we had walked away from in frustration and despair years ago? Just what is going on here?

Why Are They Singing?

A young woman I had known earlier, a seminary graduate still unemployed and unordained by the church of her rearing, came up to me and whispered one of the questions I had been asking myself, her words lost in the rising clamor of the crowd facing the gunmen. "Why are we here?" she asked. I couldn't recall her name, so I addressed her as "Pastor." It proved to be an appropriate title. I told her I didn't know. She seemed less puzzled than I; like she did know. She drifted away.

Someone was trying to make a statement. I assumed that it was for the press. I couldn't hear much of what he said. Something about Al and Dan each being offered five minutes to defend their work over the years for Baptist Press. I made out that as journalists and as Baptists they were refusing to participate in this secret meeting. Instead, they stood near the guarded door — their trial, with neither stated charge nor defense, continuing inside.

I watched the woman who had spoken to me. She moved from one person to another, whispering as she went. "Roger Williams." She mouthed the words, turning in my direction and then to others. Yes, I thought. That's why we're here. For Roger Williams. He who stood against the intolerance of another religious establishment of another day, bent as surely as this one on stopping the free flow of religious communication. Roger Williams, who gave us our beginning in the new country: the first Baptist church of America. The lone courage of Roger Williams. Of course. For him we are gathered.

The woman drifted away again, then caught my eye as she formed the name of Isaac Backus on her lips. Yes, yes. Isaac Backus. He who stood against king and court in defense of religious liberty, and saw his mother spend thirteen weeks in prison for refusing to pay a church tax. This would be a familiar scene to him, watching Caesar's centurions guarding the Faith. The raw fortitude of Isaac Backus. We are here for him. And for his mother.

I watched as the young woman whispered another name. "John Leland." Ah, yes. I remembered. The Baptist preacher of Virginia, who would grant no peace to his neighbors, Thomas Jefferson and James Madison, until the First Amendment to the Constitution spoke of religious liberty and separation of church and state. Without him those rights would not have been. I thought of Bill Finlator, a Carolina preacher, asking why every Baptist in America is not a card-carrying member of the ACLU, since it was a Baptist notion from the outset. I heard someone say that we were there in honor of, and with apology to, John Leland. And to a host of Baptist martyrs besides.

"What does this mean?" a journalist from Fort Worth asked me. "It means that the Baptist movement is over," I replied. "Over. Done. Gone. Dead."

"Then why are they singing?" he asked, scribbling hurriedly on his note pad, then moving through the crowd. I had been so occupied with my own thoughts, and the names spoken by the young woman, that I had not heard the singing at all. Now I listened. Two hundred people, barred from participating in, or even hearing the business of their church, lifting their voices in disruptive hymn-singing, surely stopping the proceedings on the other side of the secured door. Young and old, male and female, standing there. Some smiling as if in jubilation. Some sobbing as if in deep mourning.

I had second thoughts and searched the area for the Fort Worth journalist. I wanted to amend my answer to his first question. And try to answer the second. When I couldn't find him, I spoke to the woman who had moved back beside me. "What do you think, Pastor?" I asked her.

"Maybe history is all we have left," she replied. She seemed somehow joyous. "But there is something here in which to exult as well. For so long as a little band of believers stand huddled together facing armed guards, in a house allegedly built for the glory of God; standing, singing, smiling, weeping, hoping, the historic Baptist notion of freedom will never die." I asked her to write down what she had said. It seemed important to remember.

At about 1:30 it was announced that Al Shackleford and Dan Martin had been relieved of their duties with Baptist Press. Effective immediately.

Part 7

Christmas/Easter/Christmas

Much of what has been presented in this book involves analysis, reporting, reviewing, reflection, and commentary. These words have often, but not always, presumed a dimension of faith. But they have not been confessions or meditations in the devotional tradition.

The essays that follow move into the exploration of faith. They are contemporary attempts to address the core celebrations of the Christian faith, Christmas and Easter, common events on the U.S. calendar, uncommon in their meaning.

Christmas and Easter have elicited multitudes of responses in word and music. Too often they fail to move those mysteries into the broader questions of how we seek love and do justice.

C & C's founder, Reinhold Niebuhr, caught some of the complexity of these central affirmations of the Christian faith in an essay in the first issue, February 10, 1941:

However difficult it may be to give a fully rational account of what Christ's atoning death upon the Cross means to Christian faith, this mystery, never fully comprehended by and yet not wholly incomprehensible to faith, speaks to us of a mercy that transcends but also satisfies the demands of justice.

Six people who have been regular contributors to C & C seek out the meaning today of the mystery we express when we talk about God visiting the earth in the form of a human, who met and overcame death on the cross. Because God so loved the world.

For those who believe history is transcended, our lives have meaning, and love is unlimited.

Dialogue at Christmas

December 11, 1967

Amos N. Wilder

Amos N. Wilder, who in 1923 won the Yale Series of Younger Poets annual prize, in 1991 at age ninety-five published his latest book, The Bible and the Literary Critic. *Hollis Professor of Divinity Emeritus of Harvard Divinity School, he is the oldest living person to have played center court at Wimbledon.*

ONE OF THE *minim* burst in on the Rabbi and exclaimed: "The Messiah has come!" The Rabbi went to the window and looked out, and demurred: "Nothing has changed."

> "As of old,
> seedtime and harvest, cold and heat, day and night;
> a generation goes and a generation comes
> but the earth remaineth the same.
> What is crooked is not made straight.
> As of old,
> a time to weep and a time to laugh,
> a time to mourn and a time to dance,
> a time to love and a time to hate,
> a time for war and a time for peace;
> there is nothing new under the sun.
> The king tarrieth.
> What is wanting is not made up."

·

> *Nevertheless,* the Kingdom has come;
> Behind the scenes, a clandestine irruption;
> A fission in the world's grain,
> A benign conflagration.
> O Lord, open the eyes of thy servant:
> Behold, the mountain full of horses and chariots of fire.
>
> Nothing has changed? But listen:
> Tellurian tremors,
> Convulsions at the earth's core,
> The silent collapse of parapets.
> Moorings have parted
> And we are carried away into new latitudes.
>
> The Kingdom cometh not with observation,
> But it has overtaken us
> Dispelling old obsessions.

Therefore this dancing through iron doors,
This singing our way through blind walls,
This mocking of old hierarchic dooms,
Levitation across impassable wastes.

Therefore these hilarities, against all reason,
And charities welling up for no cause,
Righteousness appears from nowhere, like dew,
The earth opens and joy springs in the furrows
And the angels acclaim it from pole to pole.

Awakened by Easter

March 20, 1989

Gayraud Wilmore

Gayraud Wilmore, a contributing editor, recently retired as professor of church history at the Interdenominational Theological Center in Atlanta.

I AM WRITING this guest editorial on a red formica-topped table in the small kitchen of my mother's quiet, early morning house. It is several weeks before Easter, but resurrection is on my mind. Upstairs the floor creaks as the elder of my two younger brothers gets out of bed. Otherwise, this old brick house in the Nicetown section of North Philadelphia is empty and soundless. Somewhere over southern Africa our youngest brother is flying west and north, hastening to mother's funeral two days from now. Earlier this week, after a long illness, Patricia Wilmore slipped away only a few weeks from what would have been her ninety-fifth birthday.

There is a reason why I could not sleep. It has to do with more than the nagging reminder of a promise to write this editorial. It is the fact that this old house, so recently bereft of its gray-haired matriarch, is full of the glow of the resurrection this morning, and the thought comes to me that it is just not possible to sleep enveloped in the glow and glory of the Risen Christ. One has to be up and doing something worthwhile, something that draws strength from the resurrection, something related to the victory over death.

This house, this little space on God's earth, so inseparably connected to other spaces around the world where our extended family resides, is the center of the strange phenomenon I am experiencing this bright February morning. This emanation, this something inexhaustible that streams from this place, the navel of our world, I cannot explain except to say that it energizes, awakens, fills everything with force and vitality. I believe it can only be the mystical effulgence of the resurrection left by my mother's departure from this temporary haven and her arrival in a new and more permanent, eternal home.

It seems almost too unctious to say that we, all of the old C & C fire-fighters who may read these lines, need this power of the resurrected Christ to get off our duffs. I don't mean to be overly romantic about it. There is nothing very romantic about the desperation some of us feel when we try to operate in this crazy world outside of the gravitational field of Easter. It rather takes cold, pure logic to recognize, here at the beginning of a new year and the Bush administration, that we Christians — Protestant, Catholic, and Orthodox, black and white, men and women, liberals and conservatives — are dying. The United States of America is sick and the churches of this nation, no better off, are a most unlikely source of healing. I cannot remember a time, either before or after the 1960s, when we Christians were more confused, more demoralized, and in greater disarray — a rudderless ship in a heavy sea. In fact, the whole society seems caught up in a paralyzing ennui, except perhaps the new and very rich who rode into power eight years ago with six-shooters blazing and white sombreros waving, behind a Hollywood cowboy who sanctimoniously and effectively represented their interests in the name of "less government means better government."

They Ate the Cake

It strikes me with something akin to terror to think how we permitted ourselves to be taken in, silenced and neutralized, by the boyish grin and a trickle-down prosperity while resurgent racism, Rambo militarism, cultural philistinism, and unregulated, let-them-eat-cake capitalism swaggered across the stage on an eight-year run. If I were asked what in the world happened, how did we let ourselves get into that situation, I should only reply that most of us Democrats, who were out there battling twenty years ago, fell asleep at the switch. While we were dreaming Martin's dream and waiting for some new messiah to arrive and save "the gains of the '60s," this new group of middle-aged, increasingly well-off stock- and bondholders, corporate managers and their cadres of young urban professionals who never had it so good, were walking away with their loot and leaving the nation with a deficit which in 1990 will probably be in excess of $154 billion. In the meantime, our new leader is proposing to deal with the unprecedented problems of the city, child-care, education, homelessness, and the environment without raising taxes. An economic policy that will surely have to out-voodoo anything that Ronald Reagan was able to conjure up.

If Easter does anything for us this year, let it rouse us from our apathetic slumber and give us the energy to build some fires under George Bush and the 101st Congress before this new four-year period gets very far along. It is past time for us secular humanists, wimp liberals, and unborn-again spoilers of the American Dream to wake up.

Since rereading 1 Corinthians 15 during these days of quiet bereavement I have been more than usually sensitive to the New Testament image of death as sleep, to the several connotations and implications of words in the Bible that speak of sleeping and awakening, perishing and quickening, death and resurrection. The Scriptures have nothing to do with somnolence and inactivity. They call us out of sleep into wakefulness, out of darkness into enlightenment — eyes wide open, fists clenched and punching, poised on tiptoes like high-strung boxers bobbing and weaving before the bell.

Why do the cults and sects make so much better use of these images and metaphors than the church? I remember how often Jehovah's Witnesses, Scientology, and the late Honorable Elijah Muhammad spoke about being awake! clear! rousing "a race of dead men and women from their sleep of death," and getting them "on the battlefield against the Devil!" Such talk feeds on the idea of resurrection. The sleep of death is understood to have been banished and the true believers are called to awake, full of energy and vitality, strengthened to do what they have to do — in Jerusalem, in all Judea, in Samaria, and "unto the uttermost parts of the earth."

New Morning

It is undoubtedly bad exegesis, but a useful — if eisegetical — application of 1 Corinthians 15:6b, "but some are fallen asleep," to describe what has happened to the forces of progressive Christian action in recent years with such a metaphor. Some of us who were so deeply involved in the urban mission, the fight against racial segregation, opposition to the war in Vietnam, the struggle for the rights of Native Americans, Hispanic Americans, and women, freedom in southern Africa, and hands off Central America, badly need to hear Paul's exclamation in verse 34, "Awake to righteousness, and sin not!" For it is as true of us as it was of the Corinthians that we have shamefully lost the knowledge of God and must renew our faith in the resurrection and the claim it lays upon the church of Christ before we can get on with the mission of liberation.

Sitting here this morning, I am aware of a great loss, but also of a great encouragement — personally and in terms of our common struggle for a more just and responsible society. I have a keen sense that this quiet house that seems so empty is really full of power and life as never before, and that this is also true of the world at Easter, 1989. Life! Obviously I am not talking about the mechanical motion of the planets or the rumpus of atoms and molecules, but about the eternal beingness of intelligent, purposing, seeking life. That is what the church and the nation need today as we blunder into a world in which the desire of Americans for wealth and power has been the source of so much benevolence, and yet so much anguish and death.

Life! Life that breaks through denial, negation, and oppression to freedom, justice, and peace, not only for Americans, but for every person on earth.

Life! Life that posits, affirms, and defends all we believe in and hold dear — loving justice and tenderness against all attempts by the Enemy, who always appears as an angel of light, to wipe them out and return the world to the power of death, to the anarchy of "might makes right" and "only the fittest deserve to survive." But life will not be suppressed. Death is swallowed up in the victory of Christ who stands against such an insensible, dying world and, through our ambassadorship, raises it from the dead. Easter calls us to wake up. Wake up and choose life!

God Newborn

December 12, 1988

Elizabeth Bettenhausen

Elizabeth Bettenhausen learns and teaches feminist theology and theory at the Women's Theological Center in Boston. She is a contributing editor of C & C.

I

"GOD'S MY SIZE!" The three-year-old girl jumped up and ran to tell her mother. "Mom, God's my size!" She got the idea while lying on her stomach looking at the creche beneath the Christmas tree. Eye-level with a baby is a good position from which to do theology.

At Christmas God is newborn, less like Michaelangelo's muscular men and more like an infant in wet diapers sucking milk from its mother's breast. God is less like an equation in theoretical physics and more like a hungry three-year-old in a refugee camp. At Christmas God is less like a come-of-age, postmodern adult and more like the toddler laughing at being able to walk.

II

ADULTS LOOK AT the baby and say, "This can't be God! This is a bawling baby!" The protests are diverse. "This can't be God! This baby is Jewish. This baby is poor. This baby is illegitimate. This baby is male. This baby is traditional. This baby is a refugee. This baby is, well, a baby."

Children look at the baby and say, "God's our size!"

Adults look at the baby, shuffle their feet in the straw, and mutter to each other:

"Adoptionist Christology is preferable to Incarnation."

"The Ancient Near East was full of Incarnation myths."

"Doesn't Mary look well, theologically speaking?"

"This wouldn't be necessary except for sin."

"This would be necessary even without sin."

"When he's older he'll amount to something."

Meanwhile, children touch and say, "God's our size!"

III

CHRISTIAN THEOLOGY is done by adults for adults; it is God-talk which usually neglects children. Whether as Lord, Liberator, or Lover, Jesus is portrayed as an adult for adults. We judge our Christologies by how well they suit adult needs only. We write our anthropologies as if being human begins at adulthood. When we accuse someone of "playing God" or urge them "to God," it is not a gurgling infant or a three-year-old refugee we have in mind.

Christmas celebrates God as newborn, wholly dependent. This baby is not just a preview of the real thing: an adult. Dependency does not mean decreased or incomplete humanity. Adults uneasy with their own dependence on each other and on children hasten to warn against "sentimentality" at Christmas, and rush to make this liturgical season only a prelude to adult history.

IV

HOW CAN WE TALK about God in this age? Is it feminist to talk about God as a human baby? What does a crying baby have to do with the federal deficit, not to mention the debt? Will the mainline churches grow or shrink if they say God has wet diapers? If God is a child, does the Vatican need a new study on the representative nature of the priesthood? Isn't the God question more related to charmed and colored quarks and quantum mechanics? Why not attend to the preborn God? How does liberation take place in a manger? How can you posit an incarnate God in a situation of religious pluralism and interfaith dialogue? Doesn't celebrating Christmas reinforce codependence? Why not engrave a baby on this crystal pyramid? The blizzard of questions muffles any good news.

But at Christmas adults are offered again grace abundant in the newborn and embodied in three-year-olds. Theological sophistication will have its day. Ethical complexity will have its place. Working for justice will have its season. But at Christmas it is all right to lie on the floor — dirt or carpet, prison or home, office or shelter — eye-level with a baby, listening to a three-year-old, near or far, call out, "God's my size!"

God's Last Laugh

April 6, 1987

Harvey Cox

Harvey Cox is professor of divinity at Harvard Divinity School and a contributing editor of C&C. Author of the influential The Secular City *(1964) and many other books, he has drawn on his broad ecumenical experiences and travels to write about important developments in religious experience and their relationships to social and political change.*

IN A PASSAGE in Umberto Eco's *The Name of the Rose*, one monk furiously upbraids another one for presuming to think that Christ ever laughed. We may dismiss his rigidness as excessive, but the question remains: Why does laughter hold such a meager place in our religion?

In the church I attended as a boy, a snicker during the sermon was ample proof that you must have been thinking of something else. Laughter and faith seem incommensurate. But are they really? It has not always been so. In his *Divine Comedy*, Dante Alighieri reports that after he had made the tortuous ascent from hell to purgatory, and had then drawn close to the celestial sphere, he suddenly heard a sound he had never heard before. Stopping and listening, he then writes, *"me sembiana un riso del universo."* It sounded "like the laughter of the universe."

True, on Easter Sunday 1987 there appears to be very little to smile about in God's universe. Wars still tear at the flesh in Central America, Afghanistan, and Lebanon. Wide-eyed Iranian boys, roped together in platoons lest they lose heart, are urged forward into Iraqi mine fields. Hunger chokes children's lives every day while our gifts of imagination and inventiveness go into fashioning ever deadlier missiles and

countermissiles. American agents kill and burn in Nicaragua while being paid by funds gathered from arms sales by shadowy figures who
act in our names. The concept of "the consent of the governed" sometimes seems almost as inoperative as it was when a Caesar imposed
his will by fiat. All in all, there seems to be little room for laughter.

Yet the Bible teaches us that in the face of proud claims of rulers
and the cruelty of despots, "The Holy One who sitteth in the heavens
shall laugh" (Psalm 2:4). God laughs at oppression and meanness? At
first the idea sounds irreverent, surprising. With suffering and evil so
rampant, how can a loving God laugh?

The Easter story gives us a clue to this baffling riddle. A small
and precarious clue, perhaps, but a clue nonetheless. God laughs, it
seems, because God knows how it all turns out in the end. Further, the
laughter of God, as the passion accounts tell us, does not come from
afar. It does not emanate from One who can safely chortle, from a safe
distance, at another's pain. It comes from One who has also felt the
hunger pangs, the hurt of betrayal by friends and the torturer's touch.

Perhaps Easter Sunday 1987 provides us with just the right occasion to reclaim the holy laughter that fell on Dante's astonished ears
as his steps drew near God's dwelling place. On the Christian calendar
Easter is a feast of gladness. Grief turns into jubilation. Bitter defeat
becomes exuberant hope. Even those who walk in the valley of the
shadow of death know they need fear no evil. But, without a trace of
irreverence, can we not also say there is something genuinely comic
about Easter? Could it be God's hilarious answer to those who sported
and derided God's prophet, who blindfolded and buffeted him, and
who continue to hound and deprive God's children today?

I hope so. On Easter, after all, we retell an unlikely tale that —
were it not so profoundly true — would have to be passed off as a
lame joke. Without even so much as a stop-me-if-you've-heard-this-
one (since most of us already have), we recount the tale of a man
who sided with the disinherited and the heartbroken, who became the
hope of those who had lost all hope, who was tortured to death and
sealed in a tomb. So far there is nothing terribly noteworthy because
so many others have gone through so much of the same.

But the punchline of this tall story is that this same man — so his
friends insisted — was once more alive. The Romans and their local
supporters had thought they had rid themselves of the rabble-rousing
rabbi for good. Against the clear counsel of the wisest Pharisees, a
clique of the Jerusalem elite, fearful that Jesus might provoke a bloody
Roman reprisal, conspired with the imperial occupation authorities to
push through a drumhead trial. Unable to concoct a credible religious
excuse to condemn Jesus — who remained a pious Jew — they advanced a political charge. Jesus claimed, they said, to be a king, and

"we have no king but Caesar." So, they warned Pilate, "If you release him, you are no friend of Caesar's."

Silence and After

This was too much for Pilate. Like all underlings clinging to the middle rungs of power before and since, he feared nothing more than a negative report to headquarters. So he confronted Jesus with the accusation. Having such a charge brought against him, Jesus held his silence. Yes, he had spoken of a new reign that was already arriving in the midst of Pilate's world. But it was a kingdom neither Pilate nor Caesar had the spiritual capacity to discern. Indeed how could the rich and powerful understand that he was talking about a kingdom that bore no resemblance to the one Rome had imposed on his people with its fearful phalanxes of legions?

If his accusers had not already grasped the Message — that the reign he was talking about was one in which peace would hold sway and the hungry would be fed — how could they understand it now? But Jesus' tormentors knew only the kind of power that paid them. So it was ironic that when they designed a nasty sight-gag by handing him a phony scepter and placing a crown of thorns on his head, they inadvertently hit closer to the truth than they knew: Jesus' kingdom is one that comes only when people risk the pain that results from speaking inconvenient truth to spurious power. So Jesus was put to death.

For a while there was no laughter. The joking was over. The raucous howls of the executioners stopped only when they finally grew weary. The obscene hoots of the passersby ended at last when the figure on the cross would not rail back. The sneers of Pilate and the jeers of Herod also subsided when, their official duties finished, they returned to their palaces having rid themselves once and for all — so they thought — of this troublemaker.

Now there was no laughter. Only silence.

But then came Easter morning. And if we listen carefully to the silence of that dawn we may also detect, dimly and at a distance, what Dante heard when he came within earshot of the *Paradiso*. We hear a gentle murmur, ethereal yet earthly, angelic yet terribly human. It begins as a whisper that as we listen begins to sound like laughter. But if we fine-tune our hearing we notice it bears no resemblance at all to the screeches and howls we heard during the trial at the cross. It sounds more like the laughter of eight-year-olds doing cartwheels or of old friends savoring a birthday, or of a gray-haired couple chuckling at the antics of a grandchild. Yet it is more, much more.

Holy laughter is a gift of grace. It is the human spirit's last defense against banality and despair. Sometimes I think that comedians —

those of the gentle type — can be God's emissaries in a mean-spirited time like ours. Woody Allen depicts neurotic people who, despite everything, somehow succeed in being compassionate. Garrison Keillor reports regularly from a forgotten little town on the pedestrian virtues and unspectacular goodness of ordinary people. Rightly rendered, the comic spirit transcends tragedy. It steps outside the probability tables and enables us to catch a fleeting glimpse of what might be, even of what — ultimately — already is.

Some people, no matter how hard you try to explain it, simply don't get a joke. The Easter Story is like that. There is no point whatever is trying to explain it or make it more plausible. Easter is that moment when the laughter of the universe breaks through. It fades, of course, like a distant radio signal on a stormy night. A lot of noise and static crowds it out. But once we have heard it we know from then on that it is there. It is God's last laugh.

From Creche to Crucifixion: A Pilgrimage

December 23, 1985

Howard Moody

Howard Moody, a contributing editor of C & C *and senior minister at Judson Memorial Church in New York City, is known for his involvement in a host of struggles for progressive social and legal changes, especially women's rights and health care. He was among the champions of women's legal right to abortion in the 1960s and 1970s.*

NO MATTER HOW MUCH we may anticipate or enjoy the Christmas season, there has got to be a little Scrooge in all of us. There are times when the spirit of that bitter old cynic attempting to block out the overzealous conviviality and joviality of the season strikes a chord.

One of the reasons that people suffer hives, crying jags, drinking bouts, and plain orneriness in the Christmas season is the *rules:* Everyone has got to celebrate, renew family ties, exchange gifts, and above all "be happy." Most people really can't manage it, and they suffer the psychic disease of the season — depression. But the church and Christians haven't handled the celebration much better. We are always tempted to gild the story over, covering its hard paradoxes with tinsel and glitter. We want to see only the joyful celebration, feel the warmth of the stable, and hear the angels' glorious song. We don't want to think about rejoicing at the birth of one who will suffer and die. Our need to remember the joy and forget the pain of this celebration may be due to the world we live in, a world threatened by all kinds of catastrophes — some we know, and some we cannot name. Who has not wanted to put aside misgivings and uncertainties when a child is born into the world?

A few weeks ago I was in San Salvador, standing with some friends down by the railroad tracks where the poorest displaced people had built shelters with sticks and mud and a piece of corrugated tin, that familiar material symbolizing wretched poverty all over this world. Beside these hovels a Palestinian stable would look like a palace. In the midst of it all, suddenly surrounding us, were small children with upturned faces full of innocence and curiosity, looking for some sign of caring approval, a smile of recognition from these "gringo strangers," and shouting *"toma mi foto"* — take my picture. It's those children's version of the slogan "I am somebody."

If only I could have basked in the sunlight of the shining faces of those children whose state of being almost has the power to wash one clean! But I couldn't. For a shadow hangs over their young lives, making it more than likely that a number of them will die of malnutrition or bombs or be made orphans when their parents disappear.

Can we handle the paradox of it all? Birth, new life, coming into existence in the midst of physical squalor, economic impoverishment, and daily terror. Christmas is so full of innocence and wonder and glory that it makes the pulse pound and the heart beat fast. But if we really experience the Nativity we are faced with the heartache and suffering embedded deep in the nature of the event: No decent place for his birth, the fear of discovery by the wrong people, all the children who died because he was born, the anxious flight into a foreign country.

Christmas is a symbol of joy and hope and love in the world. But it is also a reminder of another truth: There is no deliverance unless someone suffers and sacrifices. Isn't that the meaning of the anguished and painful cry out of Mary's "insides" that brings the child into the world? And what about that other cry of forlorn abandonment on the lips of the baby who grew up and hung on a cross? Is this not a truth that sometimes escapes us — that the rough-hewn cradle in the beginning and the "old rugged cross" at the end are made of the same wood? This symbolizes that at the heart of things is a hard and unacceptable reality that another is always suffering that we may live, someone always going to prison that we might be free.

The campesinos of San Salvador will celebrate Christmas with all the joy and festivity of their faith, but they would be the first to admit that because of the death of Archbishop Romero, many more of them are alive today. The challenge of a real celebration of Christmas is to make the connections between that wonderful story and "our story," whoever we are and wherever we live. We need to understand the relationship between a desperate housing shortage for low income people in New York City and the story that there is "no room in the inn"; between the fearful flight of Mary and Joseph and people fleeing from war and repression in Central America; between the "slaughter of innocents" and millions of children dying of starvation in Africa; the incredible innocence of the babe in the crib and our cynical, worldly-wiseness that taught us we could be bought for the right amount of money, the right opportunity, or the right cause.

The pilgrimage to Christmas is not an easy one for people of intellect and learning, to find their way to a stable and bow before some Truth wrapped in humble clothes. But even if we get there we'd like there to be joy and adoration without thinking of the outcome. Our dilemma is how to rejoice in the Nativity without sentimentalizing it; how to praise with the angels this new Beginning without forgetting the tragic ending. No one speaks of this enigmatic celebration with more insight into the mystery than T. S. Eliot in his poem "Journey of the Magi":

> All this was a long time ago, I remember,
> And I would do it again, but set down
> This set down
> This: were we led all that way for
> Birth or Death? There was a Birth, certainly
> We had evidence and no doubt. I had seen birth and death,
>
> But had thought they were different; this Birth was
> Hard and bitter agony for us, like Death, our death.
> We returned to our places, these Kingdoms,
> But no longer at ease here, in the old dispensation,
> With an alien people clutching their gods.
> I should be glad of another death.

If only we could have kept the baby in the creche. But he grew up and spoke the truth and got hounded and harassed, tried and convicted, and put to death. Somehow the end was there in the beginning. But we don't want to see it. We would flee from the hard truth that just as death follows birth as surely as night day, so the Christian promise of rebirth is inseparable from, even dependent upon, the very death we fear.

So in spite of the beauty and joy of this celebration, we are troubled and afraid. But if we can embrace the whole story of Christmas, holding on to the anguish as well as the glory, we may yet experience a truly faithful celebration.

Easter: The Demand and the Promise

March 17, 1986

Robert McAfee Brown

Robert McAfee Brown, whose name is symbolic for engaged theologian and ethicist, is perhaps best known for being able to write clearly, for example, in Theology in a New Key: Responding to Liberation Theology *and* Saying Yes and Saying No: On Rendering to God and Caesar.

IT'S A FEW DAYS after your leader has been captured, roughed up by the jail keepers, tried in a kangaroo court, and then (to employ the currently favorite CIA euphemism) "neutralized."

You had been captivated by him that day when he appeared over the hill and caught you working on your fish nets. He shared a compelling vision of a new world. So compelling, in fact, that almost on the spur of the moment you turned your back on the fishing business, left your wife and kids who were perplexed if not put out at your departure, and went off with the wandering teacher.

In the beginning, as you glimpsed what the teacher not only talked about but lived, as the crowds responded enthusiastically, your rash decision to follow him seemed almost reasonable. But then the crowds had tailed off, and the new world didn't seem to be coming quite on schedule. So you and the other disciples had followed him down to Jerusalem, at the height of the holy season and the tourist trade, in an effort to force the issue.

You had forced the issue, all right. By the time you got there, the opposition was well orchestrated and finely tuned, and in less than a week your leader was strung up, and you were smart enough to head for the hills. You made it back to the lakeside up north, and had taken a few days getting things squared away with the family, which had remained unenchanted during your impulsive leave of absence.

You had been particularly careful not to tell friends and neighbors what you had actually been about during your absence, not only because you felt you'd been taken in and made to look three parts the fool, but because you knew the authorities had an all-points warning out on you. You felt distinctly uncomfortable at the thought of being fitted for a cross of your own, nailed there on a "guilt by association" charge. So you had nursed privately your embarrassment and fear, vowing that the next time a wandering prophet came down the pike you would be smart enough to be looking the other way.

And then — just when the fishing business was picking up again and your family beginning to let you back into its good graces — Bartholomew had come over the hill and found you down by the lake shore mending the fishing nets. The following conversation had ensued:

BARTHOLOMEW: "Hey! He's risen!

YOU (*out loud*): "Oh, no!"

YOU (*continuing to yourself*): "Oh, no! If he's risen that means he was right all along. It wasn't just a dream. And *that* means back on the road, back into the midst of trouble. Why couldn't he have stayed dead? Just when I'm beginning to get my life together again, this has to happen."

It probably didn't take place that way. And then, again, it might have. But even if it didn't, the episode reminds us that the resurrection story is not just a happy ending tacked onto an otherwise gloomy tale. "If Jesus' death is the end of the story," we are usually informed on Easter Sunday morning, "then we're in big trouble. All our hopes have been defeated."

The message really ought to go, "If Jesus' resurrection is the end of the story, then we're in really big trouble. All our hopes could be realized, and we're being enlisted to make them come to pass. The bottom line is no longer Business As Usual, but Everything Is Up for Grabs. The lid is off: Neighbors are to be loved rather than mistrusted. Enemies are to be loved even when we oppose them. How inconvenient."

That's about where our lakeside conversation ended, the Easter message seen in the form of a *demand*. And if that's not the full message, at least it is the only condition within which the full message can be heard. The full message is one of *promise*. But only those who have heard the demand can rightly hear the promise.

How would the conversation continue? Then or now? It might become a monologue that would go something like this:

If he has beaten death, then everything changes. If he calls us to spread the word around — in Jerusalem, or right here by the lakeside, or off in Thessalonika, in Washington or Chicago, or off in San Salvador — we won't have to do it alone. We'll not only have each other; we'll have him too. It doesn't mean we are safe — any more than he was. But he'll somehow be with us, lending his strength and help. *We won't be alone.* And — my God! — if he has somehow even beaten death, that's his promise that nothing can really separate us from him.

You know, I think it's worth another try....

Afterword

A FEW YEARS AGO, I returned to my native home in "grassroots" Kentucky armed with several issues of *Christianity and Crisis* to give to one of my friends from high school days. This would be her first introduction to *C&C*. I told her some of the history of the journal — its years of publication, the reason it was born. She read all the issues. Then she asked me: "How can a magazine so small be so big?" In response to my query for interpretation, she said she was asking how "this little magazine" had stayed in print so many years, given what looked like a history of bold reporting, a hard stand against oppression and being on top of critical issues.

Responding to my friend, I said something about the kind of audience that keeps *C&C* alive. But today, when I reflect upon her interpretation of the journal as "small and big," I try to imagine the kind of future in America *Christianity and Crisis* might have to face with its characteristic boldness, advocacy, and critique.

More than twenty years ago, Martin Luther King posed the question that is apt to plague Americans for years to come. "Where do we go from here," he asked, "chaos or community?" If some of the signs of the times be reckoned with, it seems that America is headed in both directions, i.e., toward the possibility of affirming perpetual chaos and simultaneously toward the possibility of creating real community (at least in some quarters).

As I see it, the looming chaos is indicated by at least one major trend now prevalent in American culture. That trend is the great media "dupe." This is the growing tendency of news media and television to join with power structures. This union deceives Americans into either ignoring or accepting something other than the truth about America's involvement in the creation of destructive chaos. The recent Persian Gulf war is a case in point. Television coverage, along with military reports, presented the war as sterile and as "clean" as possible: no blood, no bodies, very few American casualties. Therefore many Americans failed to ask significant questions about the number of Middle Eastern Arab or Islamic casualties of the war.

Apparently some of the most realistic news came from sources beyond the media and military. At the March 1991 meeting of the Women's Inter-Seminary Conference held at Union Theological Seminary in New York, for example, a Palestinian woman working out of the UN reported that more than one hundred and thirty thousand Iraqi people had been killed by America's "carpet-sweeping" bombing. Many of those killed were civilians. She also said that large numbers of African-American soldiers were put in stockade in Saudi Arabia by the American military because the African-Americans protested the racist statements white American soldiers were making about the Iraqi people, calling them "sand niggers." At a convocation sponsored at Drew University by students and faculty against the war, I heard the keynote speaker — a journalist from an organization critiquing the way the media was managing the news about the war — say that the American government was using racism to "inspire" American soldiers to want to fight.

It seems to me that *C & C* faces a future in which it must constantly test its advocacy stand by raising the question of the role racism plays in the media's and the military's attempt to cover up the chaos America creates in other countries.

However, racism is not the only cover-up strategy. Nor was it the only one used in the Gulf incident (to hide from the soldiers the extent of American greed for control of the world's oil supply). Watching the war on TV, I noted that reporters and commentators did not question the way military officials used language that avoided or neutralized the idea of chaos. For instance, military officials reporting on TV spoke of "a target-rich environment" in reference to the Iraqi-Kuwait area America was constantly carpet bombing. Thus the image of massive, cruel death was avoided as the image "rich" came to consciousness, suggesting something pleasant and possibly good.

Also, the media and the war-machine manipulated and reinterpreted symbols that distracted American consciousness from associations made in everyday life. An illustration of this was the yellow ribbon phenomenon that became such an important symbol of support for some aspect of the war effort. I watched one of the morning news shows associate the yellow ribbon with such pleasantries as the love song about "a yellow ribbon in her hair." Nobody on the show mentioned the fact that in our everyday world, policemen use yellow ribbon to mark off a crime scene where death has occurred. It seems to me that this everyday usage and symbol indicated more appropriately what the American-led war in the Gulf was: a crime scene of massive death, disease, destruction of property, and homelessness.

What this suggests is that *Christianity and Crisis*, the church, and all Americans face a future of mind control where the manipulation of language and traditional symbols plays a major role. This kind of collusion between media and military may dupe Americans into accepting the values of a completely technological world — like the one described in the 1930s in Aldous Huxley's *Brave New World* — a context where humans value life and nature only to the degree that life and nature support and fit into a technological worldview. The horror is that many Americans may already have become so captivated by television that they cannot distinguish its provision of "simple" entertainment from its involvement in mind control.

Maybe some questions *Christianity and Crisis* and the church should ponder as they chart future directions are these: Does this new method of warfare introduced by the Persian Gulf War evidence that George Orwell's world of technological mind control and constant surveillance (described in his book *1984*) have arrived in North America? In the "new world order," is the Third World the place where we will vividly see "Big Brother" watching for the purpose of controlling the minds and movements of Third World people and exploiting their natural and human resources? Will the terrible racism and sexism lodged deeply in the American soul keep Americans so oblivious to Big Brother's atrocities against dark, Third World people that Americans will not recognize surveillance and mind control taking over their own lives? Journals like *Christianity and Crisis* will have to be the vanguard constantly showing how language, symbol, and ordinary life are being twisted by the media–power-structure alliance in order to shift values and establish control.

There are, however, a few rays of hope in the distance. *C & C* will no doubt alert its readers about the progression of these good things. In some quarters, people are struggling to reach beyond racial, sexual, class, and homophobic boundaries to create real communities of action that subvert some of this movement of mind control. Among these people are feminist (white) and womanist (black) women beginning to come together to discover the foundations upon which they can build dialogue and communities of action for social justice work.

The first of these "comings-together" happened recently at the Cardinal Spellman retreat center in the Bronx. United Methodist clergywomen (black and white) gathered to begin identifying and ferreting out those things impeding the development of community and commitment among feminist and womanist Methodist clergywomen. The group plans to publish these first proceedings so that a network can develop between feminist and womanist women struggling together to create community.

These kinds of groups, struggling to have community across oppressive boundaries, are our hope for an American future in which mind control, the affirmation of instant chaos-producing war, violence, and complete technological value systems are *not* commonplace. Though the struggle for community across barriers is painful and demands that people give up something, the reward is a more humane society in which people respect rather than hate difference, a society where "shared privilege" becomes a philosophy of human relations.

No doubt *Christianity and Crisis,* as the journal "so small and so big," will — in its reporting and advocacy — support these efforts by human beings struggling to achieve community. Perhaps the church will also place high on its priority list support for these efforts. This kind of community building is a vision of the future. But without this vision, the reign of God on earth can never be realized, and Christians have no good news to report.

DELORES S. WILLIAMS